AF480755

IGNORANCE
SINS
SUFFERINGS

TEACHINGS OF
SADGURU SRI SRI ARJUN

ENGLISH VERSION BY
RABINDRANATH MOHANTY

ISBN 979-8-88883-955-3

Sadguru Sri Sri Arjun

(1933-1989)

"Oh, mankind!

☞ Forgetting your True Self and mistaking this stage for your abode and unreal role for your Self, how long will you continue to be tortured in the frying cauldrons of lust and greed, pride and prejudice?

☞ Arise! Enkindle the flame of awareness within.

☞ Get ready to return to your peaceful, immortal and heavenly abode and get back your eternal, true and pure Self. Then only you will free yourself from all miseries and fears.

☞ Remember! You are immortal and free."

కు★కు

Contents

Acknowledgement

I prostrate myself at the lotus feet of Sadguru Sri Sri Arjun, my spiritual master who is the exponent of Divya Darshan, The Philosophy Divine. From Him only I learnt the alphabets of this great philosophy that presents Advait siddhanta in a simplest possible manner for the benefit of mankind.

Self is the only knowable essence which is to be realised by the Self. Not knowing the Self is ignorance that breeds sins and sufferings. Therefore, realisation of Self is Dharma of all human beings. Sadguru says,"Without self-knowledge it is impossible to attain freedom. Dharma brings us bliss and freedom." But where is bliss and freedom? Our sufferings unmistakably indicate that there is breach of Dharma or the Law of Eternity.

In order to spread Sadguru's teachings far and wide, a modest attempt has been made to publish English versions of His teachings. The first project was "Divya Darshan, The Philosophy Divine" (2017) followed by "Diamond in the Hills" (2019), a biography of Sadguru Sri Sri Arjun. Only a couple of months back, the first volume of Sadguru's teachings under the title of "Truth Knowledge Bliss" (2022) was published. The fourth in the series is the present book titled "Ignorance Sins Sufferings." I would say that while doing this, I am only learning and experiencing Sadguru's grace.

Regular enquiries from my sisters and brothers of Divya Darshan Sangha inspired me a lot to accelerate. Our President Sri Gurudip Singh Ji has all along been boosting my morale which has acted as a favourable wind to my sail. Respected senior members of our Central Committee, namely, Ratnakar Bhai, Biswanath Bhai, Sunaram Bhai, Sadananda Bhai,

Satyanarayan Bhai, Keshab Bhai and others have been guiding and encouraging me in my endeavour. I am grateful to all of them. I am grateful to Divya Darshan Charitable Trust for sponsoring this project.

I must make a special mention about Er. B. P. Mishra, Bhubaneswar. He has been my first reader of all four books. He has spent a lot of time to meticulously examine the manuscript, edit and reshuffle the topics.

It has been a satisfying experience for me to get the professional services of M/s Notion Press Chennai for their promptness and cooperation at different stages, from publishing to other support services. I am grateful to all the readers for their kind words of appreciation.

Let noble thoughts come to us from every side.

Rabindranath Mohanty

Bhubaneswar (Odisha, India)

mail-rnmiob@gmail.com

mob: 9439749074

છ—✦—છ

Foreword

Life we live is a great puzzle or mathematical problem full of actions and reactions, rights and wrongs, hopes and frustrations and so on. Finding out a right answer is a continuous challenge for all of us. We all are surrounded by people and different creatures of varying levels of knowledge and qualities. We come across different trying situations and circumstances from which we have to wriggle ourselves out to reach our divine destination.

The secret formula or the guiding principle to face different situations is observance of Dharma in its true spirit. Therefore, we must know first what Dharma is so that we can observe the same perfectly well in order to reach our goal.

Here is Divya Darshan-The Philosophy Divine, propounded by Sadguru Sri Sri Arjun, that presents for the benefit of entire mankind true knowledge based on Advaita Siddhanta in a very lucid manner by which man can arouse his inert powers within, blossom latent divine virtues while observing the Law of Eternity for taking care of not only his own existence but also ensuring a happy and harmonious social living ultimately to get rid of all illusions together with the associated sufferings.

We are glad to say that Sri Rabindranath Mohanty has been doing the English versions of Sadguru Sri Sri Arjun's philosophy which was originally in the Odia language. He brought out first the English version of Sadguru's complete philosophy under the title Divya Darshan-The Philosophy Divine in the year 2017. Sadguru's complete biography was brought out by him under the title of Diamond in the Hills in the year 2019. A couple of months back he made the English version of Sadguru's discourses under the title 'Truth Knowledge Bliss'. The present book titled 'Ignorance Sins Sufferings' also contains Sadguru's discourses arranged properly for an easy understanding of the deep philosophical thoughts.

We place on record our sincere appreciation of the noble efforts of Sri Mohanty in reflecting the divine knowledge of Sadguru in English which, we are confident, would reach a wide range of readers.

Central Committee

Divya Darshan Sangha

6th Nov, 2022

❧⋆❧

Sadguru Sri Sri Arjun (1933-1989)

His Holiness Sadguru Sri Sri Arjun (1933-1989), was born on 18.07.1933 at Gudiabandh (a village near Gunupur of Rayagada District in Odisha) to Sri Odiya Gomango and Srimati Chandrama Devi. His original name was Arjun Gomango.

He had studied up to class VIII in Gunupur High school of Koraput Dist (Odisha). He was very sharp, intelligent with an analytical mind and unusual inquisitiveness with excellent grasping capacity. He had a strong inclination towards science and technical studies. But he was not interested in the routine syllabus-bound school education. He was good in carpentry, drawing, dance, music, painting, sculpting, drama and theatre, astrology, palmistry, Ayurveda, magic, sorcery etc.

After his school education, he underwent training on Turner trade at ITI, Cuttack, but could not complete the course. He worked as carpentry teacher at different schools of Koraput district for about 7 years. Then he set up a furniture shop and electric appliance repair shop. From 1967, he worked at HAL Sunabeda as a carpenter till his demise in 1989.

Once while reading a science book, he came across a topic on X-ray. A scientist had written, "On passing electricity through a vacuumed tube, he had observed a feeble ray inside the tube. He could not cognize it fully. But he had a conviction that there was a fourth state of matter." This term, "fourth state of matter" made Him inquisitive. There are normally three states of matter, i.e. solid, liquid and gaseous. The fourth state, if any, is not discussed or clearly comprehended. He started inquiring into the fourth state of matter. He had tremendous respect for knowledge. Once his mind was inclined towards fourth state of matter, he got inclined towards the subtlest subject of spirituality. He reasoned that, behind the Creation, there is some invisible power. This thought haunted him again and again. All his previously nurtured obsessions slowly vanished. He became keen to know about the Eternal Truth.

In the year 1948, when he was 15 year old, he came across Socrates' words; **"Ignorance is a great sin."** At that time he was a student of class VIII. This statement spontaneously triggered an awakening in him. He accepted Socrates as his Guru. He heartily concurred with this statement of Socrates and repeated the same several times as if it was a great *mantra* for him. He was convinced that by acquiring knowledge only, ignorance could be dispelled. That means, not acquiring knowledge is a sin. Sins are committed due to ignorance. By welcoming divinity, man can get rid of all sins and attain divinity. By knowledge only man can raise himself to a greater height, i.e. to the stage of Supreme. The divine knowledge is therefore essential. He accepted and adored him as his spiritual master (Guru).

In 1963, while going through the Bible, he was greatly impressed with the teachings of **Lord Jesus** and accepted him as his Guru. **"Ask, you will get; Seek, it will be revealed; Knock, the door shall be opened."** These sermons of Lord Jesus Christ inspired him to ask, seek and knock which were essential for any seeker of knowledge to go further and further.

In 1965, he happened to come across **Lord Buddha's** teachings. He could understand and appreciate what is truth. Lord Buddha had envisioned sorrows and sufferings everywhere. Sorrow is entangled with birth and death. Sorrow is there with decay or disease. Sorrows according to him follow everyone just as the wheels of the bullock cart follow the hooves of the bullocks. According to Lord Buddha there are four noble truths. First, there is suffering. Second, there is a cause behind the origin of suffering. Third, suffering which has come shall also go. Fourth, as there is a cause for the suffering, there is also a cause for its cessation. Once the cause is known the sufferings shall vanish. He stated that, "Craving is the cause of sufferings." Annihilation of cravings will lead to cessation of sufferings. Annihilating cravings means extinguishing the fire of desires. That is the state of *Nirvana*. Hence Lord Buddha's first discourse at Sarnath is known as the Fire Discourse. He accepted Lord Buddha as his Guru.

In a nutshell, Socrates represented knowledge and truth; Jesus represented Love and Forgiveness; Buddha represented Truth and non-injury (love). He appreciated and realised the essence of these teachings. He accepted the three masters as his Guru and drew inspiration from their words.

He had also accepted various sages, Vedas and Vedantas, Prakriti and Param Brahman as his Guru. By seeing, hearing and deeply meditating, he could go deep into any subject. Thus out of his seven Gurus, the last Guru is God. God being Omnipresent, Omniscient and Omnipotent, makes everything possible.

He got the insight that the universe is full of energy; knowledge is energy and by knowledge-power all other powers are understood, appreciated and acquired. Whether it is energy or matter, the fourth state of matter must be identical and homogeneous. He developed a conviction that the higher state of consciousness starts from this stage. Why it happens? How it happens? Who is the cause behind all these happenings? All these questions repeatedly haunted him and he started inquiring into these questions.

Normally the scientists who deal with physical science do not believe in God. According to them, the matter is converted to energy and vice versa. This is the natural law which is final, they believed. According to them there is no need to believe in another power called God. There is no such existence as God.

But Sadguru Sri Sri Arjun's thinking was different. He did not want to put a stop to further enquiry. He wanted to unfold things more and more. According to him, it is true that matter is converted to energy and vice versa. But how does this conversion take place? For this process of transformation, there has to be some independent principle, law or some power that is at work. That principle, remaining independent of matter and energy but residing in the matter and energy, must be governing the process of transformation. In other words, there is some external impressed force that remains internally but independently to trigger the process of change from matter to energy and vice-versa. The spiritualists call it God, Brahman, Atman or Self. The energy that is talked about in the domain of physical science is termed by spiritualists as *apara shakti* (lower power). There is still a higher power called *para shakti* which causes and controls *apara shakti*. With such inquisitive mind, he continued on his spiritual pursuits, till he realised the Truth.

He was a house-holder and yet by his persistence inquisitiveness and continuous spiritual practice, attained enlightenment in the year 1967. Post realisation, He propounded his unique philosophy, namely, **Divya Darshan** which focuses on consciousness, knowledge, Truth, love and bliss, other concepts like Theory of Change, Theory of Colours, Theory of Rebirth etc. He established Divya Darshan Sangh and started accepting disciples from 1976. He toured extensively in the interior districts of Odisha to spread the knowledge of Oneness. Divya Darshan stands on three pillars. First, one should do his duties diligently to the best of one's abilities; Second, one should practice divine qualities like (Thyaga, Sanjama, Sadhana, Seva, Satya, Prema and khyama) to live harmoniously in society; Third, one must develop an intense longing for self-knowledge which alone will lead to self-realisation. Sadguru is not asking to do Asana, Pranayama, Dhyana, counting of beads, idol worship, reading of scriptures etc. He has shown the path to be a good house-holder; to live in society and at the same time realise ones' Self.

Sadguru Sri Sri Arjun says, "If you want to be free from sins, change your mind. Because when the mind changes everything else changes. It is ignorance that breeds sins. Sins breed sufferings. Therefore acquire the light of knowledge to dispel the darkness of ignorance. If you want to live, be dutiful; if you want peace and happiness, possess divine qualities; if you want liberation, acquire self-knowledge. Without self-knowledge, liberation is impossible. You have forgotten your Self which means you have lost your Self. Regain your lost paradise. You are forever immortal and free."

❦ ⋆ ❦

Prologue

[1]Today's man is at the peak of material enjoyment and luxurious living style, but there is constant decay in the moral standard of most of us. Character building seems to have been given a good-bye. It is not a priority today. Therefore, despite all prosperity there is increase in sufferings and mental unrest. Whatever we are doing is for earning peace and happiness, but the result is temporary. Suffering is the rule rather than exception. Whatever steps we take to enhance our level of happiness are ending up with misery, pains and sufferings. We are not able to know the actual source of happiness. We are unable to understand the basis of peace and bliss. With limited knowledge or out of ignorance whatever we have been doing ultimately brings us sufferings, although we always crave for happiness.

It is said that the people of Satya Yug were living in peace and happiness. At that time the material science had not developed so much and there was limited scope for material enjoyment. Real happiness can be had from out of spiritual knowledge. If we distance ourselves from spiritual knowledge we cannot get peace and happiness. Freedom shall remain still farther.

Sadguru Sri Sri Arjun, to guide mankind for getting rid of sufferings, has presented Divya Darshan in a quite simple style to suit one and all. Divya Darshan lays stress upon the basis of peace and happiness which is nothing other than spirituality. It means pursuing true knowledge and divine virtues by which he can move on the right path. By acquiring true knowledge, he can do away with the lacunae or misconceptions and take corrective steps.

By means of divine qualities he can live in peace and happiness in the society and move faster towards his goal.

Man must be good first. Thereafter he can do good to others and experience goodness within. Consequently he can get rid of all sufferings and realise Self. Self-knowledge is essential for peace, bliss and freedom. Without self-knowledge freedom is impossible. Man has been adopting different types of difficult practices for God realisation. But he is not conscious of knowing what goodness is and who God is. Hence, he is neither able to live peacefully nor attain God. He, who would try to know what goodness is must take recourse to goodness and conduct himself properly so as to live in peace and happiness, get rid of all sufferings, and realise God.

It should be remembered that human life is a secret and silent journey from humanity to divinity. Divinity is our destination. A thorough reading of the book can make our journey strategic and straight. Commonly, life is chaotic, full of digressions and dilemma without any specific purpose. It is as if we possess speed bereft of direction. We are intrinsically divine but have taken human form temporarily, which means our human appearance is only a passing phase. By our spiritual efforts and ingenuity, we can regain our lost paradise. This book shows the highway to a successful and worthy divine life which is our true nature where there is total absence of ignorance, sins and sufferings. In this context, Sadguru Sri Sri Arjun's famous gospel is worth mentioning. "Ignorance breeds sin. Sin breeds sorrows. Hence welcome knowledge and get rid of sufferings."

ೞ★ೞ

Ignorance and Sufferings

[This is a compilation of discourses of Sadguru Sri Sri Arjun. The main aim of all the discourses has been to make one aware that 'Ignorance is a great sin' and all efforts must be made to eradicate this ignorance and realise True Self. In this context, it may be mentioned that ignorance does not mean absence of knowledge; it refers to incomplete knowledge and incorrect knowledge. Here, knowledge refers to self-knowledge. In the course of His discourses, we find that we are in a journey of discovering our own Self; discovering our true identity. For this purpose, He is not asking us to undertake any strenuous practices or construct temples or visit forests for meditation; He is only asking us to develop the urge to know and understand True Self. He has explained the intricate concepts relating to Self with simple and day to day examples.]

[2]*["You never want sufferings, but your ignorance brings them to you. You are divine. Therefore, possess divine knowledge; desire for divinity and hold on to divine thoughts. Then only you can enjoy divine bliss."*

(Amritbindu-2)]

From the standpoint of the highest spiritual knowledge, the Creation is a manifestation of Brahman and as such it is pervaded by Brahman. But you consider yourself as jiva. Brahman's true nature is without attributes. He has manifested as Devas. Specific qualities are bestowed upon specific Devas. Through the process of transformation, Brahman manifested as Deva and thereafter as jiva with befitting qualities in them. You are all

---

divine because you have all descended from the unitary divine source. Therefore, your conscience agitates when you commit bad or sinful acts. You may consider conscience as Atman. Atman radiates as conscience in you. By your conscience you discriminate between good and bad. Buddhi is the domain of Devas. Sense organs are Tamasic and have more asuric (demoniac) tendencies. Sensing what is good or bad, is the effect of conscience. Although you are divine, you consider yourself as jiva and therefore, the impact of conscience in you becomes weaker. Jiva feeling has been entrenched in you very strongly due to the ignorance driven misperceptions and misfeasance which are carried through several births. In other words, ignorance is a chronic malady you suffer from. By acquiring right knowledge, you can correct your misperceptions and regain your divine nature.

Since your true nature is divine, you never welcome sufferings. There is no suffering in the divine nature. It is all good and just. You shun sufferings because you are eternally divine. Hence going back to Self is the only remedy for getting rid of sufferings. Darkness of ignorance has veiled all of you. Therefore, you all are committing various lapses. The demons are in deep darkness and therefore, they are so vicious and venomous. We are all suffering. This situation clearly indicates that we remain blinded by ignorance. Divine knowledge is faultless and free from ignorance. Therefore, acquire divine knowledge and get back your blissful self.

In the gross forms, made of five elements such as Earth, Water, Fire, Air and Ether, there are different qualities which are subtle. When Brahman willed to become many, He first manifested as tri-qualities (triguna) such as Sattva, Rajas and Tamas. All other qualities emanated from the tri-qualities. Every guna is a divine power which is invisible. Different gunas are latent in different objects designed purposefully with some utility value for the Creation. Quite a many do not understand the intrinsic qualities in the gross forms. Qualities were there before creation of forms through which the qualities found expression. The common people attach more importance to the gross forms because they come across the visible first. But the wise perceive the inner qualities or powers and accordingly utilize the same. A subtle body with all its qualities take a human form and considers himself to be a human being. He, who possesses divine qualities and divine powers, becomes a divine being or Deva. Brahman expresses Himself as knowledge and power. The more a person perceives these inner qualities or powers, the more he enjoys peace and bliss. Brahman has become the Devas. Hence, I (Sadguru Sri Sri Arjun) always urge upon you to acquire divine knowledge and develop divine virtues. By doing so, you shall realise that you are divine. This is the only way to get rid of sufferings.

Our parents and elders therefore always advise us to do good and be good. Divya Darshan therefore lays so much emphasis on divine knowledge. Whatever is done to acquire divine knowledge and inculcate divine feelings is called Sadhana or spiritual practice. For this, no educational qualification is necessary. An illiterate person can also realise True Self. Not by any external source but by his own potency, one can enjoy divine bliss. Everybody is an embodiment of Sat-Chit-Ananda. Scriptures reiterate this truth.

If you entertain divine feelings in you, you will not feel bad even if someone scolds you. You are already and always divine. How does it matter to you if somebody casts aspersions on you? We are not getting that divine bliss because we consider ourselves as jiva. Everyone must try to acquire divine knowledge. It is never impossible for you to enjoy the divine bliss.

೮౩★౮ౢ

[3]**Ignorance is the cause of sufferings.** It is knowledge that makes one pure and bright. Ignorance drags one towards death. Therefore, it is imperative that everyone should acquire more and more knowledge. I (Sadguru Sri Sri Arjun) do not have much education. But since I had intense craving for knowledge, I have come this far. He, who is knowledgeable, can unravel the mystery anywhere. The ignorant would commit mistakes, shall be punished and would suffer. When we fail in school examination, we feel sad and ashamed. He, who loves knowledge, can understand everything easily and correctly.

---

3   Oriya Divya Dhara Vol 10 Page 30

Knowledge is power. Knowledge is strength. The intelligent people make the less knowledgeable person work for them. The illiterate persons are subjugated and they keep on serving the educated people. Hence you must decide, whether you wish to be educated and become independent or grope in ignorance and depend upon others? He, who would take to knowledge, can enjoy freedom. The sages are free. If you look at the history of mankind, you will see that a nation plagued by ignorance is always subjugated by a nation of educated and intelligent men. Look at any animal. It cannot come out of a surrounding fence on its own. A bumble bee, if it enters into a room, cannot come out easily. It bangs its head against the window panes. Sometimes, it falls and dies after making vain attempts repeatedly.

The ignorant persons suffer. The more the ignorance, the more one undergoes sufferings. A person without knowledge or sense is as good as dead. He, who possesses knowledge, radiates life and lustre. Just as it is a shame not to know our own parents, similarly it is also a shame not to know our Creator. God is Supreme who has created everything. The man is not able to realise Him.

By knowing whom nothing remains to be known; by attaining whom, nothing else remains to be attained, He is the Supreme Lord, and everyone should try to realise Him.

It would not help you in getting success in your examination if you merely put a pot full of water at the door of your house while going to examination, considering the same as an auspicious sign. If you really evince interest in learning and make efforts, you will succeed. You must make yourselves fit to receive the blessings of your teachers. Suppose I want to hand over some object, say, a glass tumbler to you; if you are interested to receive the same from me, you need to extend your hands and with full concentration you must receive the same. Otherwise, the glass tumbler may fall and break. Guru is imparting knowledge with love wishing that the disciple should get knowledge, but if he does not receive it with interest, how would he get? Hence both the giver and taker should be sincere while handing over and receiving.

Guru is God. Guru builds the life for us. You are in darkness of ignorance. Guru would give you the light of knowledge. One should not leave or forget Guru and be like a baby monkey who clings to its mother with its tiny hands. The sages used to believe, serve and respect their Gurus. He, who does not possess faith, devotion and attitude of service, cannot be great. A student must think that knowledge is his life or vital energy and by this knowledge he is going to attain God. Some persons ask, "Why should one try to think about God from childhood?" It is to be remembered that from childhood if we start learning, we will acquire complete knowledge at a matured age. Otherwise we shall repent in old age pondering why we did not acquire knowledge from the childhood. Whole life may be spent by committing sins or wrong doings. Hence always keep in mind to experience God. He, who is truthful, evinces more interest in acquiring knowledge. I am citing an example from the Upanishad. The story runs like this. Narada was a great devotee of Lord Vishnu. Narada used to chant God's name always but in spite of that he was not having peace of mind. Sanat Kumar was a realiser although he was younger to Narada. Narada one day approached Sanat Kumar and sought his guidance to tide over his sadness and sufferings. Sanat Kumar said, "You are staying with Lord Vishnu and learnt a lot of things. How is that you are still suffering?" Narada replied, "Although I have read Tantra, Yoga, Vedas, I am still not getting peace and bliss. Hence please tell me how I can get peace." Sanat Kumar said, "Without self-knowledge, one cannot get peace and bliss."

Many persons ask the question, "What is the benefit of acquiring Self-knowledge?" Man wants peace and bliss always. Whatever is good and auspicious is Self-knowledge. Self is there inside all of us. He is Peace Absolute and Bliss-Absolute. That is why we all seek peace and bliss. We all want to live freely and with bliss. Atman is Self. "When Atman is Peace-Absolute, why I am not having peace? Why I am suffering?" So, we all must contemplate on what Atman or True Self is. We should always contemplate on all good things. A true realiser only can live in peace and bliss. But since we are ignorant about Self, we say that self-knowledge is not necessary for a good living. It is to be remembered that other material objects cannot give us peace. Peace is not available outside like any other commodity.

We must acquire true knowledge to get peace from within. Unless we start learning now itself, how shall we have the same? All want to live in peace and happiness. Hence, we must acquire full knowledge in this life. At the old age if we start learning, that will be too little and too late. We must first get admitted into first standard so that we shall be elevated to post-graduate class step by step. Since we want peace and bliss, we must acquire self-knowledge. Rishi Sukadev was wise from his childhood. Jagadguru Sri Shankaracharya also acquired knowledge at a young age. Hence, knowledge about self is of utmost priority. One must know the Self by his own self. Guru must be respected; otherwise knowledge cannot be passed on to the disciple. Disregarding Guru amounts to disregarding knowledge. When we respect our elders, it means we are respecting their knowledge and experience. If you have devotion towards Guru, you would be blessed by Goddess Saraswati. All Devas are with Guru. Hence the sages were praying," Guru Brahmaa Guru Vishnu Gurudeva Maheswar, Guru sakshat Param Brahman tasmai Sri Gurave namoh." Like this none other has been adored. With this *bhava*, if Guru is prayed or respected, one will get His blessings.

☙✶❧

[4]Knowledge is there uniformly everywhere. There is no increase or decrease. The apparent difference is due to difference in forms and qualities. To explain this, we normally divide it into two parts such as sentient and insentient. There is no knowledge expressed in and through the insentient. But knowledge is expressed in varying degrees through the sentient. Man possesses more knowledge than animals. Different men possess different levels of knowledge.

Knowledge that is expressed in the humans is limited only. But man actually possesses a lot of knowledge. Even though knowledge acquired in thousands of previous births is stored in him, only that much knowledge as is relevant to this human birth, finds expression in him. He forgets all other knowledge. That means most of his knowledge remain in dormant state. Since man functions with his limited knowledge, there occur many mistakes in his

---

4   Oriya Divya Dhara Vol 3 Page 1

actions or behaviour. For example- a baby may put his finger into the fire not knowing what it is. Somebody may take poison mistaking the same for some eatable. Therefore, man suffers. When he is suffering, it is to be understood that he is having ignorance. Ignorance is not total absence of knowledge. It is limited or fragmented knowledge. Due to ignorance he does not understand good or bad, truth or untruth, vice or virtue. Due to his limited knowledge he cannot understand something fully and that is why he commits mistakes and sins. Sins give rise to sufferings. Where there is sin, there is suffering. Where there is sin, there is ignorance. Ignorance is likened to darkness. In darkness man cannot see things and very often gets into problems. Similarly, due to ignorance he undergoes sufferings. Lord Buddha had said, "Desire is the cause of sufferings."

Divya Darshan asks, "Why desires? What is to be desired and what not?" Man does not know the answer properly due to ignorance. Due to such ignorance, man, instead of seeking his goal, moves on opposite routes or in wrong direction. In other words, he craves for temporary pleasure and suffers thereafter. Due to ignorance he nurtures doubts, anxieties and fear only to suffer.

An ignorant person cannot see or experience things correctly, cannot speak properly and cannot hear properly. By acquiring knowledge only he improves himself to lead a better life. Knowledge in fact is his vital energy. Due to vital energy a man survives. Jnana expresses itself when he has prana (life principle or vital energy) in him. Without prana he is dead.

Therefore, he, who understands the greatness of knowledge, seeks knowledge and acquires knowledge; he can thereby lead a better life and mitigate his sufferings. Ultimately, he would enjoy eternal bliss and liberation by acquiring more knowledge. He would also get rid of his sufferings. Human life can be divided into three stages.

- ❖ Survival

- ❖ Harmonious living in society with peace and happiness

- ❖ Seeking the goal of his life i.e. self-realisation.

Man should acquire knowledge for the maintenance of his body. He should have adequate knowledge regarding his food and drinks. Even the parents fail to take proper care of the children due to want of proper knowledge on what food to eat and what food to avoid.

This body is made of five gross elements which are changeable. Body is also subject to changes. Due to change in climatic conditions also body is affected. Without adequate knowledge to handle these adverse situations man suffers.

The second stage is harmonious social living with peace and happiness. Divine qualities are essential for this. Man suffers more as he possesses demoniac qualities such as greed, infatuation, anger and crookedness. Demoniac qualities are followed by sufferings. Man's ego also brings him sufferings. It is seen that many people are not in good terms with their neighbours even. Some people are seen to be quarrelling with fellow passengers in buses and trains. Due to ignorance man suffers.

Human birth has some specific purpose. Man is different from and far superior to animals. With self-restraint and good social behaviour, he has to live with others with mutual help and cooperation. Then only he can enjoy peace and happiness. Instead of friendship, love and affection, if we create more enmity with others, they will also try to retaliate. There would be distrust and disturbances.

Due to jealousy also people suffer. Instead of being sympathetic towards others' causes, people, at times, celebrate on others' adversities. If someone flourishes, they become intolerant and jealous. This is how we invite sufferings due to mistuned mind-set.

The third stage is to realise our goal. The goal of every human being is liberation or self-realisation. Almost all of us live aimlessly. Hence whatever we are doing is fraught with faults. Everyone must try for self-development. The Greek philosopher Socrates had said, "Ignorance is a great sin".

Divya Darshan further elucidates as follows. Man commits sins due to ignorance. Due to ignorance man is not able to discriminate between truth and untruth, Dharma and Adharma, vice and virtue. Directionless, he sails whimsically. Multiple mistakes recur resulting in sufferings. Whenever there is any mistake, that means, there is some untruth. Wherever there is untruth, there is Adharma and injustice. Wherever any of these negativities is present, sins may be committed. Sins are bred and nurtured by ignorance. Ignorance is embedded with sin, not only sin but great sin. This means not acquiring knowledge or not evincing interest in knowledge is a great sin. It follows that knowledge is essential to get rid of sufferings. By knowledge we can do the righteous things. Our loopholes get plugged and we enjoy happiness.

Our goal is to go back to the point from where we all originated. This is called realisation of true self. With limited knowledge, suffering is inevitable. Limited or fragmented knowledge shall bring in doubts, despair, fear and anxieties. Liberation means freedom from all these. Our long journey shall come to an end once we realise our true self which is Bliss-Absolute. It is a state of total absence of sufferings. Why everyone automatically gathers knowledge and experience? This is because our journey is to attain complete knowledge in the state of liberation which is our ultimate and only goal.

The Law of Karma is always operative. Our good actions yield good results whereas wrongful actions yield bad results. When we are suffering it is to be understood that we have committed some wrongdoings somewhere. We cannot identify our own mistakes. We think we are right. This is due to ignorance. Due to arrogance we do not confess our faults. Rather we stubbornly stick to our guns thereby inviting further problems.

Some examples of ignorance:

If somebody says something to us which is beyond our knowledge, we cannot understand the same properly. We are not able reply also when needed.

A student of a lower class fails to understand the syllabi of a higher class.

A child commits mistakes in the childhood. At that time, he does not understand his mistakes. He comes to know his mistakes only at a subsequent stage i.e. when his level of knowledge goes up.

A student, while writing on the examination paper, thinks he has written everything correctly, but the examiner finds mistakes in his answer sheet and accordingly reduces his marks. This is because the teacher's knowledge is more than that of the student.

Wherever there is a flaw, there is suffering. But man does not realise his flaws. He only blames others or his fate.

Knowledge is there everywhere. Man does not evince interest in knowledge. He gropes in darkness of ignorance only to suffer. When shall man try to dispel his ignorance?

Different qualities are seen in different forms. Different forms are there corresponding to different qualities. Fire looks bright and has burning power. Water is a liquid. Hence it flows downward. Tree has its own qualities. Dog or cat has its own qualities. Similarly, man also possesses certain qualities.

It is consciousness that takes different forms and qualities. Every form or quality has some power which depends upon the situations and circumstances. For example- a matchstick contains fire which remains dormant. Fire would come out from the same when we strike the stick against the match box. When there is friction, sparks would come out of a stone or a metal.

By the power of consciousness or knowledge, we protect ourselves, influence others, understand others etc. To understand and explain things is also a power. This power is called knowledge or consciousness. Consciousness manifests in various forms and qualities. Man is also a form of consciousness. According to past impulses, situations and circumstances, consciousness expresses itself. Every individual has different level of consciousness or knowledge. With that level of knowledge, he acts, reacts and perceives things or happenings. He cannot understand consciousness or power of higher level. There are gradations, variations in the levels of consciousness which are again different in different persons, animals and plants etc. Hence a lower level of consciousness cannot understand the level of higher consciousness. We do not know or understand things due to our ignorance. In other words, not knowing or not understanding is ignorance.

Ignorance remains with everyone. Therefore, everyone cannot understand everything. Hence fear and doubts overwhelm a person. Ultimately, he suffers.

Even though a person remains in ignorance, he considers himself to be a Jnani (Knowledgeable) and behaves as if he knows everything. Partial knowledge is considered by him as total knowledge. This is also due to ignorance. This happens because everything is distinct from the other with regard to differences in forms, shapes or sizes, differences in qualities, properties or tendencies.

Without knowing things completely man considers himself to be very wise and experienced. Is it not ignorance? The ignorant man cannot know that he is ignorant. This is also due to ignorance.

He, who knows more and more about 'good', and comes in contact with 'good', would become good. Due to ignorance we do not know 'good' as good or 'bad' as bad. We know truly little. Had we known 'good' completely, we would have preferred 'good' and become 'good'. We would have lived life with peace and happiness. But man is not able to lead life happily. This indicates his ignorance. Neither we know completely what good is nor do we know completely what bad is. Therefore, we cannot come closer to 'good'. At the same time, we cannot distance ourselves from 'bad'. By doing good and being good we can save ourselves from sufferings. Due to ignorance we do not accept or appreciate this simple statement. Therefore, it is reiterated by Divya Darshan that ignorance is the cause of sufferings.

☙ ⋆ ❧

[5]Human birth is the best creation of God. It is an exceedingly rare and fair form craved for even by Devas. It is because God-realisation is possible only through human birth. After eighty four lakh of births, this human form is made available. Hence the sages call the humans as scions of

---

5   Oriya Divya Dhara Vol 5 Page 4

immortality. It is also said in the scriptures that when someone's virtues are more than 50% (i.e. vices are less than 50%), one gets human birth. Therefore, it can be well imagined how valuable the human birth is. Therefore, how much care and caution is to be taken in a human birth! But normally people do not pay attention to this aspect. Due to indifference and ignorance, this human birth is more or less wasted by many.

Many people are under the erroneous impression that death is the end and after death nothing remains. Many people do not believe in rebirth. In this birth if we earn more virtues than vices, we shall be reborn as humans. Virtuous people are born as sages who are superior to the ordinary human beings. If virtues are more than the vices, one would be born in a better environment where there shall be more purity, righteousness, knowledge and wisdom. The vices drag us downward. When the vices are more than the virtues, such persons are born as demons or sub-human creatures. Therefore, man should lead his life cautiously so as to have more purity and righteousness in his conduct for a better and more qualitative future life. Life is like a game of Ludo consisting of snakes and ladders. Virtues are like ladders that elevate us whereas vices, which are likened to snakes, cause our downslide. By virtues man earns happiness and peace by coming nearer to God whereas due to vices he moves farther from God. Every moment, man impelled by his nature earns either virtues or vices. The choice lies with the man. At times he is compelled by circumstances to commit vices and ultimately he suffers. At times, we deliberately commit sins and at times we unknowingly commit sins. First, we should have knowledge about virtues and vices and also about how to earn virtues and do away with sins. Sins result in sufferings. Virtues give us peace and happiness. To get rid of sufferings, we must make efforts to increase our virtues otherwise we would slip down to animal category. We are intrinsically virtuous beings but due to various desires and different circumstances, we remain away from virtues and consequently we suffer.

We serve our family and others. This is also a virtue. We help the poor. This is a virtue. If we consciously try to earn more virtues by avoiding sins, at the end we would be able to maximise our virtues. This means our future birth in still better environment is secured for us thus paving the way for self-development.

In our day to day life, all our actions yield either virtues or vices. This we are not aware of and that is why we are not able to develop much.

When we cook food, many insects are killed. Many small creatures die when we do our day to day work. The scriptures have prescribed 'Pancha Maha Yajna' as atonement for these sins committed by us unknowingly. Those are Rishi Yajna or Brahma-Yajna, Deva Yajna, Pitru Yajna, Atithi Yajna and Bhuta Yajna.

By resorting to Rishi Yajna or Brahma Yajna we can get rid of all sins. Yajna means sacrifice. Through Pancha Yajna, we make sacrifices for the lower animals and birds by feeding them. We take care of the persons who come to our place; we pay homage to our fore-fathers and different Devas to get their blessings. Because we are not conscious of increasing our punya, we are doing nothing for earning the same. It is to be remembered that due to virtues earned in our previous births we are born as humans and getting some peace and happiness. Due to sins also we are suffering. It is to be remembered that results would accrue depending upon the quality of karma we undertake. Everyone should think how to live happily and peacefully.

Many religions in the world have been preaching how to get rid of sufferings. In the past many sages were born who imparted knowledge to mankind on how to get rid of sufferings but we do not evince interest in the preaching or guidance given to us by the sages of yesteryears as a result of which we are not able to earn that much of virtues which we are supposed to earn by remaining a little more alert.

The Creation is managed and regulated by one law which is known as the Law of Eternity. Although there is elaborate preaching on how to get rid of sufferings, people are not able to get rid of sufferings. Why is it so? All religions are advocating for establishment of peace but where is peace? This means, man is not able to realise the truth (essence) of all such preaching. The people of yesteryears for example, of Satya Yug, Tretya Yug and

Dwapara Yug, had realised the scriptural instructions and were conducting themselves properly whereas now a days, we worship different Gods and Goddesses to propitiate them to get rid of sins and sufferings. Still we are not able to escape from the sufferings.

Some people believe that even after committing sins, if they approach God for forgiveness, God will forgive, and they would be saved from punishments. But the Law is that one must get the results of past actions. Good actions yield good results. This is the Law of Karma. No amount of worshipping would give any reprieve. Some scriptures prescribe atonement for some sins committed. When one repents for his wrong doings, he would learn lessons from it and won't repeat the same. This is the idea. If he repeats, he must be punished by the Law. Personal godheads are not empowered to break the Law of Karma. This Law of Karma comes under the ambit of the Law of Eternity which is the Will of the Supreme.

Man should acquire true knowledge by which he would refrain from wrong doings. In future, wrong doings should not be repeated particularly after knowing the implications and consequences of sinful acts. Why does a man commit mistakes? It is because man cannot identify his own mistakes. He considers it right even while moving in a wrong direction.

With increased knowledge, he can know his past mistakes which he had been committing.

When he would learn about Dharma and Adharma, virtues and vices, justice and injustice by reading scriptures or by meeting spiritual teachers, he can know what is right and what is wrong. Then only his mistakes would be reduced. In absence of true knowledge or right knowledge man would be erring from time to time. Now-a-days many turn out to be disbelievers. They have distanced themselves from true knowledge. They are not afraid of committing sins. As a result, they undergo sufferings of various types. Many people worship some Gods and Goddesses. They do not possess the knowledge about the greatness and specific powers of personal godheads. Even some new Gods and Goddesses with different names and looks are created out of pure imagination. We worship a specific personal godhead and ask of him/her many things at a time. But the personal godheads have specific powers. They are like the Heads of different Departments in any organisation. One department cannot fulfil all requirements. Action comes under our choice. But the results are the prerogative of God or Ishwar. The ignorant man is not interested to know the unitary God who is all powerful. Spiritual knowledge gets last priority by some people. According to them belief in God is a superstition.

Due to inadequate knowledge even the theists who worship God in different manners do not get the desired results. Their wishes are not fulfilled. The fact that sufferings are there indicates that God does not fulfil all our wishes. People carry bundle of desires. All material desires cannot be fulfilled. God of our imagination cannot help us in any way. We shall not get rid of sufferings in this manner. We must acquire knowledge and make our own arrangements to get rid of our sufferings. God of our imagination cannot give us a chocolate even. He cannot give us cooked food. But He has provided us with all materials and knowledge to cook food. We must make use of our knowledge and prepare food for our use. He cannot give us a piece of cloth. We are to make use of our knowledge to manufacture the same for our use. He cannot give us a house. All materials are there in His Creation. We are to utilise our knowledge to build our houses according to our requirement. God does not act for fulfilling an individual's wishful thinking. How can God of our imagination protect us? How can God, who is made by us, fulfil all our needs? In fact, the maker is more powerful than the made and in this case we are the makers.

The scriptures speak about the unitary, all-pervasive and all-powerful Brahman who can do everything including creation, maintenance and dissolution. Brahman is called by the sages as 'Prajnanam Brahman.' Brahman manifests as knowledge. Brahman manifests as everything in this Creation. He is both the material cause and the efficient cause. He is Energy-Absolute and Consciousness-Absolute. He manifests as knowledge, strength, vital energy etc. If man wills, he can, by dint of knowledge and intellect, do wonders and even can attain the Supreme State. One need not ask for everything from God. He has given us knowledge by which we can have anything we like to have. By knowledge and efforts everything is possible. Hence Divya Darshan emphasises on acquisition of knowledge.

A question may be asked here. How some people get their desired objects by doing idol worship? The answer is Reflection Theory. Our *bhava* gets reflected. Whatever is to happen, happens. Nothing is done by God or Goddess of the devotee's imagination.

Scriptures say that Brahman is Peace-Absolute, Bliss-Absolute and Freedom Absolute. He, who knows Him as such, also gets peace, bliss and freedom. Whatever man seeks, God has already provided all those in advance i.e. much before his seeking. Since we do not have any idea about the Reality, we are not able to know about His systems and arrangements. We are always after the God or Goddess of our imagination.

How does a man survive? To this question, man's intellect will fail to answer. By His energy only, we are doing everything; our food gets digested, blood gets circulated, heart functions; we are able to sleep and wake up from sleep. We also experience different kinds of dreams. Although everything occurs due to Him, we are not able to understand His role. The ignorant man only asks for something or other from Him instead of trying to understand Him. Every moment the humans, the animals and the plants owe their existence to God only. Whatever is required for sustenance, He has already made adequate provisions well in advance.

Before a baby is born, milk is stored in the mother's breast. Before something is created, everything is provided for its sustenance. If man really wants to know God, he can get everything, even beyond his imagination. Therefore, in order to get rid of sufferings we must know the Almighty and surrender to Him. The more we know Him, the more we get peace and bliss.

Atheists are in a sense better than the ordinary devotees who, guided by their superstitious beliefs undertake different types of rituals to appease God or Goddess of their imagination. The atheists would never worship such imaginary God or Goddess who cannot give anything. Due to this they close all doors to God. But if the atheists would try to know the Reality as described in the scriptures, they can better understand the

Almighty who is Energy-Absolute and Consciousness-Absolute. We do everything with our limited or fragmented knowledge. Mostly we do opposite things and not the right things. We are not interested to acquire true knowledge. With limited knowledge whatever is done, mistakes are bound to be there. The results of wrong doings are suffering. We carry wrong notion that by appeasing God, we shall be forgiven. That is why we have no hesitation in repeating our wrong doings. Hence there is no end to our sufferings. According to Lord Buddha, the suffering that has come has to depart. It was not there before. It has come now. It must go. We do not know when it shall go. Lord Buddha has described truth in four steps. That there is suffering is a truth. That there is some cause of suffering is a truth. Suffering has come; it shall pass away. This is also a truth. There is some cause of suffering. There is also some cause of cessation of suffering. Once the cause is identified suffering would vanish. This is the fourth truth. Lord Buddha says, when man shall realise the root cause of sufferings from that time onwards, he would get rid of sufferings.

When we do not try to understand the root cause of sufferings, how shall we get rid of sufferings? Once cause is known the remedial steps can be taken. But instead of trying to know the cause of suffering and taking remedial measures we start worshipping various personal godheads. The Law of Karma cannot be transgressed by any personal godhead. To get rid of sufferings, it is essential for the man to know God's Laws called the Law of Eternity. Man has to follow the laws to get happiness, peace and bliss.

There are three qualities such as Sattva, Rajas and Tamas. Sattva is superior to Rajas and Tamas. Tamas is inferior to Rajas. Generally, man possesses Rajas. Sattva is a divine quality. Tamas is a demoniac quality. In between there is rajas which is a human quality. Since man stands in between, he tells truth as well as lies. Hence, he at times enjoys happiness and at times he suffers. To enhance his level of happiness, he has to move towards Sattva which is a divine quality. Man survives due to Truth. But many people believe that man cannot live properly if he always sticks to truth. This is due to ignorance. Truth is everyone's life and vital energy. Without truth man cannot live even for a second. Some examples can be cited here.

When the husband comes back home for lunch from his work place, he finds his food ready and his wife dishes out the food. It is a truth that her husband would come at a specific time for lunch and therefore she keeps things ready. If the husband violates the truth or the wife violates the truth, both shall suffer and there would be disturbances in the family. This indicates that observance of truth makes our life smooth and peaceful. A thief also honours truth knowingly or unknowingly and divides the loot as agreed upon; otherwise his gang would break up. He also tells truth and takes care of his family. Due to ignorance we are not able to understand how truth brings us peace and happiness. Violation of truth would create all sorts of disturbances or chaos. Man suffers because he does not follow truth as much as he should follow. Violations are there. This is the cause of sufferings. Since we do not realise the importance of truth, we tend to violate and suffer.

Everyone craves for truth. People do wrong things, but they go to courts for judgement in their favour. In other words, they knock the door of righteousness and justice. Would it save them from sufferings? God's Court of Justice is Supreme, perfect and impartial. Sinners never go unpunished. Trespassers must be prosecuted. Therefore, observance of truth is so essential.

❧✦❧

[6]Because of divine qualities such as love and forgiveness, we maintain our families and live peacefully in the family. Without this quality, our family life would have been miserable. We would not have tolerated the wrongdoings of our children. Because our parents are having the qualities of love and forgiveness, we have grown up to this stage. All our mistakes have been forgiven. We in our lifetime might have picked up quarrels or entered into heated arguments with our friends and neighbours but we have forgotten all those without carrying feeling of vengeance. Like this, divine qualities are there in the kingdom of nature. These are all provisions by God for a smooth and orderly sustenance of the Creation. Due to

---

6   Oriya Divya Dhara Vol 5 Page 15

ignorance man is unable to know that he survives due to divine qualities. He, who possesses more of divine qualities, leads a better and more peaceful life.

From the beginning God has made all provisions for us to live in peace, bliss and freedom. But we are not able to realise this. We habitually go on begging to God for something or other. God would be smiling at our ignorance-driven implorations.

When we can understand God's perfect arrangements, we cannot ask for anything else. If we want bliss, we must develop and practise the divine qualities in us. If we love all, everyone will love us back and we shall enjoy peace and happiness. If we ask for bliss from God, we cannot get but if we love others, we can get bliss. Bliss is a matter of self experience. It is not a gross object which can be handed over to anyone. Possessing negative qualities such as malice and hatred, if we ask for peace and happiness from God is it not our ignorance? These negative qualities are opposites of love and bliss. God's arrangements are all perfect. Nothing extra remains to be offered to the man. The Creation is already enriched and complete with all perquisites and pre-requisites. We are only to know and conduct ourselves suitably by properly utilising His provisions.

A characteristic aspect of all divine qualities is that they get doubled when they come back to us. If we serve others we shall be served by thousands of people. If we love others, we shall be loved by them. By utilising the divine virtues all our basic needs can be fulfilled. Divine virtues cannot be borrowed from anyone. It is already there in us. It would never get exhausted. The more one holds on to divine virtues, the more he would have it. All these come under the purview of the Law of Eternity. As long as man is not aware of the Law of Eternity, he is bound to undergo sufferings. No personal godheads can save us from sufferings. When man would try to acquire true knowledge, and realise the indispensability of divine virtues, he would live in peace, happiness and bliss. If people conduct themselves with divine virtues, the earth we live in shall become a heaven. Divine virtues cannot be bought by material wealth.

By material wealth, we enjoy some happiness which is but for a temporary period. Material wealth is also exhaustible. But divine qualities which are abundantly bestowed upon us never get exhausted. The bliss that we get is permanent and auspicious. If divine qualities are active in someone, it is to be understood that God is getting manifested through him. The sages and seers did not possess material wealth, but they possessed the wealth of divine virtues by which they were leading blissful life. The rich people although have all sorts of luxuries and comforts at their disposal, may not have mental peace.

Sadguru Sri Sri Arjun says, "Oh Mankind! Try to understand the importance of knowledge and divine virtues and get inclined towards the same. Then only Satya Yug can return. There is no greater Dharma than inculcation of divine virtues. Divine virtues are the essence of the Law of Eternity."

Acquiring true knowledge is the most appropriate worship of God. If man tries to understand the all-perfect arrangements of God for alleviating the sufferings of man, he will understand it more and more and live in peace and bliss while getting rid of all sufferings.

⋆

[7]We all suffer. Suffering is always there. We have heard of Satya Yug and Rama Rajya in Tretya Yug. People were living in peace and happiness during those days. People at that time were not keeping their precious possessions under lock and key. But now-a-days, that environment of trust is awfully missing.

What is the difference between Satya Yug and Kali Yug? Primarily one difference is there. That is difference in knowledge level. People of yesteryears were keen to acquire knowledge on truth, righteousness, piety and justice. They were reflecting such knowledge in their conduct. Now-a-days no such education is imparted in schools and colleges i.e. how to live on the path of righteousness and truth. Now-a-days, students are taught how to earn money with the misconception that money can buy happiness and peace. How to earn mental peace? In absence of right knowledge,

---

7   Oriya Divya Dhara Vol 5 Page 19

how can anyone get peace and happiness? Hence there are recurring instances of falsehood, greed and hatred etc. which are opposite to divine qualities. Man is not able to sleep peacefully. There are doubts and anxieties, fear and despair. Man is worried and tense. There seems to be gradual degradation under the pretext of advancement. The reason is paucity of true knowledge. In the Satya Yug, people were getting true knowledge because of the favourable environment. There were Gurukul *ashrams* in many places which were imparting knowledge on truth and righteousness. Saints and sages were many. The kings and rulers were also patronising the Gurukul *ashrams* as a result of which more and more people were receiving true knowledge. Today's man does not appreciate the essential nature of true knowledge. Only a few persons are evincing interest in spiritual knowledge i.e. divine knowledge. How shall one know when one is not at all interested to know? Since we have distanced ourselves from true knowledge we are suffering. Man, with his limited knowledge, considers himself knowledgeable although he may be at an extremely low level of knowledge viewed from the point of view of true knowledge. When we are not able to live in peace, it is to be inferred that we are away from right knowledge.

The knowledge pertaining to peace, bliss and freedom is called true knowledge or right knowledge. One should therefore try to acquire that knowledge and conduct himself accordingly. In other words, by acquiring right knowledge one can discriminate between good and bad so as to live happily. A man never wants to receive anything bad. He makes his choice for good only. People think that they know what is good and what is bad for them; nothing remains to be learnt. But actually, we do not know what good is. That is why we are in unrest and anxieties. We know very little about what good is whereas we are supposed to fully know what good is. Everyone's self is good. Everyone is intrinsically good ab initio. Hence hankering for good is intrinsic to everybody.

Should we proceed towards deeper darkness and get sufferings? The common answer to this question would be 'No'. Everyone's conscience seeks peace, happiness and bliss. Therefore, God has bestowed upon man the quality of inquisitiveness. Why every human is endowed with this quality? Has God sent us here only to suffer? God is Truth, Knowledge and Bliss. Then how is it that His kingdom is destined to suffer? We are actually destined to attain bliss and freedom. But it is a matter of regret that even though we are children of God, we are suffering. Whatever temporary happiness we happen to enjoy is insignificant. Our sufferings outweigh the occasional happiness. Everyone should think, "Why am I suffering? What are the reasons?" Man should try to know the root cause of sufferings. The root cause is that man does not know the truth completely. Truth is there everywhere. Once man knows the truth, he can get peace and bliss and thus get rid of all sufferings.

We know that Oxygen and Hydrogen mix in the right proportion to form water. But the ancient men did not understand water like we understand now in this scientific age. They also did not know the multiple use of water because of their lesser knowledge about water. Similarly, earlier when electricity was invented, it was used to get only light. Now-a-days, with increased knowledge about electricity, we can put it into multifarious uses. The more we know the truth about electricity, the more are we able to utilise the same for different purposes. Hence man should acquire knowledge to enhance his happiness. There are also various truths which we must know to get peace, bliss and freedom. Since we are not aware of all such truths, we are not able to get peace, bliss and freedom. A body builder wants to remain healthy always. He chooses his food habits properly and practises different physical exercises to maintain his body and remain fit. Likewise, the right knowledge that is required for earning peace, bliss and freedom should also be acquired and practised.

God has already made all arrangements for the man to get peace, bliss and freedom. But even though man is bestowed with the power of inquisitiveness from the birth itself, man does not utilise the same to know more and more about God's scheme of things. As a result of this indifference, he suffers.

Spiritual knowledge teaches how a man can live in peace and happiness; how he can enjoy bliss; wherefrom he came; who is God; after death where shall he go and what his true self is. But when question of spiritual knowledge comes man questions the same and thoughtlessly makes adverse comments. He questions the relevance of spiritual subject matter. He asserts, "I am doing my duties and making my living."

Who does not want peace and happiness? The obvious reply is "everyone wants peace and happiness." For this, spiritual knowledge must be acquired.

⊱✦⊰

[8]We all hear about Atman. Atman resides in everybody. Because Atman is there, we are able to see, hear, speak and are able to make movements. But who is Atman? How does Atman reside in the body? How Atman expresses itself as different energy and power? A common man cannot understand this so easily. Why do we take food, why do we want to live, why do all of us want peace and happiness? All these natural instincts are there for attainment of Self or Atman. Since Atman is there in all beings, the knowledge relating to Atman is called self-knowledge or spiritual knowledge. All expressions and experiences of Atman through the gross body are called spiritual knowledge. It is about the Self. We utter the word 'I' which ordinarily denotes the body, mind, intellect and ultimately Atman. But we are not evincing interest to know about ourselves. Is it not something wrong and regrettable? Importance is given only to eating and surviving. If so, then what is the need for a human birth? Animals also eat and live. They are not required to toil for hours together. They do not carry any worries or anxieties about their present or future. Why the human being has been endowed with conscience? What is the speciality of human birth? The aim of human birth is to realise the true self. Common people cannot understand and appreciate this. To explain this truth, many ancillary subjects have to be discussed.

Why do we have eyes? The answer is to see. Why do we have ears? The answer is to hear. Similarly, why have you taken birth? The right answer is- for self-realisation.

Man has come to this world for a brief period, may be a few years. It is not his permanent abode. Man has come from Brahman. He is to return to Brahman. Since we do not know that we are destined to realise our true self

---

8   Oriya Divya Dhara Vol 5 Page 24

or return to Brahman, we go astray and undertake different wasteful pursuits losing sight of our goal.

To drive home the truth of realisation of our goal, the subject is discussed in question-answer form as follows.

- ❖ Q- Why do we eat?

- ❖ To survive

- ❖ Q- Why do we want to survive?

- ❖ To get peace and happiness.

- ❖ Q- Why do we all crave for peace and happiness?

- ❖ This is not a question. Even the questioner seeks peace and happiness. The answer therefore is so obvious. It is everyone's nature to seek peace and happiness.

The sages reiterate that Atman is Peace-Absolute, Bliss-Absolute and Freedom-Absolute. Since Atman resides in us, everyone instinctively seeks peace, bliss and freedom. In other words, since we are all intrinsically Peace-Absolute, Bliss-Absolute and Freedom-Absolute, we always crave for peace, bliss and freedom. In other words, we are living only to attain peace, bliss and freedom and for that we are to maintain our body and therefore take food.

But we are going on eating and spending days and years in an aimless manner. Our aimless wandering leads us away from peace, bliss and freedom. Sufferings and bondages always accompany us. Instead of opening the knots day by day, we are getting more entwined and constricted. Therefore, everyone should try to know his goal. Everyone should make efforts for self-realisation. We have taken birth only for this. Our eating, living and working etc. are therefore to be linked to this goal. Then only life shall move on a straight line and all knots would be opened one after another. All sins and sufferings shall vanish on self-realisation.

There are many ways to get rid of sufferings. I am now highlighting only on one part. We do not know what good is. Everyone should know what is good. God has gifted everyone with divine qualities like renunciation, restraint, spiritual practice, service, truth, love and forgiveness. To believe someone and to love others is a divine quality. Why has God bestowed upon us all these divine virtues? Because by these qualities, we can get peace, bliss and freedom that everybody instinctively seeks.

If we go a little deeper, we can find that we are able to live because of divine qualities. Our mother loves us and extends her desireless services to us as a result of which we are alive. Had we not got the services from mother we would not have survived. The entire Creation is sustained by divine qualities. The society would have been distressed, had there been no divine qualities. Every animal is able to live because of divine qualities. Tigress is a ferocious animal, but it breeds and brings up the cubs with so much care and love. The thieves also love their families and children and maintain them. When we go to any shop, the shopkeeper hands over the item to us, even before we make payment. He hands over the item first to us with the belief that the stipulated price would be paid by us at the end of all transactions. He also gives things to us on credit. This belief or trust is also a divine quality. From work place when we return home for lunch our wife serves us the food. She is sure that her husband would come home to have lunch. This is trust. Likewise, knowingly or unknowingly we all make use of divine qualities. If we consciously make use of the divine qualities, our sufferings shall go away, and we would lead a more peaceful life.

Man suffers due to demoniac qualities. The opposite of divine qualities are demoniac qualities. Due to increase in demoniac qualities, sufferings are on the rise in the society. We must give up the demoniac qualities and possess divine qualities to live in peace and happiness. Absence of divine qualities makes things difficult for us all around. There is absence of love and respect between the husband and the wife even. There are several instances of conflicts between father and son. Only when the demoniac qualities are given up and divine qualities are honoured and inculcated, Satya Yug shall reign. Divine virtues shall lead us to our divine destination. Divine virtues cannot be lost or stolen, burnt or dried up. The more one distributes, the more one shall have it.

All sages and seers had known the value of divine qualities and therefore they possessed these qualities. The greatness of divine qualities cannot be expressed in words. If someone possesses one divine quality, the other divine qualities would automatically be expressed in him. In other words, all divine qualities shall blossom in him simultaneously like the petals of a flower. While Lord Buddha had laid stress on truth and non-injury, Jesus had upheld love and forgiveness. Sri Chaitanya Dev and Meera bai had upheld love and devotion. A person in whom all the divine qualities blossom, what would happen to him is beyond our imagination. A spiritual mendicant should try to develop the latent divine qualities in him to reach the goal.

Even though the sages have been trying to impress upon us the importance of divine virtues, we do not listen to them but at the same time we seek peace and happiness. How can we get?

At times we say that we have lot of devotion towards God. But we do not evince interest to know anything about God. We simply make images of God out of our own imagination or dreams. Mentally we create some form with head, hands, legs, eyes and ears and name it as God. But we do not bother to know about the formless and all-pervasive God who is Consciousness-Absolute as described in the Vedas.

A renunciate takes shelter of God. A worldly person, if asked to take shelter of God or to have devotion towards God, would say, "Where is time for me? I am spending all my time for taking care of family. I am already overloaded." It is to be remembered that a householder gets more sufferings than a renunciate. The renunciate does not carry any burden of samsar; he has no worries; he is not entangled with the affairs of the society. But a householder encounters problems from different directions. Therefore, a householder should, to get rid of sufferings, pray to God and take shelter of God more than a renunciate does. But on the other hand, he says, "I have no time for God." Is it not opposite to what he should do?

If we go through the life history of some great devotees, we find that many wonderful things happened to them. People in general do not believe those things or take interest in such things. Many such examples of great devotees are cited which indicate that God is ever ready to come to our rescue. He is always beside us. But due to ignorance we are not able to experience His presence. The mythological character named Bhakta Prahllad had confidently replied to his father Hiranyakashyap, a demon king that God is there in the stone pillar also. Hiranyakashyap vehemently reacted to this and hit the pillar with his sword. Then and there, God came out in the form of Nrusingha and killed the demon king.

It is to be noted here that even though Prahllad was a small kid, he could confidently assert that God is everywhere. But we people ask, "Where is God?" Sri Ramakrishna Paramahansa used to give the example of a grinding stone. The lower stone remains fixed whereas upper stone revolves round the shaft because of which grinding of grains becomes possible. The grains which remain away from the centre are ground to dust whereas the grains which remain near the centre remain unbroken. Similarly, if one takes shelter of God one will not be torn by sufferings. If one distances oneself from God, suffering is inevitable. God is so powerful that he can manifest at His sweet will in any form he likes. The sages did not consider God as any form or or quality. They said, "Truth is God. Dharma is God."

God is all perfect and good. He, who takes shelter of goodness, is a true worshipper and would attain God.

Normally people are under the impression that one must renounce home; he has to go to jungle; he has to sacrifice even his food and water to maintain an austere life. But the truth is, one need not enter into fire; one need not stand single-legged or dip himself in water. The sages and seers were not doing this type of 'Tapas'. Only the demons were inflicting pain on their bodies and taking to very crude methods to appease God. The wise people know that God is all-pervasive. One can worship God from anywhere he likes. God would be happy with him, who would cling to Truth, Dharma or righteousness. One need not renounce one's family and go to jungle to attain God. "I am also a householder. Like you, I have family. One must try to know if any simpler way is there to attain God. Due to God's Grace, I could know those truths and am able to explain the same to you. Be sure, you need not go to any jungle and lead the life of a recluse." (Sadguru Sri Sri Arjun speaks about his own experience)

The question is whether only a renunciate would attain God? Whether the rest of us all would remain deprived of peace and happiness? Are we all destined to suffer like this? God designed His Creation for everyone's peace and happiness. God wants that everyone should come back to Him. Hence God has given two invaluable gifts such as inquisitiveness and divine qualities to everyone. Another great gift of God to man is 'Knowledge'. In absence of knowledge we would not have known anything; even our mother, father, the Sun, the Moon and the society. There would have been no possibility of knowing God. By knowledge we can understand and explain things. By knowledge we can communicate with others. Due to divine virtues we can live in peace and happiness in the society. Due to inquisitiveness, we can know more and more. God has bestowed upon us these qualities so that we would ultimately go back to Him. God has created everything we need. There is no deprivation anywhere. But due to want of adequate knowledge we are not able to understand the divine designs. We are not able to realise the importance of inquisitiveness, knowledge and divine virtues. When in danger, we bang our heads and pray to God for our rescue.

God has created everything for our well-being. If we commit any mistake en route and become desperate, God will help us. The devotee should say. "With my limited knowledge I am not able to understand you. Please give me more knowledge and patience to understand you." Then only God may help us.

We shall discuss here how God has made all sorts of arrangements for us. Before our birth He has made sky, air, fire, water and earth. He has made the plant kingdom and filled it with fruits, flowers, roots and herbs. Before a baby is born, he has made provision of milk in the mother. God has thus made complete arrangements for us to live in peace and bliss and to go back to Him. But man is not able to understand God's arrangements. By making proper use of inquisitiveness, knowledge and divine qualities in his daily life, man can go ahead and ultimately attain God.

The law by which man is created from Brahman and can merge with Brahman is called the Law of Eternity. The sages and seers experienced Him in and through the Law of Eternity. We are born; we live, and can get peace and happiness due to the Law of Eternity. If we do not try to know the Law of Eternity, then how shall we get peace and happiness? Therefore, lot of disturbances occur while living this life. In the scriptures such as the Vedas and the Upanishads, the Law of Eternity has been discussed well. The sages and seers impart that knowledge to the people at large in a simple manner.

We get surprised when we hear about the sages and seers of yesteryears. They were able to do impossible things. They were very powerful. Now also such knowledge is present. If anyone so wishes he can walk on water, enter fire and also can become invisible. If we evince interest to know we can learn the same at home. He, who takes shelter of God, would be protected by God. If God would not protect, He will also be at fault. But we are not able to realise that God is protecting us every moment. A person, who has faith and devotion towards God, and takes His shelter, would be protected by God.

Sometimes while walking in a lonely place, we have some fear and anxiety. Sometimes a dog would come and give company. Who knows, God might have given us company in such a form! When two persons quarrel with each other, a third person comes and convinces both for reconciliation. Who knows, the third person is sent by God for resolving the issues! We might have experienced many such things. Since we do not have any idea about the powers of God, we question His Existence.

Due to God's Will, we all have come into existence; we are able to survive; we are able to know so many things. But we question, "Where is God?" At times, I (Sadguru Sri Sri Arjun) ask a question, "Anybody is there who disowns his own existence?" Can anybody raise his hand to assert that he is not there? If somebody raises his hand I ask him, "If you are not there, then how could you raise your hand?" The power, by which you are able to say, "I am there, or I am not there", is God.

The power, by which we survive, speak, hear and experience, is God. If He won't be there the Creation also won't come into existence. He, who would know all these, can experience God every moment. He, who is not trying to know God, simply wastes his life. Those, who are trying to distance themselves from God and are not interested to know God, are bound to suffer.

To protect the human society and to know everything, God has given us knowledge and divine virtues. These two things are essential to get God's Grace and realise Him. The society is moving towards darkness due to want of true knowledge and divine qualities. When man would honour and inculcate divine virtues and right knowledge, world peace is bound to come. When we are all facing towards darkness, how shall we get peace and bliss? We must acquire true knowledge. Then only the earth can become a heaven. Satya Yug would be there all over. If man remains ignorant and possesses demoniac qualities, the society would undergo sorrows and sufferings. We must bring in Satya Yug. We have to change ourselves. Everyone is having truth and all powers within. But we are unaware of this invaluable gift of God. I have come to remind you of your latent knowledge and virtues. I have not come to give you anything new or extra. I have come to remind you that you are all divine and thereafter you have to activate the latent divine qualities.

It is God's will that everybody should get rid of sufferings and come back to Him. He, who would attain God, would be free from all sufferings. That is called liberation or emancipation. He, who would make use of inquisitiveness and divine qualities, would attain God in this birth itself. Many people set aside this subject being under the impression that one has to renounce the world and lead the life of a recluse. But it is not so.

I (Sadguru Sri Sri Arjun) never ask anybody to renounce anything like garlic, onion or non-veg food. I ask only to acquire true knowledge and inculcate divine virtues. When one would acquire higher knowledge, he would know the difference between poison and nectar. He would set himself right by acquiring divine virtues. He would possess more sattvic qualities. He would become more and more powerful day by day.

Oh, immortal souls! Try to delve deep into spirituality, synchronise your living style in accordance with God's Will and get rid of all sufferings.

✧

[9]We all undergo some kind of suffering or other. Suffering is always there. But in the Satya Yug and Tretya Yug, people were living happily. They were not even putting any lock on their door or on the box. But now-a-days, things have come to such a pass that thieves are active to break the lock and steal things. It may be seen that although they are same human beings, their thoughts (knowledge) are different. The people of Satya Yug had more knowledge in the sense that they knew well about Truth, Dharma and Righteousness. But now-a-days, there is no such subject in our syllabi. Our education system at best helps us to get a job and earn money. The knowledge by acquiring which we can earn peace and happiness finds no place in our syllabi. Therefore, the knowledge about truth, Dharma and righteousness which is essential for our well-being and harmonious social living is almost absent in our system. Therefore, we frequently come across more falsehood than truth, more hatred than love, more greed than sacrifice, more disservice than service and more arrogance than humility. The above negative qualities breed sufferings every second. Therefore, we move with fear, sleep with disquiet and remain worried about the uncertain tomorrow. In many areas, things are degenerating so fast that prospects appear bleak.

Divine knowledge or scriptural knowledge is almost on the verge of oblivion. During Satya Yug and Tretya Yug, there were *ashrams* where true knowledge was imparted regularly. People were having opportunities to get glimpses of true knowledge. They were also interested to learn. But people now-a-days, remain indifferent to spiritual knowledge. Rather they spend more time and energy for fulfilment of their basic needs. Therefore, we remain away from spiritual knowledge. In such a situation, how shall we get rid of sufferings? People consider themselves knowledgeable with their limited knowledge. That a lot more remain to be learnt does not occur to

---

9   Oriya Divya Dhara Vol 14 Page 3

them. He, who is knowledgeable, will attain peace, bliss and freedom. But people do not live in peace and happiness. This indicates that they are still ignorant. Freedom from bondages remains far away from such people. This is because we are yet to acquire true knowledge. We do not know what Dharma is. We do not know how to lead a righteous living. If man acquires spiritual knowledge, the same will be reflected in his conduct and he will very well be able to discriminate between good and bad. He will choose the right path and avoid the wrong one. People are suffering which indicates that they are dipped in ignorance. Ignorance does not mean total absence of knowledge. Ignorance means a little knowledge or distorted knowledge.

We suffer. This indicates that we do not know what good is. We therefore fail to choose good ways. We know a little but that does not help us earn peace and happiness. Everyone wants good things in life. But ways being faulty, the result is sufferings. In such a case, shall we move towards darkness? Our conscience always prompts us to move towards light (knowledge), know what good is, be good and do good. Inquisitiveness is a great gift of God to the mankind. Why has God given us inquisitiveness? God is Sat-Chit-Anand. His Creation cannot suffer. That is why we all want peace and bliss. That is our true nature. His children cannot suffer. But due to our ignorance we suffer. Whatever occasional happiness we get, is only for a temporary period. Man has not been able to utilize the inquisitiveness given to him to acquire more and more knowledge. Hence even if man is Bliss-Absolute, he is not experiencing bliss. Man is yet to unravel the mystery of this Creation. That means he is yet to know the truth about the Creation. He does not know how this Creation is full of truth and is made of truth. The more we know about truth, the more shall we enjoy and become happy. An appropriate example is electricity. The more we know about electricity, the more we can put it to use in our multifarious activities. Likewise, the more we come to know about truth, the more we are benefited. We must possess the right knowledge that will bring us happiness, peace, bliss and freedom. In absence of right knowledge, we are bound to suffer. By knowing things and accordingly conducting ourselves, we can ensure good living; by possessing divine virtues, we can live in the society harmoniously with peace and happiness. But since we do not utilize our inquisitiveness and do not evince interest in acquiring knowledge, we do not get the happiness which we are entitled to. By acquiring spiritual knowledge, we come to know our origin, our destination and our identity. The subject matter of happiness, peace, bliss and freedom is there in spiritual knowledge.

Atman is present everywhere. Atman is in the body. Because of Atman, we can speak, we hear, and we see. Whatever is done by us it is all possible due to Atman. Because of presence of Atman, this body is sustained and all systems inside are running perfectly. Spiritual knowledge covers everything including the forms and qualities, visible and invisible. Spiritual knowledge is all about the self. It covers mind, intellect and conscience. We very often use the term 'I'. It is regrettable that we do not evince interest to know what that 'I' is. Man is the highest creature in the ladder of evolution. He is different from animals. Animals also eat and survive. They sleep and take rest. They procreate. They have fear. Man has all the traits that are present in the animals. What is extra in man is his quest for knowledge, divine virtues, truth and Dharma. Then only he can attain perfection. The very purpose of human birth is that he must realise his True Self. He must be free from all bondages and sufferings. Peace and bliss is his birthright.

Man must realise that this Bhuloka is not his permanent abode. He has descended from Satya-Loka and taken myriads of births before. He has experienced myriads of deaths before. Man must go back to Satya-Loka from where he has come. That is the permanent abode of rest and peace. Man has come from Brahman and shall ultimately go back to Brahman. But he is neither aware of his divine nature nor his destination.

Why do you take food? The answer is- To survive.

Why do you want to survive? The answer is- To get happiness.

Why do you seek happiness? In this case the answer is a little difficult. Everyone wants to be happy. It means, this is the very purpose of our living. Essentially, we are Happiness-Absolute, Peace-Absolute, Bliss-Absolute and Freedom-Absolute. That is why we seek happiness, peace, bliss and freedom. This craving is common to everybody. That is our True Self.

Therefore, we take food so that we can live and go back to our Self. Devoid of direction or destination, we restlessly continue our tiresome journey on zig-zag ways with many hurdles and hindrances, trials and tribulations to finally find ourselves wandering or encircling. Our purposeless actions create new bondages for us. We create more and more knots in our lives making things complex, simplification of which becomes more and more difficult. Only by acquiring right knowledge, the knots can be cut off and we shall be free from all bondages. This means, True Self which is simplest of the simple and subtlest of the subtle, can be realised. This is the state of eternal bliss, freedom and perfection.

To get rid of all sufferings, there are many ways one of which is to be good. We should acquire knowledge about what good is. From our very inception, God has endowed us with divine qualities. Divya Darshan says that there are mainly seven divine qualities such as Renunciation, Restraint, Spiritual Practice, Service, Truth, Love and Forgiveness. To tell truth, to believe, to serve others, to sacrifice, to love are all divine qualities.

Sadguru asks a fundamental question. "By what, you are living?"

By way of answer he explains thus. "You all live by divine qualities. When you were born, your mother accepted you as her child and brought you up with love and affection. She served you day and night. That is why you are a grown-up person now. Without these divine traits in your mother, you would not have survived. All humans and the lower creatures are coexisting because of the divine qualities which are gifts of God. However ferocious a tigress may be, she loves her cubs and feeds them. The nature with all its flora and fauna exists because of divine qualities. In fact, divine qualities rule the whole Creation. They are ever present in the nature."

He further explains - When you do some transaction in a shop, either you hand over the money first, or the shop keeper hands over the commodity to you first. It is because of the trust you have on the shop keeper and shop keeper's trust on you.

You go out to work. In the noon, when you come back home, your wife has kept the lunch ready for you. This is because, you are having trust on her and she is having trust on you. She is sure that you will come for lunch. You are sure that your wife must have cooked food for you. Things will be disturbed if there is no belief or trust. Belief and trust are divine qualities. Divine qualities are there in all human beings, but people are not able to understand that the whole Creation is governed by divine qualities. We get peace and happiness by divine qualities. We get sufferings by demoniac qualities. Demoniac qualities are opposed to the divine qualities. In the present society, demoniac qualities are on the rise. That is why, we suffer. Since we all want peace and happiness, we should give up bad tendencies or demoniac qualities and take to divine virtues. If a husband does not believe his wife and the wife does not believe her husband; if a father does not believe his son and a son does not believe his father, domestic disturbances are bound to occur every now and then. In such circumstances, how can one expect peace and happiness?

In Satya Yug, people were truthful. They adored truth. God has bestowed upon us divine qualities. We must utilize the same otherwise, we cannot get peace. The sages have attained the highest by possessing divine qualities. They are in peace and bliss. By Guru's blessings, they have reached the highest state. By possessing a single divine quality also, you can be great. Lord Buddha's conviction on Truth, Love of Jesus, knowledge of Socrates, Sri Chaitanya's devotion and love made them great. Likewise, there are many great devotees who attained greatness by their true devotion. He, who possesses divine qualities, shall get rid of all sufferings and shall get happiness, peace and bliss. This is sure and certain. "Satyam bada, Dharmam chara"- This means, "Speak Truth and live up to righteousness." This has been the instruction to the mankind by the sages and seers from inception. But people do not attach importance to this great teaching. In such a situation, how shall we get peace and bliss? As told earlier, devotion is a divine quality. He, who possesses faith and devotion towards God, will come to possess more and more divine knowledge and divine virtues. But faith and true devotion are scarce now-a-days. While occasionally worshipping God, samsar comes first to our mind and thereafter God. That is why we are deprived of His blessings. We continue with sufferings. A suffering person is supposed to remember God more frequently. But he too does not remember on the pretext of paucity of time. He, who has devotion towards God, will overcome all sufferings. There are so many anecdotes on how God has been helping the devotees in so many ways. If you go through the biographies of great saints or great devotees, you can understand the greatness of God, and also know how He responds to the devotion of the devotees.

We are not able to know; but God is helping us always. He is near us and inside us. Enquiring or trying to know God amounts to taking shelter of God.

God is all pervasive energy and Pure Consciousness. He manifests as all other energies. He can take any form as and when necessary. God is good. Truth is God. Love is God. Dharma is God. He, who is keen to be good, will become good. This is the Law of nature. Many people believe that one must go to dense forest and do lot of penance to become a rishi. We are not aware of the fact that goodness is God and Truth is God. The demons were doing tapas amidst fire, water etc. It must be remembered that God is everywhere. He is eternal. He, who takes shelter of truth, Dharma, righteousness or goodness will get blessings from God. He will live in peace and happiness. Hence it is not necessary to go to forest in search of God. I (Sadguru Sri Sri Arjun) am a householder. I was keen to know what truth is and in which way I must proceed to realise Brahman for attainment of liberation. By His blessings I realised the Truth.

Whether only the renunciates will attain liberation or Moksa? Whether the householders shall be suffering permanently? God is for all. God wills that all His children should live in peace and bliss. God wills that all should realise the true self. For this He has gifted us two things. One is inquisitiveness (Knowledge) and the second is divine qualities. We would not have known our mother, father, society, the Sun, the Moon and God without knowledge. By knowledge we can understand everything. He has given us divine qualities so that we can live in peace and bliss. Inquisitiveness is given to man because he will know things one after another and at last, he will know God and attain God. He has given us everything. He has made all arrangements for us so that we can use them and get peace and happiness.

But due to ignorance we are unable to understand all these. We are not attaching importance to knowledge. We do not understand the importance of divine qualities. That is why we are not inclined towards the same. During adversities, we pray God to save us. Even if we are saved by Him, we do not cognize God's role in it. God has given us all essential knowledge. We must utilize the knowledge properly to come out of adverse situations instead of seeking God's help in every matter.

"Oh God, with my limited knowledge I am not able to understand you properly. I am also not able to understand your beneficial plans and pre-arrangements designed for my well-being. Please bless me with more knowledge so that I can understand you and your scheme of things in a better manner. I am not able to assimilate your power with my inadequate competence and capacity that you have given me. Kindly bless me with more power and energy so that I can be well-prepared to hold on to you." This should be our prayer.

God will not give you a chocolate even. He has given you adequate knowledge to make any amount of chocolates you need. God has given you Earth, Water, Fire, Air and Space, minerals, plants and animals before your birth for your comfortable living. Before the birth of a child God has made necessary arrangements for milk in the mother's breast. God has given us family, friends and society for a peaceful and happy living. To the inquisitive mind, the whole Creation is an open book full of knowledge but for the ignorant, truly little is accessible.

There is knowledge. There are divine qualities. God has given inquisitiveness. Man would live in peace and realise God, if he follows God's laws intended for the well-being of the Creation. Those laws are followed by the Devas. The sages knew the Law of Eternity. This is called Sanatan Dharma. We were born; we survive, get peace and bliss, and finally attain liberation by observing the Law of Eternity. Without knowing and observing the Law of Eternity, how can we get peace and happiness? At the cost of repetition, it may be said that knowing the Law of Eternity is knowledge and observance of the same is Dharma. Jnana enables one to observe Dharma and attain Moksa, the goal of life. Every man should acquire right knowledge imparted by the scriptures and sages, and conduct himself accordingly. Then only, he can get rid of sufferings. There are various ways to get rid of sufferings. It is not possible to explain everything in a single session of one hour. I (Saguru Sri Sri Arjun) am giving some hints only. During ancient times, there were persons who were flying in the sky and walking on water. It is not necessary to go to forest to acquire knowledge. If someone does something new, we get surprised, but we can also do the same if we take interest and acquire that skill. I am serving you all by imparting right knowledge. I have come for that purpose. You are the scions of immortality. You are the descendants of sages. You have in you, infinite possibilities. Why should you suffer? If you acquire the qualities of the Devas, you will get rid of sufferings. You must therefore try to evolve yourselves to the state of Devas so that you will no longer lead the life full of sufferings. With this attitude, you must advance and stop not till God is realised.

On the other hand, most of the people are trying to maximize their happiness by holding fast to the demoniac qualities such as dishonesty, deceitfulness, etc. Can anyone get happiness from out of this? If you acquire divine qualities God will help you at every step. He, who takes shelter of God, will stay protected by God and shall get rid of sufferings. This is the Law of Eternity. God is protecting one and all every moment which we do not know. But a person who will surrender to God will receive much more help and protection from God which is beyond expectation even. God may take any form to help us. A stranger sometimes comes to us and extends support. When two persons are quarrelling, a third person may intervene and pacify both. God is present everywhere as knowledge. But due to ignorance we are unable to know Him and His Greatness. Even we go to the extent of telling that there is no God. Because God is there, we are born, we survive and are able to understand so many things.

Is there anybody who will deny his own existence? If somebody raises his hand affirming that he is not there, it becomes contradictory. If he is not there, how is he raising his hand? The power by which you raised your hand, the power by which you could tell about your existence or non-existence, the power by which you can see and hear, the power by which you can speak, that power is God. Without Him, nothing is possible. He, who knows like this, can experience God everywhere every moment. If somebody is not able to realise God, his life is in vain. He, who distances himself from God, is bound to suffer. The whole world is moving towards darkness due to want of true knowledge and divine qualities. Peace and happiness remain a distant dream for him. Due to want of divine qualities, there is disturbance in family life. Due to ignorance, people mistake poison for nectar. In such circumstances, suffering is bound to be there. By acquiring true knowledge and divine qualities, this Earth can be a heaven. We must be knowledgeable like rishis, possess all divine qualities which the Devas have. Kali Yug shall come to an end and thereafter, Satya Yug is bound to come. But if demoniac tendencies and consequently warring propensities continue to predominate, Satya Yug will remain away. Only true knowledge and divine qualities pave the way clear to Satya Yug. In other words, the ignorant must acquire knowledge and become knowledgeable, and the demoniac tendencies must be replaced by the divine qualities for welcoming Satya Yug. Everyone has the potentialities to blossom the divine nature in him. God, without any discrimination, has given inquisitiveness and divine qualities to all of you. I have come only to refresh your memory. I am not going to give you anything new. I am here to stir up your dormant power.

God wills that everyone should get rid of sufferings, live in peace and bliss, and finally come back to Him. This is called liberation or Moksa. But while moving on spiritual path, you may have to encounter some obstacles. You must give up negative qualities while at the same time blossom in yourselves the divine qualities. Old thinking must change yielding place to new. An ignorant person has weak mind-set. He will not adapt to changes so soon. He will not change his food habits so easily. He will say that without non-vegetarian food, he cannot survive. But gradually, when he acquires knowledge, his power to discriminate between what is good and what is bad will increase. He will give up the poison and take to nectar. He, who will be eager to acquire the right knowledge ultimately to go back to his eternal and blissful abode, will be blessed with the required knowledge. Hence, I never advise anybody for not eating garlics, onions, fish or meat.

I emphasize always on true knowledge and divine qualities which will cleanse them automatically. How have some people left gambling? How have some people refrained from meat and wine? They have left all these old habits by their inner strength. That is God's blessing.

಄✶಄

Sins

[10]Divya Darshan teaches us how to observe Dharma. In other words, it teaches self-knowledge. If man knows what Dharma is and observes the same properly, he can attain divinity. Ultimately, he can realise the divine Atman within.

Man craves for happiness and peace, but he mostly gets sufferings. This indicates that man does not have proper knowledge about peace and happiness. He does all his works in order to earn peace and happiness, but all his efforts end up in sufferings. In this situation what is the duty of man? Man should acquire knowledge about how to earn peace and happiness. In other words, he must know what is good and how to get the same. Then only he can live well. By doing good and being good, he can fulfil all his basic needs including peace and bliss. Ultimately he can realise his true self. God is there everywhere as 'good'. Divya Darshan teaches the knowledge about 'good'.

Everything has a basis. For example, the basis of fruit is a tree. Similarly, there is some basis of happiness, peace and bliss. Since we do not know the basis we are deprived of happiness, peace and bliss. And therefore, we suffer. Goodness is the basis of happiness, peace and bliss. Hence, one must know what good is; one must be good and express goodness in one's conduct. Then only one can get happiness, peace and bliss. But instead of knowing the basis first, we straightaway seek peace, happiness and bliss. We do not get it. Secondly, we should know that, if we mingle with bad people, bad qualities shall be transmitted to us. On the other hand, if we mingle with knowledgeable persons, we would become knowledgeable. Through contacts we get influenced. Unnoticeably, the other person's attitude or conduct may get superimposed on our mind.

God is really the Goodness-Absolute. The divine qualities shall get activated in him, who keeps contact with God. God is divine, pure, sacred and Bliss-Absolute. The question is how to maintain contact with God? God is full of everything good and precious, divine and permanent. He, who entertains divine thoughts and divine qualities, really maintains contact with God. He, who is keen to know about God, praises God, prays God, remembers God, worships God, offers his devotion to God and loves God, is in contact with God. If we love God, God would love us. When somebody reads scriptures, reads about God, hears about God, meditates on God and contemplates on God, he is in contact with God. Any person who does as mentioned above, can live in peace and happiness. Since we are not interested to know who God is, we are not able to get peace and happiness. When the basis of everything is God how is it possible to get peace and happiness without knowing Him? We must know what is 'good'. We must be good and maintain contact with 'good'. This is our duty. This is our Dharma. In other words, uphold what is good, support what is good, become good, do good, and maintain contact with good. The people of Satya Yug had known well about 'good' and conducted themselves accordingly. There is absence of such knowledge now. Hence suffering is on the rise. Those, who have interest in spirituality, should be told to inculcate goodness.

We have heard about vices and virtues. It is told that after the death the sinners go to the lower regions whereas the virtuous go to Deva-Loka by Deva-yan. Many people not only suffer here but also hereafter. As long as unfulfilled desires remain, man's suffering would not come to an end.

Man, instinctively craves for peace and happiness. He, who is more knowledgeable, is more powerful. The ignorant man is weak. The ignorant are easily mastered by the knowledgeable. The ignorant man goes to pitrulok whereas the knowledgeable man goes to devlok by Deva-yan. The sages advised mankind to increase or accumulate their virtues but in Kali

Yug while the common men try or increase their virtues, they are exploited by the greedy middlemen. Many people believe that if virtues are to be acquired money must be spent on different rituals and activities.

Divya Darshan preaches how to earn virtues easily without getting cheated or spending money on expensive rituals. The deeds that bring us peace and happiness and help in gaining self-knowledge are called virtues. The deeds that cause sufferings and take us to the dark region are sins. To remember God's name is virtue. There is no need for money here; no physical labour is involved in earning virtues.

The Supreme Goal of man is liberation. So, whatever is done to attain liberation is virtue only. Anything that is done which impedes self-development is sin or vice. Karma is divided into three parts such as physical, mental and vocal. If somebody entertains good will towards others, it is a virtue. If somebody speaks some good words about others, it is also a virtue. We get divine blessings from out of that. By doing such small acts, we can increase our virtue second by second. By thinking and discussing about God, listening to the sages and wise men, we earn virtues.

He, who contemplates on God's lila, His greatness and True Self is doing the greatest punya and acquiring virtues. No sin can enter the mind when the mind is preoccupied with divine thoughts. We are to only change our mindset, attitude and approach to multiply our virtues. It does not cost anything. But due to ignorance, in our efforts to be free from sins and earn virtues we get cheated by clever persons in the society. Due to ignorance we do not have clear idea about vices and virtues. Nothing should be done blindly. Knowledge must be acquired. By inquisitiveness and knowledge man can very easily increase virtues which would bring him peace, bliss and freedom. A person, who acquires self-knowledge, becomes pure very quickly. The best thing is Jnana Yajna through which virtues can be earned. There is no greater gift than dissemination of knowledge and there is no greater virtue than acquisition of knowledge.

∽∗∽

[11]The virtuous go to Deva-Loka by Deva-yan. There also, they would reap the results of their actions and after that again they would come back to the physical world. The sinners would go to the lower regions. The sinners suffer here and hereafter. Man suffers every moment. It is because he carries a lot of desires. In the Preta-Loka, there is no physical enjoyment.

Everybody wants to be happy. One's goal is to get happiness, peace and bliss and ultimately to attain God. He, who acquires more knowledge, becomes more powerful. The weak remain as subordinate to the powerful persons. Knowledge is the real power. Hence that kind of knowledge must be acquired which would elevate us to Deva-Loka where more peace and happiness is there. A virtuous man lives in peace and happiness. A sinner always suffers. To get into Deva-yan (divine vehicle) we must acquire more knowledge and virtues. For increasing our virtues, the sages have prescribed many ways. But we are not trying to acquire virtues. In Satya Yug, without spending anything people were earning virtues. We must know what virtue is and what vice is. That, which takes us on the path of self-development and gives us peace and happiness, is called virtue. That, which leads us towards sufferings, is called vice. For example, to chant God's name or contemplate on Him is a virtue. In other words, that which gives us happiness, peace and bliss and ultimately leads us to liberation is virtue.

To serve others and even to wish well of others is a virtue. The sages have taught us to pray, "Sarve bhabantu sukhinah, sarve santu niramaya". To wish like this is also a virtue, that is earned free of cost. If opposite feelings are harboured in the mind, it is sin or vice. To earn virtue, one need not go to any specific place. God is everywhere and He knows everything. The personal godheads also bless us if we do good things or entertain good feelings. If we wish ill of others, the personal godheads will also wish ill of us. Every moment virtues can be earned. But because we do not know the method, we are going on committing and accumulating sins on a regular basis, whereas virtues are earned by us occasionally through some occasional rituals or spiritual practices.

---

11 Oriya Divya Dhara Vol 7 Page 23

He, who contemplates on God gets purified fast and becomes eligible to travel in Deva-yan. Moment to moment virtues can be earned by constant remembrance of God and by divine thoughts, divine expressions and divine actions. Who is God and how His lila is going on? If someone contemplates on this, he has really fixed his mind on God. He would be purified very soon. Because he is remembering God always, his virtues shall increase. By taking God's names and serving others one can easily earn virtues. Even if a husband serves his wife or the wife serves the husband, virtues shall accrue. To help the animals or plants is also a service which would earn merits for us. By accumulating merits, one would be eligible to reach heaven, the abode of peace and bliss. Even by words of consolation offered to the suffering or bereaved person, punya (merit) shall accrue. Thus, by good actions, good expressions and good thoughts one can earn virtues, which would help one's self-development. Cheating others is a sin. But as we do not have adequate knowledge on either virtue or vice, we are more likely to commit sins rather than increasing our virtues. When a man acquires knowledge about God or acquires divine knowledge, he approaches divinity and shall reach divinity. Hence, the sages and the seers were regularly conducting Jnana Yajna which is stated to be the best oblation. What can be greater than the knowledge by which we can realise Brahman, the Supreme? Hence everyday a man should go through at least some lines from the scriptures. Here there is no scope for spending money or getting cheated while acquiring virtues or making atonements. Therefore keep a small pocketbook containing spiritual thoughts with you which you can go through in your leisure time.

☙✶❧

Law of Karma or Reflection Theory

Karma, Karttavya and Sadhana: Actions performed skilfully and piously to accomplish a goal smoothly in shortest time with minimum cost and labour is known as sadhana. Spiritual practice or sadhana is enhanced by renunciation and self-restraint. Renunciation, self-restraint and spiritual practice constitute Karma Yoga. By spiritual practice, self-restraint also gets strengthened. Therefore, self-restraint and spiritual practice are complementary to each other. According to Divya Darshan, whatever karma a man performs in his day to day life, constitutes sadhana or spiritual practice although he is not aware of the same. We work for earning our livelihood; we undertake some work for others too i.e. for the cause of the society. These are all parts of our spiritual pursuits. There is no need to perform any fearsome spiritual practice to attain one's true self. Only if all our activities are streamlined towards a particular goal, success is bound to come our way. On the other hand, if karma is performed in a whimsical or haphazard manner, there are more chances of failure than success. We may end up with committing more sins than acquiring virtues. Sins drag us backward while virtues take us towards our goal. We should therefore be more cautious while undertaking any karma. We must remember that wrong action yields bad results and good action yields good result. This is the Law of karma. The results that accrue come back to us in course of time and thus we are bound to enjoy the fruits of our actions. At that time we call the same as our destiny. Since the results of our actions come back to us as our destiny, it follows that our past actions are our present and future destiny and the present actions are our future destiny in preparation. In other words, we are the authors of our own destiny. If we seek happiness, we have to perform good karma from now itself. We must be well intentioned throughout our karma i.e. to serve others with sincerity. As human beings, we are fortunate that we have got an elevated status in the ladder of evolution. We must cautiously choose our actions. Animals cannot do that. They go according to their instincts. On the other hand, we are endowed with adequate knowledge and conscience. We should therefore perform our actions with knowledge and skill so as to accomplish all our duties to reach the destination. Then only our living can be purposeful. Living without a purpose is no living. Once we know the purpose of living and take to the path of duty, we are truly performing our Dharma and shall reach our goal. Hence karma should be transformed into purposeful duty and not just end up with a purposeless drudgery. Knowing the Brahman who resides as our self-consciousness within is our primary duty (Karttavya). That means karttavya is always interlinked with our goal. Attainment of goal is always our first and foremost duty.

Sadguru Sri Sri Arjun says, "If you want to live, be dutiful; if you want peace and happiness, possess divine virtues; if you want liberation, acquire self-knowledge. If all your actions are seva (service) oriented and get synchronised with duty, the attainment of goal is certain." Knowledge and skill is essential for proper performance of duty. This automatically becomes sadhana (spiritual practice). Three elements of sadhana are knowledge & skill, practice and the goal. Karma is sadhana, karma is life and karma is bliss. This means a person who undertakes karma as karttavya and sadhana, he synchronises all the above three. This is what his Dharma is. No other compartmentalized action is necessary to be undertaken for the practice of Dharma. All actions become righteous if one is mindful of one's supreme goal. It may be remembered that there is no karttavya without truth, righteousness and justice. Karttavya is always linked to the divine virtues.

Therefore, untruth, injustice or any other vices should not be resorted to under the pretext of karttavya. Man being the most gifted being, he must choose his actions carefully with application of mind, intelligence and conscience so that Dharma is observed in true spirit. Observance of Dharma should be his karttavya and his karttavya should be to observe

Dharma. In other words, his action should be a total package of seva, karttavya, sadhana and Dharma. Then only the distance to the goal shall be shortened. On the other hand if they are not synchronised properly, if they are contradictory to each other and if there is no rhyme or rhythm in his actions, his progress shall be retarded and goal would remain unreachable. Whenever we go to market to purchase some materials for our use, we are selective and make transactions after much scrutiny and consideration. But we do not pay sufficient attention to select the actions we undertake even if they bring us sins and sufferings or peace and happiness. In other words, we become mindful while buying mundane things but mindless while collecting things of permanent value. We forget that gross things we collect here are to be left here. What we can carry with us are subtle things such as good intentions, good actions and good contemplations. Karma becomes Sadhana when karma consciously linked to the goal is performed skilfully in an unattached manner. The essence of Sadhana is 'skill in action' linked to the goal. Animals and birds etc. perform their activities with their latent skill. Birds build their nests so skilfully. The white-ants build the anthills so beautifully. Similarly the honey bees build their hives with so much of skill. Man is endowed with the discriminating faculty to know what is good and what is bad. It is man only who can enquire about his goal. He gets inspiration and encouragement from within. Good works enhance divine virtues in him. That is why it is said that karma is the cause of bondage. Karma is also the cause of freedom. Man becomes more powerful by dint of spiritual practice through karma, bhakti and jnana. It is relevant to mention here that Divya Darshan makes a perfect fusion of apparently three different paths such as karma, bhakti and jnana. Jnana only remains predominant as the basis of all the three. Without knowledge karma cannot be done properly. Karma bereft of jnana shall bring forth unpredictable results without any direction. Similarly Bhakti shall be superfluous without knowing whom we worship. All our offerings may be of very little value if we do not know what we are offering and to whom. Spiritual practice culminates as divine virtues which ultimately lead to attainment of true life. In other words, spiritual practice is a path of self-development and the goal is attainment of True Self. Sadguru Sri Sri Arjun says, "By knowledge and spiritual practice, the impossible can be made possible. If anything remains impossible, it is to be inferred that there is inadequacy of either or both." He further shows the process of divine life through the words, "Divine thoughts, divine expressions, divine actions." This means, all our actions, expressions and thoughts must be harmonized and directed towards the divine goal of liberation.

We all perform some karma or other. Whatever all we do is karma. But the most pertinent point is- "What should we do?" The answer is – Actions performed with the goal of attaining true knowledge and realising True Self is the highest karma. In other words, desireless karma for the sake of God becomes worship. Here all our actions are transformed to duty i.e. Karttavya. Here all our actions become truly Sadhana. This is our true Dharma. Here there is perfect synchronisation of seva, karma, karttavya, sadhana and Dharma; all in one straight line that connects the goal of Self-knowledge. This, being a straight line, is the shortest route. The spiritual aspirant thus leads a divine life and attains divinity which is eternally established within.

⋄⋄✦⋄⋄

[12]Everything we come across is changeable in this Creation. Everything is functional. Be it a pebble or plant, be it an atom or an animal, they are all operational or active. In the atoms, the electrons are moving fast without any rest. They are actively involved in the creative process. A piece of wood or iron will not break into particles easily. The atoms by their inherent powers bind each other to maintain their forms. A plant is always active trying for survival and growth. When there is a cut in its skin, it gets repaired. A plant needs light and air. That is why a plant gets inclined or extends itself towards light. Its roots go into the soil more and more to collect minerals and water. Its branches grow to all sides to get more air and light. An animal is more active than a plant. It wants security of survival. A human being not only wants to live with security, he also seeks prestige,

---

12 Oriya Divya Dhara Vol 18 Page 26

power and status; he carries on his quest for peace, happiness and freedom. Without jnana he cannot get any of these.

Man, as he sows, so he reaps. There are three types of karma; physical, mental and vocal. Physical work is done by the help of eyes and ears, legs and hands etc. The moment we open our eyes we see something or other, whether we like it or not. Accordingly, we react. When we hear melodious music, we get attracted. When somebody scolds us, we get angry. When we meet with any accident, our body as well as mind gets impacted by that. We are also affected by the changes taking place all around us. For example, if fire burns in the nearby place, we get light and heat. When it rains, we get drenched. If the weather changes, we are bound to feel heat or cold. Our actions are also hindered due to various environmental factors because of which the desired results do not come forth. Due to this, man's belief in the Law of Karma gets shaken. He does not hesitate to perform bad actions. He does not feel the urgency of good or noble actions. Whether by nature or by the jiva, any activity will yield some result or other. If you go to a cave and shout, the same will come back to you by way of echo. If the head of the family suffers, the members of family will also get affected in some way or other.

It is true that man reaps the results of his actions. Sometimes, the results come immediately and sometimes late. The results of karma are like shadow of an object that clings to it. Courtesy begets courtesy; love begets love. If you scold someone, he will also scold you. If you stand in front of a mirror, a reflection of your image will be there in the mirror. Good actions bring good results. Bad actions yield bad results. This is the Law of Karma.

Lord Buddhadev also upheld the Law of Karma. Lord Jesus also advocated for loving others so that others will love us back.

When we hold a pen and write something on a piece of paper, we get the result simultaneously. The more we write, the more we get words or sentences. Here there is no gap between our action and the result. A line or a letter comes then and there along with the movement of the pen. Due to lack of awareness, we are not able to understand the intricacies of karma and its results. That is why we do not understand the importance of good karma. At times, we unnecessarily blame God for the bad results. We get reward or punishment according to our karma. By acquiring right knowledge, man can discriminate between good and bad, and accordingly he makes his choice of karma. Ignorance brings sufferings.

☙✶❧

[13]Karma is always going on. Results also accrue according to karma. This is not easily understood by many since things occur beyond our knowledge. Some results accrue very quickly whereas some come late.

Since karma sometimes yields results late, they go unnoticed or unidentified. People do forget these past deeds. They are not able to correlate the same with the present sufferings, but the sages and seers understand the same very well.

Karma and results are interlinked. Every result of karma comes sooner or later. With increase in level of knowledge, one can know this better. If I get angry with someone, immediately he will retaliate. We also get results according to our thoughts. If I think of going to a village, the village comes to my mind. Whatever man thinks everything gets recorded. For some actions happened in our past lives, results are experienced by us in this life. Therefore, we should not do injustice to anybody. Let us be fair and just to others so that future shall be good and filled with happiness. Therefore, let us consciously try to store good results for future by good actions now itself.

Divine Virtues: By divine qualities, man can attain immortality. Persons with divine qualities are sattvic. Lord Vishnu is maintaining everything in this Creation. Goddess Laxmi is His consort. Vishnu plans to make different arrangements for the maintenance of the Creation. For this, many ingredients are necessary.

Lord Vishnu's power being Laxmi, she supplies all provisions including food and clothing. The decision is made by Vishnu. Where there are demoniac qualities Laxmi does not stay. Many kings due to their demoniac

---

13   Oriya Divya Dhara Vol 3 Page 45

qualities have lost their kingdoms. But where divine virtues rule, peace and happiness remain there. Where there is crookedness and deceit, Laxmi quits that place.

Wealth is of two types. The gross wealth and subtle wealth; gross wealth is normally called Laxmi whereas the subtle wealth is called Vishnu. We normally worship gross wealth (Laxmi) more than we worship subtle wealth (Vishnu). Gross wealth gradually diminishes but there is no end to subtle wealth such as divine qualities. If we adore divine qualities, along with Vishnu, Laxmi will also remain with us. Where there is Vishnu, there is Laxmi. They never part. Love, forgiveness, truth and service are the divine qualities among others which grow even after spending whereas the gross wealth gets diminished when spent. When we go to any shop to buy anything the shopkeeper hands over things even before we pay him. This is called trust. Trust is also a divine quality. The family and the society are running smoothly due to divine qualities. Where there is any aberration there is disturbance or chaos. In the satya Yug, without money also they were able to live properly due to mutual help, care and respect for each other. Subtle wealth cannot be stolen. It cannot be burnt by fire. It cannot be wetted by water. But on the other hand, gross wealth cannot bring permanent peace and happiness to the possessor. By possessing divine virtues man can go on the path of self-development even up to his goal i.e. realisation of True Self. Realisation of True Self means overcoming death and enjoying Supreme Bliss. Divya Darshan lays stress on divine virtues. By Practising divine virtues man can lead a divine life. Whatever path may be chosen for happiness, peace, bliss and liberation, without divine qualities any effort in this direction shall be futile. Bhakti will not be there without practice of divine virtues. Chanting God's names will not work if divine qualities are not inculcated. Hence Satya Yug can come if and only if divine virtues prevail everywhere. It will benefit one and all.

ଔଓ★ଔଓ

[14] *["Humbleness is strength. The more humble a man is, the more powerful he is. Therefore humbleness is the ornament of a powerful man."*

(Amritbindu-103)]

There are different kinds of powers as seen in this Creation. For example, serving others is a power. Forgiving others is a power. Humbleness is a divine quality. Each divine quality is a power. Opposite of divine qualities are the demoniac qualities which are nothing but poison or weakness. True, it is difficult to remain humble in all circumstances. Humbleness can be seen in a person who has conquered anger, violence and crookedness etc. In other words, humbleness can be seen in a person who has completely won over the demoniac qualities. This means, a person with divine qualities such as kindness, service, and righteousness possesses humbleness also. Unless a person becomes humble, he cannot attain life's goal i.e. Bliss and Freedom. The opposite qualities of humbleness are- ego, pride, arrogance etc.

Three qualities such as sattvic, rajasic and tamasic are present in everybody. The lower qualities such as tamasic and rajasic have to be subdued by sattvic quality. It may take a long time to attain sattvic quality. It may take thousand years or several births even. But the person, who takes to spiritual path and continues his spiritual efforts, can elevate himself to sattva in this birth itself. While proceeding on the path of spirituality, he leads a disciplined life with devotion and knowledge that makes him humble. His behavior changes to a remarkable extent. It is to be understood that he, who is not yet humble, has not progressed much on the spiritual path. In other words, his spiritual efforts have not been effective.

Humbleness is strength. By this strength many hurdles on the spiritual path can be crossed over thereby ensuring faster progress towards the goal. By humbleness, even the hearts of sworn enemies can be changed. Humbleness works as catalyst for all our spiritual efforts. He easily attains

---

14 Oriya Divya Dhara Vol 19 Page 36

purity of heart and comes closer to God. A humble person is a fit recipient of God's Grace.

God is great and most powerful. To attain Him, one has to make himself powerful. To be powerful, one has to be simple, humble and submissive. God's grace will be bestowed upon him. A weak and faint-hearted person cannot attain God. All divine qualities are stored in you but those are lying dormant. You have to awaken those latent qualities and apply them. A humble person, enriched with divine qualities, becomes calm and cool. He does not react to external happenings. He faces the adverse situations without getting perturbed.

There are people who go on talking. In the process, so many lies creep in knowingly or unknowingly. Things come out distorted or exaggerated. It is advised therefore to speak less. It is said that an empty vessel sounds much. A humble person speaks less and speaks respectfully. He is loved by others. Divine qualities are like ornaments. He, who possesses divine qualities, looks more beautiful by his endearing personality. God is the humblest Being. He is Supreme. He is all powerful. His greatness is ineffable. He is infinite and eternal. He is simplest and yet strongest. There is none other to compete with Him. Yet He is the humblest of all. He remains everywhere in all beings yet remains unnoticed and unpublicized. He creates and sustains the whole Creation yet He owns nothing. That means He remains unattached.

Attainment of God is your goal. You have to make intense spiritual practice to reach the goal. To make your spiritual practices more effective, you should join satsang for listening to spiritual discourses. In course of satsang, you will have opportunities to mingle with persons of divine qualities which will have positive influence on you.

[15]Divya Darshan lays emphasis on seven divine qualities. They are Renunciation, Restraint, Spiritual Practice, Service, Truth, Love and

---

15   Oriya Divya Dhara Vol 2 Page 47

Forgiveness. These qualities are represented by seven different colours, (VIBGYOR).

The seven colours greatly impact our life. We get more happiness due to the presence of colours. In absence of these colours, the Creation would have looked dull. These seven colours also signify seven divine qualities which are essential for a peaceful living. Without divine qualities the Creation would not have come to exist. Man is able to survive due to love and not due to hatred or violence. Man is surviving due to truth and not due to falsehood, deception or treachery. Both good and evil have got their effects on the people in a society. Goodness leads to peace, bliss and freedom whereas wickedness leads to sorrows and sufferings. In a nutshell, the Creation exists because of divine qualities which are unnoticeably present in the kingdom of nature. The Creation is colourful. Everyday the Sun rises and sets. Everyday the Creation wears new colours. Man gets happiness from out of that. Everything is provided by God for survival as well as peace and happiness.

In the list of seven colours (VIBGYOR), we do not see black and white. They remain at the background and express themselves as seven colours. Black and white colours are present in all seven colours. Black is invisible, unknown and unknowable. Black means darkness. Black signifies nothingness but it has its own existence. Due to ignorance we are not able to know the same. Brahman remains in black colour. Therefore, He is invisible. White is the manifestation of Brahman. Manifestation starts from white which gets diffused as seven colours.

Just as all the seven colours have emerged from out of black and white, similarly the colourful Creation has emerged from Brahman. He is present in everything although remains invisible. Due to ignorance we refute His Existence. The Creation appears new and fresh always because of His Existence. We feel refreshed to see the changing Creation. The ocean looks vast and blue as if emerging from the horizon. Waves are created one after another, dash against the shore and again they retreat to merge in the sea. We all stand, watch and enjoy the turbulent waves. Thus, changes take place incessantly in the Creation. Brahman is attributeless and formless, but He manifests through colours and divine qualities.

Divya Darshan ascribes seven virtues to the seven colours as follows. In any one colour, all other six colours are present.

- ❖ Violet-   Renunciation
- ❖ Indigo-   Restraint
- ❖ Blue-   Spiritual Practice
- ❖ Green-   Service
- ❖ Yellow-   Truth
- ❖ Orange-   Love
- ❖ Red-   Forgiveness

When violet gets blended with blue, it becomes indigo. When indigo and green get blended, it becomes blue; when blue and yellow get blended, it becomes green. When green and orange are blended, it becomes yellow. When yellow and red get blended, it becomes orange. When orange and violet get blended, it becomes red.

Yellow colour is nearest to white colour. It is Brahman's first manifestation. It is the place of Truth. Truth signifies goodness and its opposite signifies sorrows and sufferings. Then orange colour is placed, which is the place of love. We should try to know the Creation, know the process of generation, operation and dissolution, and also know the cause behind all these changes who eternally exists without changes. It is said that, He is there in the beginning, middle and end. Brahman very clearly manifests but we are unable to notice Him and all His doings. We talk of His beginning, middle and end after experiencing some of His lila, but He is beginningless and endless. In other words, He is eternal. We cannot understand or know anything in black (dark). Black means nothingness. It is nothingness with all inherent potentialities. Black is a state which cannot be explained or narrated. It is darkness.

Renunciation is the place of Brahman (in unmanifest state). The colour is violet. From there the Creation began. After violet the colour is indigo which represents restraint. It is the seat of Omkar. It is the origin of Triguna. Triguna simultaneously evolved sequentially, scientifically and systematically as the Creation by the Law of Eternity which is based on certain truths, principles and properties.

When Triguna is in equilibrating state there is no Creation. Only after disequilibrium among the three qualities there starts the dynamics of the Creation. Man is endowed with lot of powers but as he is not applying self-restraint those powers do not flourish in him. For example, if anyone talks too much and in an unrestrained manner, exaggerations or false statements may creep in which is bound to trigger controversy and criticisms. This would dilute his whole talk. Likewise, even if truth is there in everyone, due to lack of self-restraint truth gets diluted and is expressed differently by different persons. Similarly, due to lack of self-restraint if someone eats in excess, he is likely to be lazy. Where there is no restraint, there is bound to be deviations and distortions. Since it is the seat of 'Om' the Creation begins from there. All latent divine qualities become functional from there. This quality inspires and impels noble thoughts. He, who possesses divine thoughts, shall have divine qualities. He will be self-restrained.

He, who possesses the quality of restraint, can possess truth and love. He, who does spiritual practice, would be strong and powerful. He only can forgive others. One can engage in vigorous spiritual practice if one possesses the quality of restraint. He, who engages in spiritual practices, comes to possess more and more powers.

The third segment is Spiritual Practice which is next to Restraint, comes in blue colour. This is the place of various personal godheads. Hence their qualities and powers would be seen here. The godheads or personal deities are always engaged in spiritual practices. The godheads are different powers of Brahman through whom different activities pertaining to the Creation are executed. The mineral kingdom is followed by vegetable kingdom and animal kingdom. The personal godheads execute the activities relating to their departments.

First is the place of Brahman who is formless. Second is the place of 'Om'. Everything is unmanifest there. Gradually, sequentially and systematically thoughts followed by things manifest. Everyone in this universe is on the path of spiritual practice knowingly or unknowingly. Those, who consciously undertake spiritual practices, will make faster movement. They are blessed with divine powers and can know the personal godheads. They can know 'Om' and ultimately realise Brahman. Bhuloka is the visible universe. There are other lokas such as Bhuvah, Swah, Mahah, Janah, Tapah, and Satya. Above the Bhuloka the Creation is invisible. These are all dark areas for us. We are not able to know them. By spiritual Practice when our knowledge shall be enhanced, we can gradually know them all.

The blue colour (colour of spiritual practice) is characterised by affection, goodness peace and purity etc. The wise are more empathetic. The sages preach the importance of all these qualities. The sages possess those qualities and observe the Law of Eternity. Hence, we call them divine souls. The personal godheads are possessed of different powers by which they control, guide and manage the Creation in proper way.

By spiritual practice, love develops in one's heart. By spiritual practice, one realises truth; one would also possess all divine virtues. Thereafter only he would be able to forgive and ultimately realise Brahman. Spontaneously the qualities of truth, love and forgiveness would appear in him, who does spiritual practice; he need not make separate efforts to acquire the qualities of truth, love and forgiveness. In other words, by spiritual practice, everything is possible; even realisation of Brahman. Without spiritual practice realisation of Brahman or self-realisation is impossible. Without spiritual practice, the inspiration for service and respect for truth would not come. If one takes the path of falsehood, one would not be able to possess love and forgiveness. Hence spiritual practice is so important.

How shall we reach our goal? Why are we born? We are to know the answers to these questions. Then only we would reach our destination. Hence all divine virtues should be developed within by spiritual practice. This is the place of Devas. They are always engaged in sustaining and regulating us. He, who would reach that stage, would become Deva and shall ultimately realise Brahman.

After spiritual practices comes 'service'. It is in green colour. The visible universe is manifested in the green colour. Mostly the Nature is green. We may observe the visible universe in two stages. Brahman willed to be many. He manifested as 'Om' and thereafter as personal godheads. The visible universe comes thereafter. In the visible universe everything is useful and is engaged in service for something or other. We serve our parents, children, kith and kin. The animals, birds and the plant kingdom are all serving each other. In other words, the mineral kingdom supports the plant kingdom as well as the animal kingdom. They all subsist by mutual help.

By seva (service), relationship is established between the person who serves and the person who is served. The more somebody serves another the more he comes to know about the other. In other words, through service, man can know the various truths behind everything. Brahman is Truth-Absolute. 'Om' is also Truth. Everything such as 'Om', Ishwar, Deva and jiva are manifestations of the unitary existence.

Service is followed by truth and truth is followed by love. Where there is truth, there is peace, happiness and bliss. Whom do we love? We love Truth who is our Self.

We like the truth that is there in the forms and qualities. But the wise not only like the forms and qualities, they also like the Consciousness inside the forms and qualities. They also like the operative Laws and principles or processes in the kingdom of nature and they love the Creator known as Brahman. Therefore, between our love and a wise man's love, there is huge difference. Form is a truth. Quality is also a truth. The characteristic of the orange colour is reactionlessness. He, who loves, is free from reactions. He, who attains love, would not have greed, infatuation and cruelty etc. We say we love but our love is limited to forms and qualities. A sage is the truest lover. They love more because they know the intrinsic truth in everything they love. The sages love the self within. They remain in that state. That is why they do not see anything except the self. Atman is there everywhere. Where Atman is not present? Hence the sages love the whole Creation realising and treating the same as divine manifestation. Their love is without any boundary.

He, who attains this stage of love, can forgive everything. He cannot take revenge as he loves all. After going to the stage of forgiveness, he can realise 'Om'. The state of forgiveness is the state of reactionlessness.

At the beginning and before the beginning there was 'Om'. Various manifestations took place thereafter. Ultimately man came into being. Man first realises Devas, thereafter 'Om' and ultimately Brahman. This Creation is governed by the Law of Eternity. According to the Law, man must again realise the Supreme he has come from.

The question here is- How would man know and get elevated to the stage of the Deva? The answer is- When he would know the Law of Eternity, the purpose of the Creation, he would be elevated to divine stage and shall move on to realise Brahman ultimately. The Creation is sustained due to mutual service or inter-dependence.

Everyone in the Creation has some relation with the other. There is no mismatch or inconsistency. The Law is operative in such a manner that everything is complementary to the other. Nothing is unwanted or unnecessary. Everything is there for a reason. Everything is getting influenced by the other. That is because the unitary consciousness named Brahman is present everywhere and in everything. His lila is incessantly going on, but we are not able to understand the same due to our ignorance. The moment we unravel the mystery, we shall enjoy everything, and we shall be blissful. All sufferings shall vanish forthwith. We can know the wonderful architect of the Creation. One would marvel at how the vast Creation is operational in such a disciplined manner.

☙✦❧

Emblem of Divya Darshan

[16]Ignorance is great sin. This is written on the top of the monogram of Divya Darshan. Sins bring in sufferings. Man suffers due to ignorance. In other words, sufferings originate from out of ignorance. By acquiring knowledge, all sufferings will go away. Knowing the truth is knowledge. Knowledge is Truth-Absolute. Truth is divine. He, who realises and expresses Truth, is divine. In order to get rid of sufferings, one must acquire knowledge on truth. This means, one must acquire knowledge about God to do away with sufferings. Not knowing the truth is ignorance. Ignorance leads us to sins but at the same time we do not know that we are committing sins. Hence, Ignorance is a great sin.

Not to know anything is sin. When we are not interested to know it indicates that we prefer to remain ignorant. Therefore, we undergo sufferings. Divya Darshan says, it is a great sin to be without self- knowledge. Once one surrenders to God, who is the Truth-Absolute, his sufferings shall go away.

If we do not evince interest to learn, we are bound to suffer. Living ignorantly is sin. One must, therefore, surrender to Truth. God is there as truth. To evince interest to know Him or to welcome Him means taking

---

resort to God. How can we surrender to somebody if we do not know Him? If we do not surrender to Him, how shall we get His blessings?

The monogram of Divya Darshan represents this Creation. It is a flower embellished by seven colours. 'Om' is the saffron of that flower. This flower represents the entire Creation. He, who gets attracted towards this flower, can reach the flower and enjoy the nectar from its saffron and get immerged in 'Om'. This flower has no reed, no support. It is the void (Shunya) which is all-pervasive.

There are seven colours in the monogram. At the centre, there is 'Om'. Light contains all the seven colours (VIBGYOR), but they are hidden. If the light is made to pass through a prism, we can clearly see all the seven colours.

Seven colours represent seven divine qualities. God expresses Himself through the seven divine qualities. By possessing divine qualities, one can know Brahman who is Sat-Chit-Anand. By possessing demoniac qualities, one cannot know Brahman. He, who knows Brahman, realises Him and attains liberation.

The first colour in the monogram is violet, which is the place for renunciation. When Brahman willed to express Himself, He first assumed violet colour. This means violet colour is the nearest colour of black. In the violet colour black is present in an invisible manner.

The black colour remains unmanifest. Brahman remains in unmanifest state and at the same time He manifests as the Creation consisting of various names, forms and qualities. White colour is the first manifestation of Brahman.

This Creation is made beautiful by the seven colours in various combinations. These seven colours together with white and black make nine colours. This Creation is a seven coloured flower which is beautiful. In the monogram there are seven divine virtues. Each colour represents one divine virtue.

Divya Darshan says, "Satyam sharanam gachchhami, which means -I am surrendering to Truth." Surrendering to Truth means surrendering to God and heartily welcoming Him. God is Truth-Absolute. Without knowing about Him, how can one surrender to Him? He, who would surrender to Him, can know Truth and become a true recipient of God's blessings.

At the bottom of the monogram, there is a boat named Divya Darshan. At both the ends of the boat, there are flags. One flag represents knowledge and the other, divine virtues. The flags are of saffron colour which is the symbol of renunciation. Renunciation does not mean renouncing homes and hearths but renouncing the bad qualities from within. This world ocean can be crossed by this divine boat. In the monogram, there is a equilateral triangle emanating from the centre. Sky colour of the triangle indicates that He is as infinite as the sky or space. The three angles of this triangle represent Sat, Chit and Anand (Existence, Knowledge and Bliss). The divine existence expresses Himself as Consciousness and Bliss. By consciousness, the divine existence is realised. By consciousness, Bliss is experienced. In other words, by Him only, He is known and experienced.

Man is not able to know this truth. He, who knows this, enjoys bliss. Therefore, the sages so emphatically tell us, "You are all scions of immortality; you are Self-Absolute; you are Bliss-Absolute."

Everything in this Creation is well-controlled and disciplined. The ignorant man is not able to know this. He, who knows the greatness of God, will get bliss. God is Bliss-Absolute. All His machinations and manifestations are also blissful. We suffer because we are ignorant about the all-inclusive and wide-ranging provisions He has already made for us. This triangle is of blue colour which means He is all-pervasive like the sky.

As told earlier, Brahman is Sat, Chit and Anand (Existence, Knowledge and Bliss). He expresses Himself as divine virtues and through divine virtues. To realise Brahman, one must possess the divine virtues. Any quality opposite to the above divine qualities will stand as deterrent to God realisation. In other words, to realise Existence, Knowledge and Bliss, divine virtues are essential. He who realises, Sat, Chit and Ananda, is liberated. Hence divine virtues are the only divine route to divinity.

The monogram of Divya Darshan represents complete Yoga with Karma, Bhakti and Jnana embedded in it. Renunciation, Restraint and Spiritual

Practices are all bracketed by Divya Darshan as Karma Yoga. Seva or service is Bhakti Yoga. Truth, love and forgiveness represent Jnana Yoga.

Shrimad Bhagavad-Gita lays emphasis on karma, bhakti and jnana. By karma, man can survive. Without bhakti, man will become undisciplined and waylaid. By Bhakti he will be restrained and shall get peace. By knowledge he can discriminate between good and bad, transient and permanent. All these three are essential for a man to live properly. This is called complete Yoga. Absence of any one of the above would make yoga incomplete.

Divya Darshan upholds karma, bhakti and jnana while it lays more emphasis on jnana. According to Divya Darshan, karma is necessary for survival; for harmonious social living with peace and happiness, bhakti is necessary. To attain liberation, there is need for jnana (knowledge). Hence Divya Darshan lays emphasis on "Divine thoughts, Divine expression and Divine action."

ᘓᕒ★ᕒᘓ

[17] **Seven Colours and their Interrelationship:** The monogram of Divya Darshan contains seven petals or segments, each representing a particular colour. The lila (divine play) of the Creator takes place through the seven divine qualities and becomes livelier by the spectrum of seven colours. The colours not only add to the beauty of the Creation but also carry special significance. Out of all colours, three colours are primary and therefore very important. They are black, white and orange. From out of these three colours, other colours have emerged. Although present in all colours, the black colour remains unseen. Brahman is not an object of vision. Although inexpressible, He expresses Himself through white and then through the seven colours. In and through orange colour, Brahman's greatness manifests.

Although Brahman ever remains in His unique state, the jiva comes to know about His manifested forms only when He expresses Himself through His lila. This is the self-expression or self-illumination of Brahman, which is spontaneous. Had there been no lila, there would not have been any

---

17 Oriya Divya Dhara Vol 14 Page 28

Creation. The basis of lila is Prakriti (the female energy). Prakriti is normally contemplated as feminine. The Purusha (The Consciousness Absolute) and Prakriti are the Supra-Causal and causal factors responsible for designing this splendid Creation with different colours to appear lively and lustrous, renewed and refurbished. It is relevant to mention here that Lord Jagannath, Lord Balabhadra and Goddess Subhadra represent these three fundamental colours i.e. black, white and orange respectively. While black signifies Brahman, white signifies His self-expression.

The orange signifies His lila, which is the manifestation of female energy. Orange colour is the symbol of love, benediction and blissfulness. Lila contains and carries the beauty of the Creation. In other words, the existence of Brahman gets self-expression through lila or the divine play.

In the manifested universe, seven colours are experienced and if the two colours viz. black and white are considered, total colours become nine. These nine colours are present in this multi-coloured universe. In this context, it can be said that the processes of generation, operation and destruction of this universe incessantly carry the nine colours. When Sun rises, the sleeping plants and flowers open up. The Sunflower turns to the east. The animal kingdom wakes up from slumber. Through these colours, the visible universe becomes more attractive and gets activated. The spectrum of seven colours is nothing but the self-expression and manifestation of Brahman, the Almighty. These seven colours are interrelated and mutually dependent. The monogram of Divya Darshan is characterised by seven colours in a particular order, i.e. (VIBGYOR).

These seven colours are linked with seven divine virtues such as renunciation, restraint, spiritual practice, service, truth, love and forgiveness. Renunciation is represented by violet colour. Restraint is represented by indigo. Spiritual practice is represented by blue and service is represented by green. Likewise, Truth is represented by yellow; love by orange and forgiveness by red. Each colour is linked with the other. Therefore, it is not possible to tell which of the seven colours comes first and what comes last. However, since Brahman's place is represented by violet, this colour is reckoned as the beginning for the purpose of expounding the subject stage by stage. In all these seven colours, there is invisible presence of black and white, but still the seven colours maintain their own specialities and distinctness. In the violet segment of the monogram, the black colour is also present. Black means darkness. Black signifies nothingness. Black is unknown and unknowable but it has its own existence. From the black colour, slowly the intensity of darkness diminishes and brightness gets saturated until it is reflected as yellow (Truth) in and through which there is total self-expression. Yellow colour represents truth, which indicates that Brahman eternally reveals Himself as Truth. This colour completely expresses the manifested state of the Brahman. Further, the radiance of the yellow colour gradually diminishes till it is merged in the violet colour. In other words, Brahman expresses Himself in varieties of colours and thus carries on His lila in His manifested states. Before we discuss about the manifestation of Brahman through various colours it is relevant to discuss about the development and effects of different colours. Violet is the resultant colour when red is blended with indigo. Indigo is derived from violet and blue. Blue is the resultant colour of indigo and green. Green is derived from blue and yellow; yellow is derived from green and orange. Orange is derived from yellow and red; red is derived from violet and orange. In other words, each and every colour is inter-mingled as a result of which the marvellous form of this Creation has been so alluring and enchanting. By the combination of seven colours, the varieties in this Creation are expressed, though the three colours, namely, black, white and orange remain as the background colours as well as the causal factors of lila. Even though the seven colours appear to have separate entities, when they collectively express themselves, they lose their identities and appear as white like the sunshine, which appears bright (white) although seven colours exist in it. These seven colours are Brahman's manifested state whereas black is inexpressible. The Law of Eternity is operational in the process of manifestation. If we see the operation of the Law of Eternity, we will have peace, bliss and love. Then we can realise that by God all these divine qualities are made functional for the generation, sustenance and transformation of the Creation. In fact, God manifests as all these divine qualities.

Brahman manifests as this Creation. Man gets peace and bliss due to divine qualities. Colours add charm and beauty to the Creation. Brahman manifests as colours and qualities. If we wish to know the background truth behind all these apparent colours and qualities, we can know the Supreme Truth who is attributeless and formless. When the Creator assumes qualities, He becomes white. He is attributeless when He is black.

Brahman is unmanifest and inexpressible. No specificity can be ascribed to Him. Rishi Yajnavalkya finally said, "Neti Neti". Although Brahman is all-pervasive, none can see Him as He is dark in colour. None can say what is inside darkness. Still darkness has its existence. That is why we can experience it.

Violet: Renunciation is placed on the violet segment of the monogram. It is as if the entire spectrum of seven colours and all its qualities are ingrained in the violet colour and the entire universe remains hidden in it. It has been said earlier that it is the place of Brahman and the segment of renunciation. Through and by renunciation, the process of self-expression starts and through the same renunciation, self-realisation is also attained. In other words, until and unless one renounces the samsar (samsaric obsessions), one cannot realise Brahman. Opposite to violet are green and yellow which stand for service and truth respectively. This is the manifested state of Brahman (gross state). Matter, men, Devas, and demons are all here. All their powers are seen here. It should be noted that a person who possesses renunciation also possesses the qualities like truth and service. Conversely, he who possesses truth and service also possesses quality of renunciation. In other words, these three qualities such as renunciation, service and truth are complementary to each other.

Indigo: The second segment of the monogram is indigo. It is the manifestation of Brahman. By His Omnipotence, He becomes many or reveals Himself as many. This is the place of 'Om'. From here He manifests Himself first as Triguna (tri-qualities) which is also known as primordial energy. From here Para Shakti expresses itself as Apara Shakti. The quality of indigo is to create divine thoughts, inspire, encourage and to do good.

In this segment, there is restraint because for blossoming of all the divine qualities, restraint is a precursor. The manifested universe is created from here and by the quality of restraint, everything is controlled and regulated. He, who possesses the power of restraint, can get the blessings of Shakti. In other words, to awaken the dormant energy in everything and also to make everything blossom fully, power of restraint is essential. It is relevant to mention that when Brahman creates this well coordinated and integrated universe by inter-linking and balancing one with the other, the quality of restraint is indispensable. Therefore each and everything contains the divine gift of restraint. All the great incarnates show lot of self-restraint.

(It is pertinent to mention that Brahman has no beginning; no end too. He remains everywhere uniformly and homogeneously. His lila operates everywhere. In other words, creation, preservation and destruction are continuously carried on by way of His lila. The realiser having realised Him indicates Him by various methods and this is one such method.)

Opposite to restraint are the two qualities, namely, truth and love. He, who restrains himself, possesses the qualities of truth and love. Conversely, he, who possesses truth and love, possesses the quality of self-restraint.

Blue: The third segment of the monogram is coloured blue. It is the colour of sky. The quality of this colour is affection, courtesy, purity and peace etc. This is the place of the personal godheads (Devas). Within the ambit of Apara Shakti, the personal godheads remain and regulate everything to execute the lila of Brahman. In other words, whatever is required for the processes of creation, preservation and destruction, is regulated by the personal godheads. It is the segment of Spiritual Practice. From spiritual point of view, the different powers of Brahman are named as personal gods. By this power only, His lila is carried on. Through lila, He expresses Himself. By spiritual practices, the latent divine power is awakened. Wherever there is spiritual practice, there is love and affection, peace and purity. Opposite to this colour are orange and red. A spiritual seeker will gradually develop the divine virtues of love and forgiveness in him. A spiritual seeker is a lover of truth. As he acquires strength by dint of spiritual practices, he will be strong enough to be in a position to forgive. The weak cannot forgive others. A person who is a lover of truth and possesses the quality of forgiveness is undoubtedly on right spiritual track.

Green: The fourth segment of the monogram represents service, which is green. This colour represents liveliness, freshness, inspiration, promptness and softness. This segment is the gross universe, the place for lila. This is also the place of actions of the jiva. Because of the above qualities, man generally remains active. As a result of his spiritual practice, he also possesses the qualities of courage, inspiration, love for peace etc. Each and every living being has got the instinct of service. Man from his birth till his death has been getting services from his mother, father, brother, sister, friends, relatives and even strangers. That is how he survives. It is God's design that man by means of service and spiritual practices should go ahead and regain his lost paradise i.e. attain his True Self. Opposite to this colour is red and violet. Violet represents renunciation and red represents forgiveness. A man who possesses this quality also possesses the twin qualities such as renunciation and forgiveness. He who can renounce can also forgive. Conversely, he who possesses the qualities of renunciation and forgiveness also possesses the temperament of serving others.

Yellow: This colour remains at the fifth segment of the monogram. The qualities of this colour are- restraint, virtues and helpfulness. This colour is brighter than all other colours. The splendour of the visible universe of invisible Brahman is fully expressed here. This segment represents complete manifestation of Brahman as Truth. Yellow colour stands for benediction, peace and goodness. This is the place of Truth. Truth manifests through yellow colour. The play of Brahman culminates here. When jiva possesses the sattvic qualities, he realises the greatness of Truth and the importance of yellow colour. He comes to know about the personal godheads. Here he gets supersensuous knowledge. His spirit of inquisitiveness is boosted up. He develops a strong urge for insight and introspection. As he realises Truth, his jiva feelings fade away and consequently he attains divine state; he becomes Truth personified and experiences Truth everywhere. He transcends Apara and attains Para knowledge.

Orange: The sixth segment of the monogram is of orange colour. The characteristics of this colour are simplicity, faith, devotion and sattvic qualities. This is the place of 'Om'. This colour is dear to everybody. Love is the ruling virtue of this segment. He, who understands the significance of this orange colour and love, can love one and all. He will not discriminate. This is the place of the tri-qualities. He, who is aware of the equilibrium state (equalities of the three qualities) Viz. Sattva, Rajas and Tamas, becomes indifferent to the worldly affairs. He can realise the Para Jnana. It may be added here that when the quality of love takes full possession of someone, the quality of renunciation also appears in him spontaneously. That is why the sages and yogis normally wear saffron robes (orange colour).

Red: This colour is present in the seventh segment of the monogram. The main characteristics of this colour are irritation, excitement and anger. Because of the above-mentioned temperaments, the qualities like violence and anger are normally found in a person. But because of the predominance of sattvic qualities in this segment, the qualities like violence and anger go away. Rather the opposite qualities such as forgiveness, kindness, helpfulness and service are seen. Because red colour is a combination of orange and violet, the qualities of both the colours such as love and renunciation are also present in the red colour along with forgiveness. Violet colour encourages self-knowledge. Because violet is present in the red colour, red colour makes one inclined towards self-knowledge and helps him proceed further. Normally the infants are simple and truthful. They like red colour. The quality of forgiveness is present in red colour. Man after transcending various stages/various colours like yellow and orange (truth and love) reaches the seventh segment which is red. At that time forgiveness becomes his predominant quality. This is a crucial state. Many spiritual aspirants fail to attain this state. He, who realises truth, will spontaneously love each and every one. As a result of love, he will become nirvikar. And forgiveness will be the ruling quality. Only such spiritual aspirants can be merged in the Brahman. In other words, he attains his heavenly abode from where he came. It should be remembered that after red, comes violet. Violet is also present in the red. In the monogram, the violet colour (renunciation) is the place of Brahman. Before coming to violet (Brahman's place) one has to be nirvikar. That is why red colour is marked by forgiveness. It is difficult to acquire the quality of forgiveness. He, who is free from all qualities, or he, who has transcended all qualities, can only forgive. Without attaining this state, no one can attain Brahman.

The foregoing paragraphs indicate the interrelationship among the seven colours and the seven divine virtues. If we realise the significance of each and every colour, we are bound to be astonished. It is as if all and sundry forms in this universe, activated by the colours and qualities, are actively serving a divine purpose and playing a divine game in a subtle and silent manner. A deeper analysis can only unravel this mystery. An incisive insight can reveal that colours and qualities influence and mould the entire universe by someone's well thought out directions and intelligent guidance.

Astrology lays great stress on the colour science. Different stars and planets emit different rays with different colours and with different effects. Tantra Sastra also lays much importance on rays and colours to achieve the desired effects. One will be surprised to know the effects of various rays, which are the fourth state of matter. During yogic practice, the yogi meditates on various chakras in the body and gets the desired results from various colours emitted by the chakras. Ayurveda also makes use of different colours to control various diseases. Even glass containers of different colours are used to put liquid so as to have different effects to cure diseases. Colours produce various effects by which we are influenced. Without colours, this Creation would have been dull. The Creation being colourful, we are attracted towards the same and derive pleasure. Without colours, it would have been confusing for us to identify or differentiate varieties of animals, birds and innumerable objects. How would we have distinguished between gold and silver? How would we have identified and named different creatures? The golden beam of the rising sun captivates every one. The reddish hue of the setting Sun with its aesthetic beauty entices everybody. Colourful plants, flowers, fruits, mountainous ranges, birds and animals contribute to the beauty and bliss. All these are for our sake. What a marvellous Creation God has made for our peace and happiness! These colours are not just only colours. Colours contain different divine qualities in them so as to enrich this Creation and give happiness to one and all. But for divine qualities, we would have never existed with our various forms and colours. Divya Darshan expounds the significance of various divine virtues and presents the same before the mankind so that they can acquire the same, live with peace, harmony and happiness and attain True Self ultimately.

Seven Divine Virtues

(A compilation of various discourses delivered by Sadguru)

[Divya Darshan gives lot of importance to the seven divine virtues. If one can practice even one of these virtues he will enjoy bliss. The below mentioned article is a synthesis of various talks on the divine virtues delivered by Sadguru Sri Sri Arjun at various places and times. It is not an exact translation of his talks but a gist. It is presented here for the benefit of the readers.]

Divya Darshan lays great emphasis on knowledge and divine virtues for effective spiritual practice that leads the aspirant to the spiritual goal. With intense inquisitiveness, a spiritual seeker starts his spiritual practice and keeps on acquiring true knowledge. He also tries to inculcate divine virtues in him. Reading, listening, meditating and contemplating are the ways to acquiring knowledge. The spiritual seeker divinises himself by instinctively expressing divine qualities in his conduct. In course of acquisition of knowledge, he unveils one truth after another and purifies himself.

The entire universe owes its existence to the divine qualities. Divine qualities bring peace and happiness to life. The opposite of divine qualities are the demoniac qualities. With demoniac qualities, none can be happy. Divine qualities are inexhaustible i.e. without any limitation or erosion. The Creation is lively and vibrant only due to divine qualities. Divine qualities bring fulfilment to life i.e. attainment of the divine goal. The secret of observance of the Law of Eternity lies in the divine qualities. He, who spontaneously conducts himself with the divine qualities, is pious and he truly observes Dharma that leads him to the goal of self-realisation.

What does the spiritual mendicant gain from the spiritual practice? The answer is- 'Divine Virtues' that pave the way clear to attainment of the goal of self-realisation. He comes to know the greatness of God and His role play. He becomes keen to know and observe the Law of Eternity. Thus, he observes Dharma and realises the Supreme Truth. The Creation is a manifestation of the divine qualities. Therefore, all the divine qualities are discreetly present in and around us. When divine qualities or virtues become our way of life, we lead a divine life which is full of happiness, peace and bliss. Divya Darshan explains the importance and indispensability of the divine qualities for a happy and harmonious living and urges upon everyone to practise the seven divine virtues. They are- Renunciation, Restraint, Spiritual Practice, Service, Truth, Love and Forgiveness. Those are explained briefly in the following paragraphs.

Renunciation: Although this quality comes first, all the divine qualities are interlinked with each other. This quality is especially important because by this quality, the jiva has come from Brahman and again by this quality, he will be merged with Brahman thus completing the grand cycle. This is such a great power that all apparently impossible things can be made possible by it. Without this quality of renunciation, the system would not have been dynamic. We cannot think of a motionless Creation characterized by inertia only. No evolution would have taken place. There would have been no Creation even. Tendency of renunciation is there in every being in this Creation. Due to this tendency, a person is able to move on the path of self-development even though this tendency is not perceptible to the outside world. All scriptures in the world have therefore given importance to this divine quality of renunciation. It is true that lot of benefits accrue to the people who possess the quality of renunciation or the spirit of sacrifice. By possessing this quality man gets release from the snares of illusion. Without this quality man's progress would have halted. Due to the grace of God, man has taken birth on this earth with this great quality of renunciation. Man is lucky to have this great divine quality but due to ignorance man is not able to understand the importance of renunciation and that is why he has been suffering a lot. Had he not possessed this quality of renunciation, he would have got more sufferings; his survival would have been impossible. There are many examples of great persons who have sacrificed a lot for others. The sages have also sacrificed their comfort for the sake of God. Lord Buddha had sacrificed his family and kingdom in quest of truth. When the question of renunciation comes, people are usually afraid. They fear that if they will sacrifice everything, how will they survive? This feeling comes due to ignorance. If one thinks deeply, one will know that his survival has been possible due to this essential divine quality of renunciation. Our journey starts from renunciation and ends up with renunciation. Man moves on the path of life's journey due to this divine quality. Man is really a great renunciate. He finally relinquishes everything for the sake of others.

❧ ✦ ❧

If someone wants to go to a particular place, he starts walking. He is to lift one step after another. One foot is to leave the ground first; thereafter the second foot will also leave the ground and move forward. In other words, one has to leave the present spot to move to next spot. That means, without renunciation or sacrifice, progress is not possible. Similarly, a child must leave the mother's lap or his play kits to go to school for education. Take for example a scientist who has made so much sacrifice to invent or discover certain things for the benefit of the world. He sacrifices all his comforts, forgets about his food, and even puts his life at risk for accomplishing his task. That is why God has probably gifted man with inquisitiveness.

But the ignorant men do not realise the importance of sacrifice. For them, the truth remains veiled. Even the ferocious animals like the tigers make lot of sacrifices for their cubs and bring them up with lot of care. That means sacrifice is a natural quality in all beings. A mother bird, starting from laying of eggs to hatching and thereafter feeding and protecting its little ones makes a lot of sacrifice. Wherefrom do they learn to make such sacrifice? Throughout the kingdom of nature the principle of sacrifice can be seen. That means sacrifice is a God given quality. There are umpteen examples of people sacrificing their lives even for the sake of their kin or kingdom, for race or religion, for truth and love. Those, who realise the value of sacrifice and make selfless sacrifices win the hearts of millions and become immortal. Divya Darshan says, "Sacrifice does not bring sufferings, rather it brings happiness, bliss and divinity."

We have taken birth due to sacrifice; we go ahead on the path of self-development to ultimately reach our goal of self-realisation due to sacrifice. Man starts discarding one thing after another from his very childhood. A time comes when this world has to be renounced. Body, mind, intellect and even the Creation are to be renounced. A time comes when nothing remains to be renounced. This state is called the Supreme state. Rishi Yajnavalkya while explaining about Brahman remained silent after pronouncing 'Neti Neti' which means, 'Not this, not like this'. After renouncing everything, realisation of self is possible. Only renouncing the house property, family and children is not adequate for this purpose. Those who are at the lower level of knowledge cannot understand the true import of renunciation. One must know what all have been renounced and what else are to be renounced. Finally, renunciation has to be renounced. Then only one can move to the highest state. A spiritual seeker has to think in this line and then only he can reach the highest state. He, who realises the importance of renunciation, can advance faster.

The sages had renounced everything and that is how they could reach the Supreme state. It is to be well understood that a renouncer finally attains everything after which nothing remains to be achieved. One must possess the necessary quality or qualification before possessing big things. Entertaining worldly thoughts, one cannot enjoy the Supreme Bliss which is possible only by renunciation. Some leave the worldly life and go to jungle. But while remaining in the jungle also they may get obsessed with the worldly thoughts. Then what type of renunciation is this?

The scriptures instruct mankind to give up desires. He, who follows it, can develop himself faster and attain self-realisation. For a true renouncer, what is there to lose? Hence there is no question of any loss and consequent suffering. By this quality of renunciation, a spiritual seeker can transcend the lower truths one after another to finally reach the Supreme state.

By renunciation, self-development is possible. Renunciation brings peace and bliss. Life begins from renunciation and ends up with renunciation. Renunciation frees one from all bondages and consequent sufferings. Renunciation uplifts one to the Supreme state where nothing remains to be received, nothing remains to be renounced.

We all have been sacrificing something or other in our personal lives. Parents sacrifice so many things for the children. People will be motivated to sacrifice if they understand that they are going to get better things. Since people do not have idea about the higher aspects of life, they cling to the smaller things considering them as indispensable.

At the highest level, it will be well understood that nothing is renounced. Only there is a change in thoughts or perceptions.

Lord Buddha said, "Craving is the cause of sufferings". The common people are unable to understand or appreciate the import of this statement. Some people argue, "Whether desire for liberation is not a desire?"

The sages clarify that desire for liberation is no desire. It is one's instinct to know the Self. Whatever is done for realisation of Self is Dharma. Desire for sensuous enjoyment is desire that is the cause of sins and sufferings. That way, God-realisation is not possible.

Due to ignorance, people sacrifice certain things in exchange for something considered to be more gainful. But desireless renunciation is true renunciation that can bring infinite peace and bliss. Spiritual bliss is free from anxiety and fear. Those who are attached to worldly matters cannot attain self-realisation. It is to be remembered that renunciation is the Law of nature.

Renunciation does not mean giving up or running away from the samsar. It means living in this world but with a different understanding, with a different vision. Renunciation is practiced at every step. Any movement involves renunciation. Any change involves renunciation. Any renunciation involves a process of sacrifice on one side and acceptance on the other side. The jiva after leaving his Supreme state has been born as jiva. Again by renouncing only, he will go back to True Self which is the Supreme state.

In other words, by renunciation only he will be able to attain liberation. He has to renounce everything other than his True Self. He has to go beyond his body, senses, mind, and intellect. He has to renounce the samsar in order to realise his True Self. He has to renounce the non-self to realise the Self. Anything other than the Self is non-self. (But the reality is that, there is nothing other than the Self. Everything is Self only). When Self is realised everything becomes Self. Everything vanishes except Self. Ishavasya Upanishad says- "The Almighty pervades everywhere. Everything belongs to Him. Whatever is available to us are all for our use. But we are not the owners. Only the Almighty is the owner. We can be dispossessed of everything whenever he chooses to do so. Hence it should always be remembered that all the possessions ignorantly claimed to be ours are not really ours. Everything belongs to Him." Once the seeker realises this truth, it is said that he has truly renounced. This feeling is renunciation. In other words, it is a state of knowledge which does not involve physically forsaking anything. We breathe in because we also breathe out. We have left our childhood. We attained youth. We have to leave our youth and become old. This is the law of nature. Renunciation is the law of nature. This law is also applicable to the vegetable kingdom as well as mineral kingdom. The fruit leaves the mother tree to develop into another tree. The electrons keep on moving and join with others to form new substances. The root works day and night not just for itself but also to nourish the whole tree. Every part of the plant is engaged in a predetermined manner helping each other for sustenance. Renunciation does not mean only rejection. It also means acceptance. It means abandoning something for the sake of some other. We, as human beings, are bestowed with inquisitiveness. We must keep on reviewing our existing knowledge. We should give up our obsolete knowledge to learn newer and newer truths. Lower truths must be abandoned for the sake of higher truths. Lower goals must be relinquished for the sake of the highest goal. That only can lead us to real evolution. Low-value items must be given up for things of higher value. Our mind-set must change. Our vision must change. We must analyse which is permanent and which is not. We must hold on to the eternal and renounce the ephemeral things we come across on our way.

Self-Restraint: It comes in the second segment of the Divya Darshan monogram. Life cannot run smoothly without self-restraint. Self-restraint helps one proceed fast towards the goal. Just as a motor vehicle cannot run faster in absence of a proper brake system, similarly life journey gets obstructed and retarded if there is no self-restraint. There is an intimate relation between renunciation and self-restraint. Self-restraint is the outcome of renunciation. That means, one has to renounce certain things to have self-restraint. Renunciation also comes on practising self-restraint. That is why we find that a true renunciate is a restrained person.

Self-restraint means controlling power. Man possesses this quality from his very birth, as it is a God given quality or a divine quality. Those, who are under the clutches of their sense organs, cannot restrain themselves. That is why they suffer a lot. At times, man loses control over his sense organs resulting in lot of disturbances. As a result, many sufferings in the forms of disease, accidents, clashes and mental unrest etc. raise their ugly hoods which distract him from moving towards his goal. The wise persons understand this well. But the ignorant cannot think of the indispensability of self-restraint.

Man is endowed with lot of powers within him. In appropriate situations, these dormant powers rise and become clearly perceptible. For example, during phases of sufferings, a person struggles and many creative qualities in him come up. He may get more and more devoted towards God. His tolerance capacity may increase. But due to want of self-restraint, man's hidden qualities cannot blossom up. When a man talks more, not only he wastes his energy, but he tells many exaggerated things and even lies. He may, in order to impress others, be pretentious; as a result of which people in course of time reject him as a liar even when he speaks some truth. If a man sleeps excessively, he becomes lazy and useless. Rather he suffers from more diseases. If a man eats excessively, he becomes indisposed and suffers. As a result, he suffers physically and mentally also. Quarrels occur between individuals and groups because of lack of self-restraint. God has bestowed upon us lot of powers. It is our responsibility to conserve the same and utilise properly. That is why, even though we are strong intrinsically, we behave at times like weak creatures. Birds and animals are also seen to maintain self-restraint and discipline. They instinctively follow the natural laws perhaps more than the human beings. Self-restraint is also seen everywhere in the kingdom of nature. The sages are so powerful because they possess the divine quality of self-restraint.

Restraint helps a spiritual mendicant to move faster on the path of self-development. It must be remembered that without self-restraint, renunciation is not possible, and without renunciation, self-restraint is not possible. Both are divine qualities, and they are intertwined. Self-restraint brings balance to life. A person becomes more stable by the quality of self-restraint because of which he becomes stronger physically and mentally. Internal power gets strengthened by self-restraint. Self-restraint enables one to acquire more and more power. Self-restraint not only protects us, it also helps us attain our goal. A restrained man is a successful man.

Restraint or self-discipline is always observed in nature. The various ingredients of air always maintain their limitations and proportions. The oceans confine themselves to their shores. The fire remains sheathed everywhere until a particular situation is created to make it appear as a devouring flame. Every matter reacts in a manner consistent with its latent properties, which are pre-designed. Slowly but systematically, a seed evolves into a plant. The earth and all other planets move in a predetermined way in their orbits.

Spiritual Practice (Sadhana): In the third segment of the monogram, there is Spiritual Practice or Sadhana. Without self-restraint, one cannot do spiritual practice properly. Thus, there is intimate link between self-restraint and spiritual practice. Man cannot live without work. He is always engaged in some work or other, mental or physical, be it good or bad. According to the Law of Action, he reaps appropriate results thereof. Due to ignorance, man is very often unable to distinguish between good and bad. This brings sufferings to him. Karma is undertaken with the purpose of living a good life with peace and happiness. But that does not happen. It is due to ignorance about right action. Due to ignorance, he thinks that he has come to this world only to enjoy. He usually prefers to spend a care-free life in an unrestrained manner. In other words, he undertakes some special efforts occasionally to accomplish some goal or fulfil his wishes. Therefore one should know what sadhana is.

Some people are afraid that they may have to move to jungle or enter into fire and perform many difficult rituals for undertaking sadhana. But man does not understand that daily he performs some sadhana or other during the course of his daily routine works. In other words, we are performing sadhana daily but unknowingly. To realise God, no difficult practice is to be specially undertaken. A farmer does so much of sadhana to accomplish his farming work. Even a thief or a pick-pocket learns so many tricks for stealing. Compared to all these, spiritual practice to realise God is easier. God has gifted us with so many divine qualities. Only if we know their importance and try to inculcate those divine qualities in us, we can achieve wonders. Peace and happiness will be within our easy reach.

By doing karma in a proper manner, not only we should survive, but also we should live harmoniously in the society with peace and happiness, and ultimately realise our True Self by acquiring self-knowledge. This should be everyone's karttavya of highest order. Any other type of karma bereft of the above objective will surely bring us bondage and sufferings. Man being the best and most developed creature in this Creation, all his actions should be performed with knowledge and skill. It should be remembered that without sadhana, one cannot possess adequate strength, courage and confidence to accomplish his goal. Sadhana enables a man to lead a successful and worthy life.

Skill employed to consciously accomplish a goal smoothly and selflessly in shortest time with minimum cost and labour is known as sadhana. Spiritual practice or sadhana is enhanced by renunciation and self-restraint. Renunciation, self-restraint and spiritual practice constitute Karma Yoga. By spiritual practice, self-restraint also gets strengthened. Therefore, self-restraint and spiritual practice are complementary to each other. According to Divya Darshan, whatever karma a man performs in his day to day life, constitutes sadhana or spiritual practice although he is not aware of the unknown and distant goal. There is no need to perform any fearsome practice to attain one's True Self. Only if all our karma is streamlined towards a particular goal, success is bound to come on the way. On the other hand, if karma is performed in a whimsical or haphazard manner, there are more chances of failure than of success. We all perform some karma or other. Whatever we do is all karma. But the most pertinent point is- 'What should we do?' The answer is- The goal of attaining true knowledge and realising True Self is the highest karma, Dharma, Karttavya and Sadhana for a human being who has already been bestowed with inquisitiveness, knowledge and conscience. Hence man should unswervingly tread on the spiritual path and undertake spiritual practices to know his real spiritual identity. This is called true divine life. Karma becomes sadhana when karma, linked to the goal, is skilfully performed in a selfless manner without eyeing on the fruits of action. It is called Karma Yoga. The essence of sadhana is skill in action linked to the goal. Animals and birds etc. perform their activities with their latent skill. Birds build their nests so skilfully. The white ants build the ant-hills so beautifully. Similarly, the honeybees build their hives with so much of diligence and skill. It is their sadhana. Man is endowed with the discriminating faculty to know what good is and what bad is. It is man only who can enquire about his goal. He is endowed with conscience. He gets inspiration and encouragement from within. Good works enhance divine virtues in him. That is why it is said that karma is the cause of bondage; karma is also the cause of freedom. Man becomes more powerful by dint of spiritual practice through karma, bhakti and jnana. Spiritual practice culminates as divine virtues which ultimately lead to attainment of Moksa. Spiritual practice is a path of self-development and the goal is attainment of True Self. By knowledge and spiritual practice, the impossible can be made possible. If anything is considered impossible, it is to be inferred that there is inadequacy of either or both.

Service (Seva): It is in the fourth segment of the monogram. Service is God gifted quality which is always functional in this Creation. Nothing is a separate entity. Everything works in tandem with something or other. Everything is integrated with the other. One serves the other. One depends upon another. The plant kingdom draws its sustenance from the mineral kingdom. The animal kingdom cannot survive without the plant kingdom. Multifarious natural ingredients constitute the mineral kingdom. They are at the service of the natural flora and fauna which in turn are engaged in the service of the animal world. The herbal shrubs are a great boon to us. Even earth, water, light, air etc. always render their services. Without the Sun and Sunlight, the Earth would not have come to existence. We would not have been there; the plant kingdom and the animal kingdom would not have been there. Be it day and night or seasonal changes, everything we get due to regular and timely rotation of the Earth round the Sun.

Service or Seva is so important for our survival. Even to maintain our bodies, we must take care of them regularly. To live harmoniously in the society with peace and happiness to complete the life's journey, we require so many services from others at each stage. Otherwise, our living would have been impossible. We are also expected to serve others when needed. Particularly in old age or while in the hospital for treatment, the indispensability of service is well-experienced. Man is born to move on the path of self-development for which he must possess divine qualities. There are many who, in order to earn virtues, dig wells and ponds for the benefit of others. Some build rest houses, schools, orphanages and hospitals for the service of the people. Thus, people render services to others in several ways. The goal of human life is realisation of True Self. This is liberation. For attainment of this highest goal, all must consciously strive in whatever religions or professions they may be. Therefore, reading scriptures and spreading spiritual knowledge for the self-development of others in the society is also a noble and important service. We should not only walk on the path of Dharma but we should also motivate others to walk on the path of Dharma which is so important for the attainment of life's goal. It is said that service to mankind is service to God.

In our own bodies various limbs work in a mutually supportive manner to serve a common interest. Various systems, which are for blood circulation, food digestion and respiration etc., function so perfectly and incessantly. Most sophisticated parts like brain, heart, liver, lungs and kidney etc. work flawlessly in all of us for which we survive and are kept fit. The parents, however big they may be, serve their children. Even the ferocious tigress feeds her cubs and protects them. Nature provides the life-saving milk in the mother's breast before a baby is born. Sun gives us light, heat, life and energy. Moon sprinkles the subtle and soothing beam and lights the whole earth. The plants consume the carbon di-oxide and release the oxygen for our use. From all these examples, it is quite evident that service is the underlying essential principle in this Creation. Through service, one will be able to get oneself acquainted with higher and higher truths. People serve the nation whether one is a farmer, defence personnel, scientist, teacher, researcher or an artisan. While an educationist educates others by his knowledge, a soldier keeps the whole country secure. Through service, one will be able to get acquainted with higher and higher truths that bring him more knowledge and experience. For example, a scientist carries on various experiments in his laboratory and does so much research, even sacrificing his food and sleep at times. Even if he may not be successful in all his endeavours, his knowledge gets enhanced at every step. That is how he moves on from matters to atoms, and from atoms to protons and from protons to god-particles, thereby unravelling truths one after another. Service is the culmination of Karma Yoga. Therefore, in service, there are both karma and *bhava*. Sattvic qualities develop in the man who serves. Bhakti Yoga begins from seva. Without seva, the life of the living beings would have been miserable. Nature is so bountiful that she feeds one and all and provides all minerals and vitamins for our sustenance. Nature is God's manifestation. God assumes different forms and names, and appears before us as nature, serves us every day by providing refreshing morning, sunshine, colourful flowers, varieties of flavoursome fruits, vegetables, and food grains with so much care and love.

A mother renders desireless service to her children. Services rendered with some motive or with expectation for some return become less effective as they cannot give pure happiness to the recipients. The desire to serve others should come from the core of heart. This is pure and sattvic. The spiritual seekers can very quickly take to desireless service while most of the people render services with desires. One day or other, they will also come to the level of desireless service. As explained in the Shrimad Bhagavad-Gita,

Karma Yoga means giving up sense of doership, surrendering all karma to God and finally giving up desire for any fruit. This is called desireless action (karma).

Divya Darshan says, karma in order to be qualitatively better and more productive, must be backed by knowledge and skill. Karma becomes service or seva when it is intended for the well-being of others and self, with the ultimate aim of attaining one's goal of self-realisation. The term, 'others', includes plants, animals and humans. Seva-oriented karma is the karttavya or duty of everybody. In other words, such desireless karma becomes seva, karttavya, sadhana (spiritual practice) and Dharma. That means, if karma is undertaken by someone with knowledge and skill for the wellness of self as well as others i.e. with the attitude of rendering services (seva) to others, it will develop other divine virtues such as truth, love and forgiveness in him, and shall bring him peace, bliss and self-realisation which is the goal of everybody.

By seva, one can get blessings from everyone, i.e. from animal, bird, man and the divine beings. Through and by seva, a man's past sins as well as his bondages can be destroyed in this birth. The importance of seva has been well explained in various scriptures. Seva is the duty (karttavya) and Dharma of everybody. Seva brings self-development. Seva brings peace and bliss. Lord Jesus said, "Love thy neighbour as Thyself." According to Divya Darshan, service and love are complementary to each other. In love, there are seva (service) and bliss. Seva is an effective medium to establish relationship with God. Seva cleans all inner dirt and purifies the man who serves desirelessly. Service does not mean only serving others. Service also means service to the self and God. First, we have to take care of our bodies by cleaning them regularly, take appropriate food and water for their maintenance. We do Yoga and Pranayam. We also do meditation for the stability of mind and intellect. While these are essential, service to God is the best service. Service elevates one to other divine qualities like truth, love and forgiveness which constitute Jnana Yoga according to Divya Darshan. In special circumstances even God incarnates to directly serve mankind by imparting true knowledge by which they can tread on the path of Dharma, get rid of all sufferings, and attain peace, bliss and liberation. The divine quality of seva is there in everybody. It is a God-gifted quality which man possesses since his birth.

Truth: This divine quality is placed in the fifth segment of the monogram. Most of the people know about truth, but in a limited sense. It is very difficult to define truth. It is not that easy to decide what is true and what is untrue. The greatness of the term truth is unknown to many. The equivalent of Truth in Sanskrit is 'Satya' which means- "That which was there in the past, is present now and shall exist in future." In other words, Truth is that which always exists. Truth is only eternal. In this world, only truth exists for ever. All others are ephemeral. The world is there due to manifestation of Truth. Whatever is experienced, heard or seen, everything is manifestation of Truth. Therefore, Truth is eternal.

Truth manifests as forms and qualities. On the other hand, Truth which is present as the basis or cause of the names and forms is called Supreme Truth. Our world experience is mainly due to our five sense organs such as eye, ear, nose, tongue and skin. There are some invisible things which the sense organs cannot reach. By knowledge alone, we experience those subtle and invisible things.

Examples: Ice is a truth. Without water, ice would not have been possible. Likewise, water is composed of some gas molecules. This means that water has come from Hydrogen and Oxygen. Without this combination, water or ice would not have been possible. In other words, although ice, water, vapour are truths, they have come from some other truths such as Hydrogen and Oxygen. It is pertinent to note that the Supreme Truth who is there as the Supra-Causal factor cannot be explained by citing any example. Examples can be advanced for the manifested states only. But no example is possible in respect of the Unmanifest who is Unity, Eternity, Infinity and the Indivisible Whole. There is none second to Him.

The Supreme Truth manifests as innumerable truths like forms and qualities. To explain the Supreme Truth and His manifested states, different names such as Brahman, Ishwar, jiva, plants, air, water, earth etc. are ascribed. Truth is present somewhere as the cause, somewhere as karma and somewhere as the result thereof. In this way, the processes of creation, preservation and destruction happen incessantly. This manifestation is generally called as lila. In other words, Truth manifests through lila. The maker of lila is the Supreme Truth. He is the Supra-Causal force and there is none other than Him. Whatever we come across or experience, whether the same is considered by us as good or bad, everything is but truth. There are some favourable situations for the jiva depending on which he survives. When man faces unfavourable situations, according to him, he suffers. This is due to ignorance. He misconstrues something for other due to ignorance as a result of which he gets himself entangled in different situations. It is necessary therefore to know what truth is. Knowing the truth is called true knowledge or right knowledge. By acquiring true knowledge, one can get rid of all sufferings. This Creation is nothing but a manifestation of truth. The Creation is full of truth from the beginning to the end. Everything is regulated by truth. Man is born by truth and survives by truth. He gets happiness, peace and bliss due to truth. Man cannot live even for a moment without truth. Truth exists eternally. Truth is neither created nor destroyed. Realisation of Truth is the greatest bliss. Truth can be explained by truth only.

Different minerals have different properties. Different plants have different characteristics. Different animals have different forms and qualities. Those are all relative truths. The Supreme Truth is the Absolute Truth. He is Brahman who pervades everywhere. He sustains all and protects all. Truth is the life and vital energy of everybody. Truth appears as brother, father, friends and relatives to support us. Truth brings happiness, peace and bliss to everyone. There is truth behind our birth. There is also truth for our death. There is truth for our bondage; there is truth for our freedom. There is truth for our suffering; there is also truth for our peace and bliss. Realisation of truth brings bliss. Without truth, the Creation would not have been possible. Behind all changes, there is Truth which is unchangeable. Truth can be realised by knowledge in *bhava* state, but not by arguments. It is not that easy to realise Truth. By the good impulses acquired during past several births only, there arises inquisitiveness to know what Truth is. Then only one gets some indication of Truth. Truth manifests spontaneously. Not knowing the Truth is ignorance.

It is therefore our first and foremost duty to uphold truth, practise and apply truth. Truth can be realised by truth. Everything becomes possible by truth. Respecting and loving truth is the highest divine quality which one should have. Ultimately you will realise that you are the Truth-Absolute. Never ignore or disrespect truth. If one disrespects truth, the outcome is suffering.

Love: This divine quality is placed in the sixth petal of the monogram of Divya Darshan. This Creation is nothing but God's play or lila. The quality of love has made this Creation livelier and more beautiful. Some people love money; some people love matters, and some people love beautiful creatures. The play of love goes on incessantly in this world, somewhere less and somewhere more depending on the nature and behaviour of the lover and the loved. The quality of love is instinctively present everywhere and in every being. To inculcate the quality of love, no external training is necessary. Everyone has an instinct to get happiness and bliss. That is why there is love which is a divine quality. Where there is love, there is bliss (Ananda).God has gifted love to all of us so that we will be happy and blissful. But due to ignorance, man is not able to understand the value of true love. Had he known what true love is, he would have intensely loved the Creator, the Love-Absolute to enjoy infinite bliss. "God is mine. I am His. His 'Self' and my 'Self' are one and the same. I am That." This blissful state is liberation where there is no fear or anxiety.

Opposite of bliss is suffering. In other words, absence of peace and happiness is called suffering or misery. Due to ignorance of the jiva about his blissful True Self, he suffers. In order to get rid of sufferings, he makes some efforts. Thus, everyone is on his journey towards liberation.

Now the question is- why man is not able to attain that blissful state called liberation? It is because he makes some sporadic attempts lacking sincerity and focus. It must be remembered that love is an essential prerequisite for attaining the blissful state which is liberation. It is regrettable that due to ignorance, man does not understand the value of love. In his day to day life, he entertains the feelings of ego, selfishness, jealousy, anger and greed which are opposite to the quality of love. With such qualities, how can he get peace and happiness? Only by possessing the divine quality of love, one can attain peace and liberation. We are under the wrong impression that man can live happily if he has good amount of material possessions. Had it been so, the kings and emperors would have been the happiest men in this Creation. Only because of their outward splendour they appear to be happy. Even a person with no material wealth can be happy if he possesses the divine quality of love. Let us take the example of the sages who live so happily. They do not have any possession, not even a small hut. Still they live in bliss. A mother loves her child so much. All other material things are insignificant compared to mother's love. Where there is love, there is peace and bliss. So many other qualities like sacrifice, truth, restraint, forgiveness and service remain ingrained in the divine quality of love. In other words, all the divine qualities culminate as love. In absence of love, one has to undergo sufferings throughout. In other words, where there is suffering, there is no love. Due to ignorance, infatuation is misconstrued for love. The tamasic people, who are mostly guided by their mind, rarely differentiate between right and wrong. That is why they suffer. Mind being volatile makes the man restless and unstable. Accordingly, his thoughts also change amazingly fast. Man gets attracted towards a beautiful appearance that makes him happy for some time but when gradually the beauty fades away, he again becomes unhappy. Therefore, a beautiful appearance is not a source of permanent joy.

True love does not know any suffering. True love starts from love for someone's qualities. As explained earlier, love for a beautiful appearance cannot be termed as love. The same is only infatuation. Qualities are subtle and hence last longer. In other words, quality is more beautiful than mere appearance. We might have come across many great personalities who were so much adorable for their knowledge or proficiency. Those, who love qualities more than appearance, are of rajasic nature since they are guided by their intelligence. But this love is not pure love because there remains a hidden element of some expectation. Love that comes from the level of conscience is of sattvic nature. Hence it is superior to the previous ones. We must remember that Atman is more lovable than qualities. Atman is eternal. Hence the love for Atman is eternal and blissful. Further, Atman undergoes no birth, decay or death. There is not an iota of suffering too. Those who love Atman are great. They simultaneously possess the qualities of truth, service, piety and righteousness etc. Due to these divine qualities one becomes eligible to attain Atman. Where there is love but other divine qualities are absent, it means, it is not true love. Such so-called love is either pretentious or deceptive. One cannot get lasting peace or bliss from out of such spurious love. True love is therefore so important. To spread the message of love, great personalities like Lord Jesus and Sri Chaitanya descended on earth to teach mankind what love is. Love is nectar-like. He, who possesses this divine quality, lives in eternal bliss and becomes immortal.

There is nothing to get disheartened. Anybody can attain this stage of love. It is an eternal truth. The basis of bliss is love which is present in everybody. Hence there is no question of not getting the same. The Creation exists due to love. Hence it is not impossible to develop the quality of love from inside. The tigress is so ferocious. But how carefully and lovingly does it bring up its cubs! Had there been no divine quality of love in the mother tigress, the kids would not have survived. If we look at a bird, we see how sincere and careful it is while building its nest. How it broods over its eggs constantly! How it feeds and protects its offspring! Is it not due to love? How much a mother loves her children! It is a befitting example of desireless and unalloyed love. Even a thief who indulges in wrongdoings loves his kids so much. If any love is driven by selfish desires, it is not pure love.

Desireless love brings peace and bliss. Love gradually rises from the level of intelligence and reaches the level of Atman. This is the culmination of love. Bliss is the outcome. It is Supreme Bliss or Eternal Bliss. So many sages had attained this state after prolonged spiritual practices. The quality of love gets blossomed in one's heart due to God's grace. We love various matters, men and animals but we are not able to love God due to our ignorance. He, who loves God gets rid of all sufferings and becomes Bliss-Absolute.

We must recollect our mother's love and her sacrifice for us. We have survived due to mother's love. All creatures in this Creation have survived due to their mothers' love. This means, there is mother's love behind every life. Love is God gifted. It is the basis of the Creation. Everyone possesses this God-gifted quality from his very birth. By this quality of love, man can realise God ultimately. Once one attains this state, one will be loved by one and all. For him, nothing is impossible. An enemy will become friendly with him. All sufferings shall vanish. He will be the happiest man even if he leads life as a householder.

As knowledge increases, sattvic qualities also increase. By sattvic quality, love can be understood. Gradually, this love shall be transformed into universal love. At that time, the jiva will feel as if he is in the ocean of bliss. When the jiva will love Brahman, it is the highest love different from all other types of love. In this state, only forgiveness reigns supreme. There does not remain any ill feeling towards anybody or anything. Everything becomes divine.

True nature of love: Jiva is born in bliss. That is why he craves for bliss. By means of love, he enjoys bliss. Therefore, his instinct is to love. There is selfishness in mundane love. Therefore, it is the cause of bondage. When it is extended to universal love or divine love, it brings liberation. There is no selfishness in true love. In true love, there remains no expectation, no grudge, or any type of non-fulfilment. There is no desire for any wealth or fame, not even liberation. His happiness is my happiness; His wills and instructions are only to be fulfilled or carried out by me. What else is there to offer to Him other than Self? In other words, complete and unconditional self-surrender is true love. He, who loves the Truth-Absolute, becomes blissful. It is nothing but loving the Self. This highest love culminates in union with Brahman. There remains only unity without any diversity. I am Love-Absolute, Bliss-Absolute and Truth-Absolute self-manifested as the Creation. This is realisation of True Self, or liberation. The Self, through lila, loves the Self and gets united with the Self who is blissful and eternal.

The role and importance of Love: He, who possesses the divine quality of love, gets rid of all sufferings and realises True Self. All accumulated *vikaras* are destroyed at the magic touch of true love. In love, the importance of renunciation is quite evident. All disharmony and discord vanish where love rules. Love can achieve wonders that any material wealth cannot achieve. Love is the Grace of God. Hence love is so powerful. Bliss is the outcome of love. Nothing remains unattained where there is love. The Creation is sustained by love. Without it, everything would have been disintegrated and destroyed. Love is the most powerful tool for God-realisation. There is no other divine quality stronger than love.

Love from spiritual angle: Brahman has Ahladini Shakti. This Shakti has the power to attract one and all towards itself (Brahman). This force contains love and love contains attractive force. Love and attraction are one and the same. This is present everywhere and in everything. True nature of love is inexplicable or inexpressible. It can only be experienced. It is called infinite love, celestial love or divine love. Atman is unitary but manifests in different stages and appears many. There is gold but when it appears in different designs as ornaments, it looks more attractive. Love is like that. It appears differently in different beings like love between husband and wife, brother and sister, mother and child etc. Love also expresses itself through different forms and qualities. The sages had realised this and that is why they loved God as well as all beings. They loved the whole universe as divine manifestation.

The term 'love', due to ignorance, is not understood properly. The mundane love ends up with sufferings whereas the divine love is always blissful. By so much spiritual practices, a man can realise that supreme state of love. Man attains this highest state of love only by divine grace. God is Love-Absolute and Bliss-Absolute. Without His grace, man cannot love Him. He, who loves Him, attains Him. At that time, there is no end to the love and there is no end to the bliss. Man gets lost in bliss. Everything becomes still and silent. Only blissful tears roll out from the realiser.

Forgiveness: Forgiveness is placed in the seventh segment or the last step. It is the best and highest among all divine qualities. All *vikaras* vanish when the spiritual mendicant attains the state of forgiveness. As a result of all spiritual practices, the mendicant attains this state and realises his goal of self-realisation. Forgiveness is a divine quality that is spontaneous. This quality is not learnt and acquired. It is a gift of nature and therefore it spontaneously appears in the spiritual seeker. Had there been no divine quality like forgiveness, the earth would have been destroyed long ago.

A tiger is ferocious. But it tolerates all nuisances made by its cubs. It does not kill them. A mother smilingly tolerates and forgives her child who is so naughty and troublesome. It is a God-gifted instinct in the mother to forgive her children. Other accompanying qualities of forgiveness are service, truth and love. Forgiveness comes because of love. The seeker thereafter reaches nirvikar state and gets rid of all worldly sufferings.

Forgiveness is the highest strength and a supreme quality. This divine quality puts out all negative qualities such as greed, jealousy and intolerance. It is so powerful that it can captivate the whole world even. Forgiveness is a powerful asset that leads to God-realisation. Forgiveness is synonymous with happiness, peace and bliss. It qualifies the seeker to reach the highest goal which he has been craving for so long.

Instead of forgiveness, when man becomes a prey to the demoniac qualities like revengefulness, he burns himself in the fire of anger, jealousy and crookedness, and thereby he suffers a lot. His counterpart will also be reactive and revengeful and inflict pain on him. In such situation, where is peace? One must be free from all *vikaras*. By this, the way to liberation will be clear. One will have equal vision towards everybody. There is God in all beings and everywhere. This feeling will come to him consequently. To reach this state, a spiritual speaker has to make lot of spiritual practice with great amount of sincerity and love. The sages could reach such a state with lot of perseverance. Lord Jesus had forgiven the miscreants even when he was being crucified. The great Socrates forgave the persons who made him drink the poison hemlock. Swami Dayananda, the founder of Arya Samaj and a great reformer had asked the person, who poisoned him to death, to immediately leave the place lest he should be caught and punished by his disciples. Men of such heights behaved in such manner very naturally and spontaneously and not for the sake of forgiveness. A mother forgives her child. It may not be that much unalloyed. She is conscious that the child is born of her. Therefore, natural love comes from the mother to the child. This also becomes a cause of bondage for her. But the feelings of the sages are different which cannot be expressed in any language. The sages have transcended all bondages and reached this highest state. They are liberated souls. Although they appear to dwell in samsar, they do not get afflicted by samsaric Maya. They are one with the Truth-Absolute.

Now the question may arise as to whether a common man can rise to this state. The answer is 'Yes'. When the Creator has gifted these qualities to man, why can't it be possessed? One can very well observe this quality in a mother. A spiritual seeker has to learn this quality from a mother first and thereafter gradually he can reach nirvikar state. A seeker thereafter can attain liberation and get rid of all worldly sufferings. Forgiveness is Peace-Absolute, Bliss-Absolute and Truth-Absolute. This is such a divine quality that it ensures man's survival, peace, happiness and bliss. Ultimately, the jiva experiences that "I am Sat-Chit-Ananda".

It all starts from renunciation which is there in the first segment of the monogram. Man can blossom himself by this divine quality of renunciation and attain perfection in forgiveness, the ultimate divine quality free from all *vikaras*.

Just like seven colours i.e. VIBGYOR, the seven divine qualities are also intertwined and are complementary to each other.

To elucidate further, without the quality of renunciation, self-restraint is not possible. In other words, renunciation is the basis of self-restraint. Similarly, spiritual practice gets enhanced by the quality of self-restraint. Spiritual practice makes the seeker strong enough to do service to others. He will gradually understand that by 'Truth' everything happens. There is truth behind everything. Therefore, service is a means to establish direct contact with truth. Man thus realises the Supreme Truth ultimately. That is why it is said that service to mankind is service to God. Going further, Truth is the basis of love. One gets attracted towards another person after experiencing some truths in the other. Love means loving some truths. In other words, truth finds expression as love. Forgiveness is the spontaneous offshoot of love. Love is the basis of forgiveness. Where there is love, there is no malice or deceitfulness. The lover can surrender everything for the sake of the beloved. The lover becomes free from all *vikaras*.

Like this, all divine qualities are there in man. God has gifted all these divine qualities to man so that he can get back to True Self. But due to ignorance, man is not able to realise the importance of the divine qualities. Rather he pursues the demoniac qualities due to which he suffers throughout.

Light contains seven colours. Without light, there will be darkness everywhere. Similarly, without divine qualities, man will be in dark. He goes on cursing darkness instead of welcoming light. With all divine qualities in him, he can shine bright like the Sun.

The greatness of divine qualities: Man gets peace and happiness due to divine qualities. Conversely, he suffers due to demoniac qualities. Man's survival is possible due to divine qualities. Divine qualities are everlasting assets which never get lost or diminished unlike the material wealth. The impossible can be made possible by divine qualities. Man gets all his inspiration and encouragement due to the divine qualities. Besides the aforesaid seven divine qualities, faith, trust, inquisitiveness and humility etc. are also divine qualities. Man proceeds on the path of self-development and ultimately realises True Self due to divine qualities. Divine qualities are nectar-like that bring peace and bliss, life and lustre. Possessing divine qualities is the highest Dharma. Truth prevails where there are divine qualities. Without divine qualities, the family and society will stand disintegrated. Divine qualities are the light of life. Blessings, greetings, gratitude and goodwill etc. are the outcome of divine qualities. Divine qualities lead to heaven whereas demoniac qualities lead to hell. Man has the option to choose between divine qualities and demoniac qualities. All spiritual seekers, after their intense spiritual practice, gain divine qualities as a result of which they attain the supreme goal of life. Divine qualities are very much active in the kingdom of nature. The Law of Eternity works only on the basis of divine qualities. In other words, the Creation exists and is sustained by divine qualities.

ఴ★ఴ

[18] *["You are divine. Divinity is your goal. Divinity is your base. Divine is your life. Divine is your True Self."*

(Amritbindu-32)]

At the time of need we seek others' help, which means, we seek kindness, benevolence and service from others. These are all divine qualities. That means, we seek divine qualities from others at the time of need. Everything is accomplished by divine qualities. If a man acquires more and more knowledge, he can know more about divinity and divine blessings. True knowledge is divine. No dirt can remain in fire. Man is born of divinity. A mother gives birth to a baby. By the mother's sacrifice and service, a baby grows up. In other words, whatever the parents do for us are all divine. The Creation is made of five gross elements that sustain and serve the Creation every moment. The five gross elements are also divine. While explaining about 'Truth', I (Sadguru Sri Sri Arjun) have told you earlier that you are born by truth and you survive by truth. If there is suffering, it clearly indicates that there is ignorance. By resorting to divinity or divine qualities, you can get peace and bliss. You suffer because you do not know the importance of divinity. From birth to death whatever you do are all for divinity. When divinity is your origin, you are also divine. You must regain your divinity or the lost paradise. You are not able to understand me and my words due to ignorance. The Sangha is intended for your well-being. You must serve and help each other.

Divine is your True Self. You possess all divine qualities, but those should be activated. Once you know about your intrinsic divinity, you will wish for divinity and not seek any other thing. Your thoughts, expressions and actions shall turn towards divinity.

---

18 Oriya Divya Dhara Vol 18 Page 19

You can never deny your own existence. Your existence is Truth. You are the Truth. You are divine. You are Brahman or Atman. Truth remains veiled by your ignorance. The sages had realised Truth and were living happily. It should always be remembered that you are divine. While preparing food also all mothers should think that they are doing the job of cooking for a divine purpose. All children are divine. Husband is divine. With this divine thought, if food is cooked, the food will become nectar. If you think divine, you will become divine. Never try to cheat anybody or neglect your duties. Entertaining divine thoughts on a continuous basis is true sadhana. By thinking divine, you can become divine. I bless you all.

☙✶❧

[19]*[*"Love others if you yearn for goodwill; be truthful and humble if you want blessings; hold on to love if you want bliss; try to know your True Self if you want liberation (Mukti).*

(Amritbindu-123)]

Every man is divine and Self-Absolute. Therefore, everyone instinctively seeks goodness. Everyone seeks love and goodwill of others. It is a basic feeling and dictate of the conscience. But everybody cannot get it. Some qualification is necessary to earn goodwill and love from others. Since many people violate certain principles, they are bound to lose the goodwill from others. Goodwill cannot be purchased from others. If you love others, others will love you. If you are affectionate and amiable to others, others too will be affectionate and amiable to you. One must know some truth to love others. Where there is an under-current of selfishness in love, it will not last long. Unless Atman is realised, true love and affection will not come in a spontaneous manner. With that spontaneity, one will love the plants and birds also. Love will be there in one's look, gesture and speech. At that time, he will get God's blessings. The basis of goodwill and blessings is love. Without possessing love, how can one receive God's blessings?

---

19 Oriya Divya Dhara Vol 18 Page 22

God's blessing is essential in our life. Unless God is happy with us completely, we cannot get His blessings. He, who blesses us, is ready to help us in all our difficulties. He will be happy in our happiness and sad in our sufferings. If we take recourse to truth, and express truth in our conduct, others will be happy with us. Every man loves truth. Hence if one is truthful and humble, his enemies will also change their attitude towards him. If your parents and other superiors bless you, you will get blessings from the Devas. If you get blessings from the Devas, you will get blessings from the Supreme Lord. In other words, the blessings of the Supreme Lord or Supreme Truth come to us through different mediums. He, who follows Truth, gets blessings from Truth. He who realises Truth becomes humble. A person who is truthful and humble will get blessings from parents, superiors and from the Devas and the Supreme Lord. It is pertinent to note that without any educational background also one gets blessings from the Supreme if one is truthful and humble.

Blessing is a great power. It is Gurushakti. One must prepare oneself to be eligible to receive the divine blessing. Everything becomes possible for a man who gets divine blessings. That is why the sages are so powerful. Their words are power-packed.

We do injustice due to our ego or ignorance. Thereafter we suffer. Bliss is the most important goal to be achieved in our life. The sages have been imparting spiritual knowledge to mankind in order to rid them of sufferings and make them blissful. Pure bliss does not have an iota of suffering.

Man, with all the material comforts, may get some happiness, but divine bliss which is also known as Brahmananda is many times greater. (It has been quantified to be one with seventeen zeroes or 10^{17}). According to Divya Darshan, love is the basis to get infinite bliss.

In our worldly life, we misconstrue our attachment and infatuation for love. We get attracted towards some forms. Some people get attracted towards qualities. But that is not true love. True love is union between Self and Self. Atman has neither any form nor quality. Atman manifests as all forms and qualities. He, who loves all, loves Atman. He, who loves Atman, loves all. That kind of love is eternal and divine. Loving any specific object is not true love. Anything physical is finite.

Where there is love, there is bliss. That is true life where there is bliss. Without bliss, we are almost dead. The blissful is immortal. Those who possess divine qualities become Devas. Truth, love, forgiveness and bliss are seen in them. The divine quality of forgiveness comes from love. Forgiveness instead of retaliation brings in more bliss. Supreme Bliss comes from truth and love. God's grace will be showered upon him who loves one and all as divine creations. The value and greatness of love cannot be expressed in words. Realisation of True Self is Supreme Bliss. That is liberation. Liberation is not any gross object that Guru can hand over to anybody. "Realise your True Self if you want liberation (Mukti)." This is Supreme Bliss where there is no trace of any suffering. This is your first and foremost duty and Dharma. This is the Law of Eternity.

Divya Darshan

(A person keen for self-development has questions like- What is divinity? What will happen by attaining divinity? What do you mean by divine virtues? Where is the need for divine virtues for leading a life of comfort and opulence?

Generally, we advise others to tell the truth, love others, help others, respect seniors, and do their duties sincerely etc. This means, everybody should inculcate divine qualities. Divine qualities are gifts of God which are ingrained in everybody. Knowledge is essential to activate the divine qualities within and express them in conduct. Only by knowledge, we come to know the importance and indispensability of the divine qualities. That is why Divya Darshan lays so much importance on divine qualities. Knowledge and divine qualities are interlinked. Normally, people of sattvic qualities possess and radiate more divine qualities, whereas these are conspicuously absent in the tamasic people. Rajasic people also do not have much of divine qualities. In fact, divine qualities are essential for attaining the goal of human life. An uneducated person may possess more divine qualities, compassion and righteousness than an educated person. This is all due to their past impulses or samskara.

Everybody is ingrained with divine qualities which are God-gifted. But people forget or overlook these precious possessions due to various situations and circumstances. In other words, ignorance veils the divine qualities. With acquisition of true knowledge, the inert divine qualities within buoy up and get activated. Therefore Divya Darshan lays emphasis on knowledge and divine qualities. Knowledge is essential to ignite the forgotten knowledge. In other words, man will not change unless he gets true knowledge. If we acquire true knowledge, we can move to sattvic quality from tamasic and rajasic. Divya Darshan says, "By knowledge and divine qualities, one can realise his True Self." Thus Divya Darshan shows straight and shortest way to getting rid of sufferings, and realising the True Self. This is the most appropriate path for the present day mankind who is too busy to opt for any other long-drawn or strenuous processes.

Divya Darshan presents its subject in a simple and scientific manner that should be acceptable to the modern temperament. It highlights the importance and essential nature of knowledge and divine qualities on which the whole Creation rests. Without divine qualities how can one become divine? Unless one becomes divine, how can one get rid of sufferings and live in peace and bliss? How can a demon get lasting peace?

Everyone should think over this and carve out appropriate path for his own sake as well as for others so as to get peace, bliss and freedom. Everyone must therefore make spiritual efforts to acquire true knowledge imparted by the sages clearly charting out the infallible ways to transcend all forms and qualities and reach the divine destination by the grace of Sadguru.)

[20]**Glimpses of Divya Darshan:** Samkhya Darshan lays emphasis on Prakriti and Purusha. The jiva is created from Prakriti, lives in Prakriti and ultimately gets merged in Prakriti. All his requirements are derived from Prakriti.

Maya is the other name of Prakriti. In other words, jiva is created by Maya, lives in Maya and gets lost in Maya. Samkhya Darshan emphasizes on knowing the Purusha that controls or manipulates Maya.

Vedanta dilates upon dualism and non-dualism. A common man cannot understand the essence of the great Guru-tattva that the Vedanta Darshan explains. Shrimad Bhagavad-Gita simplifies the subject to a great extent.

---

20 Oriya Divya Dhara Vol 10 Page 24

Samkhya Darshan says that by knowing Him, who controls the Prakriti, one can get liberation. But very little has been discussed as to how liberation would be attained. Hence it is not easily intelligible to a common man. Again, after *Samadhi* state is over, one has to come back to the fold of Prakriti. The Purusha would not be experienced thereafter.

In the Yoga Darshan, Rishi Patanjali has laid stress on Astanga Yoga (eight fold path) which is quite time consuming particularly for the present generation. Further he has taught about activating the Chakras inside the body by which the spiritual mendicant gets elevated Godward. But the all-pervasiveness of God is not convincingly explained.

People of the present generation with their changed lifestyle are mostly dipped in mundane affairs. The yoga practices that are possible for a sanyasi or brahmachari are not suitable for the worldly people whose immediate needs are different in the sense that they have to maintain their families and arrange for the essentials like food, clothing, education, health and housing etc. for parents, wife and children.

The people of the present generation are mostly indifferent towards God. By the routine samsaric lifestyle, none can realise God. Also by mechanically practicing some religious traditions God cannot be realised. In this scientific age, everyone calls for proof of God's existence. Hence many of them turn out to be atheists. Self-realisation cannot be explained to anybody. Therefore, the spiritual knowledge in the present-day society is on the decline. Gradually the number of atheists is also on the rise. Many sages have been trying to bring back the society from darkness to light. Those, who are engrossed in material science, would not follow Bhakti Marg. The present generation people must be taught spiritual knowledge as presented in the Vedas and Vedanta with more precision, with proofs and examples. They must feel that the divine existence is infinite and all-pervasive; He is the Truth-Absolute, beginningless and endless.

That God is all-pervasive is presented by Divya Darshan justifiably and convincingly. Man must take to knowledge path in order to understand the essence of the Vedas and Vedanta. The sayings and preaching of the sages can be understood by him who evinces interest in knowledge.

The realisers have tried to explain their spiritual practices and realisation employing different techniques or have their own philosophies. Many of them have founded sangha (society or association) to disseminate spiritual knowledge through satsang and discourses. But the explanations advanced by Bhakti Marg followers are not able to convince the modern men of scientific temperament.

Now the question is how a worldly person with scientific bent of mind shall be convinced about the existence of God and His role functions. A common question asked by people is, "Why feeling of devotion is not coming?"

The answer is – if a person does not have any idea about God and also does not understand the greatness of God, how would he have devotion towards God? There is darkness of ignorance all around. Divya Darshan teaches how to get rid of ignorance and the resultant sufferings, and how one can live in peace and happiness and ultimately realise God.

In yesteryears, people were worshipping the Moon. But today's people know what the Moon is. Earlier, people were having strong faith in the sayings of the sages. But today's man being more analytical calls for proof in every matter. God also cannot be experienced through only scientific knowledge. Only alternative is, to spread right spiritual knowledge in the society as it pertains to the knowledge about Self. By acquiring true knowledge, God can be realised. Our job is to go forward. The Vedas and Vedanta have inspired us and shown the path to go forward. Divya Darshan reiterates the same knowledge as presented in the Vedas and Vedanta, although the methodology and style of presentation is different. It is not only intelligible to the common man, it also convinces the modern men of scientific bent of mind. Divya Darshan while explaining spirituality takes into cognizance the latest scientific truths also to arrive at the state of non-dualism that remained as a matter of unexplainable self-experience of the sages so far. Divya Darshan says that without even resorting to any yogic practices, if one observes truth and Dharma, one can move Godward and ultimately realise God. If one tries to realise the existence of consciousness and energy everywhere in all beings, one can realise the Supreme.

A demon even can acquire the power to create storm and fire. Man can acquire power even without going through the Astanga Yoga. Therefore, by acquiring divine knowledge and observing the truth and the Law of Eternity and doing all good things, man can achieve wonders. By following the instructions laid down in the Vedas and Vedanta, man can live in peace and happiness and ultimately realise God.

Divya Darshan has not been named after its exponent, Sadguru Sri Sri Arjun. Divya Darshan teaches the mankind to observe certain principles in life so that one can while leading a divine life, ultimately realise the divine presence within. In this, there is no opinion or dogma. It does not contradict anyone. It supports and upholds the sayings and preaching of all the sages or realised souls. Experiencing the divinity is Divya Darshan. Divya Darshan lays stress on knowledge and divine virtues. By knowledge one can realise God and by divine qualities one can live in peace and bliss.

There are artisans who do their jobs well, but they may not be able to explain the intricacy of certain things to others. But an engineer, even if he does not himself do the job, can explain things in a better and more effective manner. By acquiring knowledge, we can move forward faster towards the divine goal. Truth can be realised by knowledge.

Divya Darshan asserts that the mankind can get rid of ignorance and the resultant sufferings, move towards peace and bliss, and attain liberation by taking to knowledge. After acquiring knowledge man would be elevated to divinity and ultimately attain God-realisation. First and foremost, man must repose belief in God. Knowledge plays an important role in this. The more one knows about God, the more one would have devotion and love towards God. One will go for self-surrender once one understands His Omnipotence. By this, one can realise truth one after another and ultimately merge with the Supreme Truth. This is Sanatan Dharma.

ఇ౨✶౨ఇ

[21]Man, since inception, has been always trying to get rid of sufferings and shall be continuing with his efforts in future too. God incarnates as sages

---

21 Oriya Divya Dhara Vol 8 Page 52

or Sadguru for allaying the sufferings of mankind. In the Kali Yug, people would be ensnared by ignorance and shall neglect knowledge. To enable mankind to get rid of sufferings Divya Darshan is presented in a unique style to suit the needs of present mankind. Sadguru Sri Sri Arjun descended for the same. He says, "I am born for this purpose; i.e. to relieve mankind of all sufferings."

Ignorance is the cause of sufferings. By acquiring knowledge and possessing divine virtues man can live in the society in peace and happiness. He would then be able to attain his goal i.e. liberation by self-realisation. Although the number of temples, mosques and churches is increasing day by day, sufferings and disturbances are also on the rise. Divya Darshan preaches pure monism. Divya Darshan lays more emphasis on knowledge path. Since we are worldly persons, our spiritual efforts are to begin from dualism, but dualism must be transcended to attain monism. Brahman is one; there is no second. His different powers are named as various personal godheads. Although Jagadguru Sri Shankaracharya was preaching Advaita, he was also respecting different personal godheads and had composed hymns or stotras and used to chant the same before various godheads.

Divya Darshan is a bridge between dualism and monism. Jagat, it says, is the manifestation of Brahman.

Bhakti starts from dualism and ends with monism. Karma, bhakti and jnana are all stitched together in Divya Darshan which lays more emphasis on knowledge or jnana. Divine thoughts, divine expressions and divine actions are the three basics that make complete Yoga. Divya Darshan is based on the Law of Eternity. The essence of all scriptural texts can be seen in Divya Darshan with a unique presentation style.

Everything has been created from Brahman and ultimately gets merged with Brahman. In between, we come across innumerable names and forms and qualities. Seed becomes a tree that ultimately becomes a seed. Right from creation up to deluge, the law that is at work is known as the Law of Eternity. Because of the operation of this Law, it becomes possible for something to get back to its origin. Due to the Law of Eternity different thoughts are created in us. As a result of such thoughts we are bound to go back to our origin ultimately.

Many sages have been descending from time to time and preaching various truths and divine virtues to uphold the Law of Eternity. Now that there are many drawbacks and deviations in the observance of the Law of Eternity, Divya Darshan re-presents complete syllabus of the Law of Eternity for flawless observance by mankind.

Divya Darshan lays more emphasis on karma and jnana without undermining the importance of bhakti. Divya Darshan is based completely on the Law of Eternity. Divya Darshan, presented very lucidly and comprehensively, is a vast treasure that contains the essence of the Vedas and Upanishads. According to the scriptures everything has been created from Brahman and gets merged with Brahman. The Law that is operative from the stage of creation to the ultimate dissolution is called the Law of Eternity. Because of this Law, it is made possible for everything to go back to the origin.

To know the Law of Eternity is knowledge and observance of the same is Dharma. It is the Law of Eternity that makes the necessary arrangements for teaching the subject matter of the Law of Eternity. The Law of Eternity is eternal. Hence it would never go out of existence. All scriptural instructions have been capsuled in Divya Darshan in order to shorten the way to self-realisation. In other words, it prescribes the shortest route for a quicker journey from dualism to monism. Divya Darshan is all-inclusive and hence it should not be classified as a different Darshan. Divya Darshan speaks on the Supreme Self which is nothing new. But things are explained in a different style for easy comprehension.

In the Divya Darshan monogram it is written, "Ignorance is great sin". Divya Darshan gives importance to happiness and hence the teaching starts from sufferings. Sufferings come from ignorance. If knowledge is acquired, sufferings shall vanish. Knowing the truth is knowledge. Knowledge is Truth-Absolute.

The unmanifest Brahman manifests through the seven divine virtues and seven colours.

He, who surrenders to the Truth-Absolute, gets rid of all sufferings. He, who would try to know Truth and welcome Truth, can surrender himself to Truth as a result of which he would get the grace of the Supreme.

The Truth-Absolute manifests as various truths by means of Chit Shakti. By the same Chit Shakti, we experience bliss. This means we experience Atman by Atman.

To take to spiritual knowledge is to take shelter of God. He, who ignores knowledge, ignores God. Inquisitiveness is ingrained in all of us since childhood by the Law of Eternity. God shows the path to us to get rid of sufferings but He does not himself remove our sufferings. Hence self-effort is essential to get rid of sufferings.

Divya Darshan is a philosophy for the mankind. At the same time, it is a way of life for the spiritual seekers.

☙ ✦ ❧

[22]We all seek happiness but get sufferings. We all think that we are doing our duties. Although we are all observing Dharma in someway or other, we are unable to realise that we are committing many lapses in the process. Divya Darshan says that everybody is telling truth but not to the full extent. People very often resort to falsehood. Everyone knows what truth is but only partially. Even if we were practicing truth earlier, we have forgotten it. That is why we are suffering. In Satya Yug, people were living in peace and happiness. They were leading life based on truth and Dharma. We are in Kali Yug now. If we take recourse to Satya (Truth) and Dharma, we can also change Kali Yug to Satya Yug. We at times consciously resort to wrongdoings. But how can we get happiness from out of wrong means? It is impossible.

According to the Greek Philosopher Socrates, knowledge is always there. Man has got unlimited knowledge; he has unlimited powers within. Only

---

22 Oriya Divya Dhara Vol 2 Page 3

that much knowledge required or relevant to a human is expressed in him. Since we have traversed long distances over an unlimited tract of time, we have forgotten all such knowledge. Only that much knowledge necessary and applicable now in this birth gets activated. The rest remains dormant. If you try to recollect, you can remember things one after another. Also whenever you come across something or some incidents, the knowledge pertaining to that inside you shall get activated. While discussing also, you will remember so many things which you had forgotten since long.

The Vedas say that you are the scions of immortality. You are Self-Absolute. Thou art that. But you are not able to accept or appreciate that. If you deeply contemplate, everything in you shall come out and you shall recollect it.

Hence do never underestimate anybody. Those, who can speak out or write something, are able to recollect. Those who are not able to express themselves, they have forgotten although everything is there inside them in a dormant state.

In the olden days, people were approaching the sages and seers for knowledge. They were visiting various *ashrams* in quest of knowledge but now-a-days, *ashrams* are there although in limited numbers where knowledge is being imparted. In course of time, people distanced themselves from spiritual knowledge. True Knowledge slowly tapered off. People remain satisfied with performing some rituals in the name of Dharma. We are facing towards darkness. False talks and crafty dealings are the order of the day. On one side there is darkness and on the other side there is light. Since we have faced towards darkness our movement is towards darkness, which amounts to turning our back towards light. Darkness connotes sufferings. There is dearth of true knowledge. Hence injustice and wrongdoings are on the rise. We never welcome woes. We all want to get rid of sufferings and crave for peace and happiness. It is therefore imperative that we should turn our face towards light and step forward towards light. Collectively we deviate from truth and plunge ourselves into delusions and desperations, agonies and anxieties. Nobody wants to suffer. Nobody wants to die. Divya Darshan shows us the way. According to Divya Darshan,

"Wherever you may be, whatever unjust practices you might be indulging in, whatever sins you might have committed, from now onwards turn towards knowledge and divine virtues, light and truth. Then only you shall be saved. It may take time, but it shall happen. One day you will be merged in the light of all lights."

"You are the Self-Absolute". This is what the scriptures preach. Self or Atman is always free from sufferings. But the jiva is not able to experience that he is none other than the Self. Hence the qualities of a jiva are conspicuous in him. The admixture of three qualities in the man (sattva, rajas and tamas) results in some happiness and some sufferings. If there is predominance of sattva, there shall be more happiness. If there is predominance of tamasic qualities, there will be more sufferings.

Mandukya Upanishad discusses Consciousness in four states.

- ❖ Waking state
- ❖ Dream state
- ❖ Sleep state
- ❖ Transcendental state or supra-causal state

Waking state: When some forms are created, some qualities are also bound to be present in them. In a human form, human qualities are seen. When consciousness takes the form of a monkey, the qualities of a monkey are present in that form. When fire takes its form, the qualities of fire are present in fire. When water is formed the qualities of water are present in water. This is the first step of consciousness i.e. pertaining to the form, the corresponding qualities are embedded. It is called body consciousness or waking consciousness. In other words, in the waking state, we experience the physical bodies as well as the world of matters and qualities.

Dream consciousness: In absence of physical body also, consciousness expresses itself. When we fall asleep, do we have any relation with the body? In the dream state we may assume different forms, experience different forms, witness different scenario, experience pleasure and pain. There are experiences like climbing a tree, swimming in a pool, crossing a river, passing through a desert, moving in a jungle, seeing and talking to different characters, meeting with accident and getting hospitalised, partying in a banquet hall, playing in a playground and visiting some historical place or a beautiful garden etc. We experience all these even when the physical body is lying on the bed with eyes closed.

All these indicate that inside the physical body, there is a subtle body that functions.

Sleep consciousness: When we fall asleep there is no desire, no greed, no anger, and no thought. This is real peace and bliss. In this state the mind, intellect, and conscience rest in the causal state. This consciousness is sleeping state. The stones and pebbles rest in this state. In this state the Supreme Consciousness oversees everything.

Transcendental consciousness: The Supreme Consciousness pervades everywhere and always. The Supreme Consciousness is the undivided whole that engulfs everything. The Supreme Consciousness manifests as sleep consciousness, dream consciousness and waking consciousness or body consciousness.

We all remain besieged by body consciousness. This means we are all parts of the Supreme Consciousness. But we are not able to understand this. We are also not interested in all these. Divya Darshan says, "Everything is inside you. If you develop inquisitiveness to know, you can know."

There are also persons in whom human qualities are rarely seen. In some persons, there is predominance of animal instincts. At the same time, there are also persons with divine qualities. Despite all such apparent variations in qualities, the Supreme Consciousness eternally remains unperturbed and undiluted in all categories of consciousness.

Divya Darshan lays lot of importance on inquisitiveness which God has gifted to everybody. By inquisitiveness man can acquire more and more knowledge, realise one truth after another and ultimately realise the Supreme Truth.

A blind person can also acquire knowledge by his inquisitiveness that is bestowed upon him. Why there is inquisitiveness? It is because man can blossom and express himself by acquiring knowledge. He is made to go beyond the bounds of body consciousness and realise Self. He can realise his True Self through inquisitiveness. The above discussion clearly suggests, "You are the Self, but you have misconstrued yourself for jiva."

Divya Darshan says, "Many lapses are committed by you due to ignorance. You are not able to realise this. Therefore, you never try to do away with your defects or deficiencies. If you have not acquired complete knowledge you are bound to err. How then shall you attain your completeness?"

Divya Darshan therefore lays stress on Jnana Yoga. God is Sat, Chit and Ananda. He is Truth, Knowledge and Bliss. This means Chit is knowledge-Absolute. By Chit when man shall know the 'Sat' i.e. when he would know his self as well as others, he will experience bliss. We are not able to experience bliss because we do not know ourselves. Whatever pleasure or joy we experience is only transient. The body is also transient; mind is transient and intellect is transient. One must transcend all these sheaths such as physical, vital, mental, intellectual and blissful, to be at his self.

Jagadguru Sri Shankaracharya says, "Brahman is real, Jagat is unreal".

We cannot get peace and happiness from imaginary and transient things. The nature is undergoing changes every moment. Some examples of change are cited below.

You were an infant, became youth and thereafter became old. There was no tree; a tree appeared. There was no cloud; a patch of cloud appeared and disappeared. This Creation is changeable and is undergoing changes very fast and incessantly. Since everything is in its passing phase the Jagat is said to be false or untrue. But He who governs all changes is Himself the unchangeable Supreme Truth. A spiritual mendicant, who realises this Supreme Truth, attains peace and bliss. This means, if one does not attain self-knowledge, peace and bliss would remain unattained.

A mythological demon named Bhasmasura had received a boon from Lord Shiva but despite the great boon he was blessed with, what was the consequence? He burnt himself to ashes while experimenting with the efficacy of the boon. Without proper knowledge, we cannot use or maintain anything properly and cannot get the benefit out of it. Misuse or mishandling will bring us sufferings. Without knowledge, no karma can be accomplished properly; without knowledge our devotion gets diluted. Without knowledge our worship becomes misplaced or misdirected. Without knowledge if we try to propitiate anybody, the same may be irritating and may end up with opposite outcome. Many believe that if somebody becomes simple, he will reach God. This is true but why people do not become simple? Without knowledge, one cannot become simple. We cannot call a foolish person simple. Only a knowledgeable person can become simple. Divya Darshan says – "Try to muster up knowledge without loss of time. If you do not acquire knowledge, how shall you realise the Truth? Scriptures have tried to present the truth in an exhaustive manner citing many examples for easy comprehension but if you do not study those things, how would you know what the sages and seers had taught? How did you know about God's existence? It is only by learning from others. It is by knowledge that you came to know something about God. By acquiring more knowledge, you would come to know about His manifestation. Realising the truth is knowledge. All wrong deeds are due to lack of appropriate knowledge. Knowledge results in true devotion. Once a man knows what God is, he would have some devotion towards Him. After knowing about God's greatness and indispensability, he will have more devotion. Consequent to divine knowledge divine thoughts shall arise."

What is divine thought or *Bhava*?

There is some Existence called God. This is knowledge. Strong faith in this Existence is called *bhava*. This means knowledge is subsequently transformed to *bhava*. Real Bhakti or devotion comes after *bhava*. After Bhakti, comes Mahabhava.

What is Mahabhava? By whom all these happen? Why it happens?

The *bhava* by which man will be able to understand the answers to the above questions is Mahabhava. Mahabhava starts with 'Prema' (Love). When jiva shall start loving God or Atman, then only union would be possible between the two. Love culminates in union and immergence in the Atman or God. Without enough knowledge, how can man rise to such a state! Man cannot know that this is real devotion. He is also not able to know whether he is having devotion or not. Everyone claims that he has devotion towards God. Shrimad Bhagavad-Gita says that desireless Bhakti is real Bhakti. Devotion only to get something in return, is not real Bhakti. One cannot reach God unless one has desireless Bhakti. How shall the desireless Bhakti come? Man cannot have desireless Bhakti until he acquires true knowledge. He cannot also undertake any type of desireless action. This means, for unconditional devotion and love, desireless action with knowledge is a pre-condition. By knowledge only, one can know whether it is with desire or without desire.

The children say there is God; the old persons also say that there is God; the sages and seers say that there is God. But there is gradation of knowledge in such assertions. The sages and seers know more than anybody else. It is an admitted fact that there remain gradations of knowledge. Without knowledge one cannot know God. Whatever knowledge we possess is only for our survival and to protect our bodies. But we are not able to attain peace with this level or standard of knowledge. The mind craves for happiness. We should know what type of knowledge we must acquire to get peace and happiness. Intellect (Buddhi) seeks bliss but we are not evincing interest in that knowledge which shall get us bliss. Our conscience (Viveka) craves for freedom, but we are averse to the knowledge that would bring us freedom. At times we imagine about freedom although we stay glued to our mind. To get freedom, we must move from the stage of mind (manas) to the stage of intellect (Buddhi) and from the stage of intellect to the stage of conscience (Viveka). Then only we can experience love or Mahabhava. Then only God-realisation is possible. Whatever knowledge or virtue we think we have acquired so far is insignificant. There is no worship or meditation at the stage of the Supreme Truth. There is none other than the Self. Any amount of explanation about God is not Brahman. He, who is the cause of our power of speech, is Brahman. Speech cannot reach Brahman or express Him. The power required for any expression is Brahman. Any contemplation by mind or intellect is not Brahman. The power by whom the mind or intellect can contemplate is Brahman. He is the cause of mind and intellect. He is beyond mind and intellect, but mind creates its own God and worships the same whereas He is beyond all imaginations. Mental imaginations come under the ambit of ignorance. Brahman is there in everybody. He is in you too. He is in stones and pebbles. This visible universe is only one quarter of Brahman. There are three other quarters which are invisible. Without knowing all the four quarters, knowledge can't be complete. Therefore, a seeker must know the indivisible whole, who is Brahman.

Gods such as Brahma, Vishnu and Maheswar etc. come under the first quarter i.e. visible Creation. During deluge, the personal godheads including Brahma, Vishnu and Maheswar, the Sun and the Moon etc. would be merged in the Supreme i.e. in the transcendental state. People remain complacent by knowing the first quarter only. It is nothing but our own imagination. Divya Darshan says, "Try to know Him. He, who makes spiritual practices to know Him, shall get Him. He is not for any sect or group. He is for everyone, for the whole of humanity and for the entire Creation. This is the eternal truth".

Many people say, "We do not worship. We believe in the formlessness of God". But without worshipping how can one realise God? It is impossible. Some people say, "We worship; we have realised God." This is also impossible because by worshipping they might have known the God with some forms. How can they know the formless? He, who knows that Brahman is formless but manifests as various forms, knows to some extent.

There are also people who worship the formless. They think others do not know who God is. They believe that those who worship various forms are inferior. Divya Darshan says, "To know God as only formless is not enough. His manifestation in forms has also to be realised."

Without knowledge we cannot realise Brahman in totality. Therefore, knowledge is your wealth. Knowledge is the vital energy. Knowledge is the master key that can unravel the Truth. When you can know the Truth, spontaneously love and devotion shall overwhelm you. Very often we say, we love God and we have true devotion towards God. But there are many deficiencies or drawbacks in our love and devotion.

Lord Jesus was emphasizing on love. But people are not able to understand the true import of love. Had they understood what love is, the world would not have moved towards darkness.

Divya Darshan says, "What we understand as love is not true love. That is infatuation or some kind of liking. If somebody sings well, we like him. If somebody is beautiful, we appreciate the beauty of his form. When we are attracted towards any form or quality, it is not true love. It is sraddha only."

We have six qualities (actually enemies) within us. Those are – Desire, Anger, Greed, Infatuation, Pride and Jealousy. Due to some qualities we get attracted towards something or some persons. That is not true love. There is heaven and hell difference between love and infatuation. But real love is, love between Self and Self, Atman with Atman. There is no room of any form or quality in true love. One may be lame, blind or ugly. It is immaterial. It is called true love when Self loves the Self. When such love is realised there would not be any war but peace. Lust or infatuation is often misconstrued for love. That is why we see revenge, murder and many such crimes in the society. Divya Darshan says, you are facing towards darkness. Hence suffering is inevitable. Turn your face towards light. Then only you shall be saved from desperation and devastation. Knowledge is light. By knowledge you can know yourself and know all. Then only you can understand what true Dharma is. Dharma does not admit of any fragmentation. It is total and all-inclusive. A specific pattern of religiosity is not necessarily Dharma. It may be a way to attainment of Dharma.

ॐ✦ॐ

What is Dharma?

[23]Knowing one's True Self is Dharma. On the other hand, if we are not interested to know the True Self, then how are we observing Dharma? Having lost our way, how shall we reach our destination? We have taken millions of births. We have enjoyed a lot. Now we are humans. Still our craving for enjoyment has not been satiated. In this birth we should make efforts for God-realisation without further procrastination. If we go on seeking pleasure from mundane objects, then when shall we realise God? He, who would be eager day and night for knowing his True Self, will attain self-realisation even in this birth. If not in this birth, another couple of births may have to be taken to realise self. But True Self will be inevitably be realised sooner or a little later.

Divya Darshan says, everybody seeks happiness and bliss because that is the True Self. We all want to attain our True Self. Self is Bliss-Absolute. Blissfulness is our True Self. But we are not able to comprehend that. We are living in this world only to realise our True Self. Life is a pilgrimage to divinity. We are not aware of our true destination. Without this knowledge or awareness of destination if we live ages after ages even, we cannot reach our destination. There is a straight and shortest route to self-realisation. That route is Dharma. But unaware of this, we misconstrue something else for Dharma. Dharma leads us to destination. Without the goal in mind, what type of Dharma are we observing? We must move unswervingly towards our goal. Hence this journey of life is a real pilgrimage.

Divya Darshan imparts true knowledge by which man can speedily move on the highway to reach the destination. By acquiring knowledge, we can realise one truth after another and ultimately, we can realise the Supreme Truth. But due to ignorance, we are facing towards darkness which is opposite to peace and happiness. When you shall take to knowledge, you would be able to discriminate between good and bad, evanescent and eternal. By knowledge you can know what Brahman is; what the world is and how Brahman manifests as Jagat (world).

Some persons believe that by Bhakti (devotion), everything is possible and therefore knowledge is irrelevant but Divya Darshan asserts that it is knowledge that shall get you devotion. Knowledge is the true path. At a later stage, when devotion overwhelms the aspirant, there is no need for knowledge. For example, how do we pay respect to the District Magistrate? First, we must know about his position and power so that we would be inclined to pay respect to him. Similarly, if we do not acquire some knowledge about God, we cannot pay Him respect. We cannot surrender to Him. Steeped in ignorance we call ourselves devotees. A thief also goes to the temple and makes offerings to God. Is it devotion? True Bhakti or devotion shall come only after we know the greatness and indispensability of God. When our knowledge shall increase, we can know that God is our vital energy, He is our Consciousness and therefore everything to us. This feeling is true devotion.

❧ ⋆ ❧

[24]From time immemorial man has been trying to get rid of sufferings and shall be trying in future also. God incarnates at periodic interval to help and guide mankind to get rid of sufferings. Due to ignorance, man commits sins and therefore suffers which means Dharma is not observed in true spirit. The intensity of sufferings increases. At that time God incarnates and takes human forms. He comes as Sadguru. During Kali Yug, people steeped in ignorance shall shun knowledge. To save people from sufferings, Divya Darshan has been revealed by Sadguru Sri Sri Arjun for the benefit

---

24 Oriya Divya Dhara Vol 4 Page 33

of the entire mankind. The exponent of Divya Darshan had descended for this purpose.

"I (Sadguru Sri Sri Arjun) have taken human birth for this purpose only. I got enlightenment in 1967. Divya Darshan was born in 1973. I accepted disciples since 1977. Divya Darshan was named as such in 1977. Since this knowledge leads us on a divine path towards divinity or Divya, it has been named as 'Divya Darshan."

Earlier to this, many sages have shown various ways to get rid of sufferings. Divya Darshan says that simply by quoting scriptures and getting the texts by heart would not lead to cessation of sufferings. That must be followed in practice.

More and more people are joining Bhakti Path now-a-days. Number of devotees is on the rise. Number of temples, mosques and churches are also on the rise. Paradoxically in the society, cases of injustice and inhuman behaviour are also on the increase. Divya Darshan asks a pertinent question; why have the happiness and peace gone missing when the number of devotees is increasing? Divya Darshan reiterates that ignorance is the cause of sufferings. The present level of sufferings indicates that there remains ignorance all over. Hence, Divya Darshan tries to bring the ancient knowledge preached by sages and seers to the reach of every household to help them get rid of sufferings. Out of ignorance, if one claims that he is a devotee, his conduct may not be free from flaws. The anti-social elements also visit temples and worship various deities. The scriptural texts are there as such, but people do not evince interest to read and assimilate. Hence man is suffering. If one does not acquire true knowledge, he will suffer. God manifests as knowledge. But we shun knowledge and thereby invite sufferings. Divya Darshan says, "He, who shuns knowledge, shuns God."

To get rid of sufferings one must acquire knowledge as well as divine virtues. Seven divine virtues are- renunciation, restraint, spiritual practice, service, truth, love and forgiveness. All these divine virtues are already ingrained in the man since his birth. Hence man should understand the indispensability of all these qualities and try to blossom them from inside. Man is surviving because of the divine qualities. Divine qualities are also ingrained in birds and animals. Divya Darshan explains mankind how man can ensure a harmonious social living and ultimately realise his True Self by divine virtues. Everyone should try to realise this and conduct himself accordingly.

Divya Darshan integrates karma, bhakti and jnana into one i.e. everything is a state of knowledge only. By doing actions properly man can survive. Similarly, without bhakti man would behave like an unbridled horse. Man has a distant destination to reach. He must follow some laws or principles. Knowledge is required to know the laws. Then only, he would be able to observe the laws properly. Knowledge forms the basis of all actions and devotion. Hence Divya Darshan speaks of complete Yoga by laying more stress on knowledge. Without knowledge, no karma can be done properly. Similarly, one must know about the greatness of God to have real devotion. He has also to know the Law of Eternity for proper observance of the same. By following the path of complete Yoga man can live harmoniously in the society with peace and happiness. Ultimately, he can realise his True Self. Divya Darshan expresses this as "Hride Bhav, Mukhe Naam, Haste Kaam" (Divine Thoughts, Divine Expressions and Divine Actions). Knowledge remains as the basis as well as the essence of everything.

Those, who know something about God, can only have devotion towards God. After knowing more and more, they can realise God. Those who give priority to only karma, they attach more importance to the body. God has given us this body for making spiritual practices for self-realisation. There is a subtle body inside this gross body. By physical karma, the subtle body is not benefited much. Hence all three types of yoga have been discussed in the Shrimad Bhagavad-Gita. He, who resorts to all these three types of yoga, such as karma, bhakti and jnana can realise the True Self ultimately.

୯୬✦୯୬

[25]Divya Darshan says that one can attain the attributeless state through karma, bhakti and jnana. Some people disown the path of karma, bhakti and jnana. They lay stress only on self-surrender. Man must resort to karma,

---

25 Oriya Divya Dhara Vol 4 Page 36

bhakti and jnana. One must begin with karma and thereafter satkarma (good action) from where he must move higher.

Whatever a child might have studied in the primary standard, he has to read higher subjects in the higher classes. Similarly, when a man takes to knowledge path, he must transcend the karma and bhakti stage. While Divya Darshan lays emphasis on jnana it does not overlook the importance of karma and bhakti. It lays greater emphasis on knowledge that enables a person to move on the path of spiritual practice. Divine virtues protect us. During his journey, if a person quarrels with others, he cannot reach his destination timely. Hence one must prepare oneself properly to reach the destination in time without hindrances or setbacks. If one does not tread on the path of justice and righteousness, his words will not carry value. Everyone should do his duty without depending on others. By means of Karma Yoga and Bhakti Yoga one can go up to the doorstep of Brahman. By Jnana Yoga one can merge with the Supreme Brahman. When a spiritual seeker realises Brahman or the Supreme Self, the law of action would not be applicable to him even if he lives in samsar and does all sorts of worldly activities. Once somebody attains the Supreme Self what else would he seek for?

Hence it is the first and foremost duty of everyone to realise Brahman or the Supreme Self.

Divya Darshan follows knowledge path and it focuses on non-dualism or Advaita. Since we are in the world and undertake various kinds of worldly activities, our spiritual practice starts from dualism and ends up with non-dualism. While moving on knowledge path, Bhakti is a pre-condition to self-realisation. Without Bhakti, only with superficial knowledge we cannot reach non-dualism. The worldly persons may start with dualism initially, but they have to transcend the worldly feelings in order to attain non-dualism. Various powers of Brahman are named as various personal godheads. Therefore, a spiritual mendicant must contemplate on the background existence behind the personal godheads. Jagadguru Sri Shankaracharya even after being firmly established in non-dualism used to compose and chant hymns before personal godheads and used to pay respect to them. But at the same time he was aware of the unitary, all-powerful Existence that manifested as different personal godheads. Hence, he was not considering anyone small or less important. Divya Darshan integrates dualism with non-dualism. In this way one can realise Brahman easily and faster. The question of devotion comes in dualism. When there is end of dualism and devotion, it becomes non-dualism. Karma and bhakti come under dualism.

We wail and mourn due to our desires. We crave for luxuries of life. For that we are to depend upon others. If we can reduce our desires, we can be self-dependent. He, who is self-dependent, is a happy man indeed. The spiritualists who do not depend upon others are self-dependent. This dependence on others is the main cause of bondage. That means we are not free. If we reduce our material enjoyments, we can be happy. We can become powerful godheads and thereafter attain Brahman.

❦

[26] Jiva and Ishwar are two names but from the point of view of True Self both are one and the same. They are in different states. Hence two names have been ascribed separately. A form of water is named as ice. Ice and water are basically one and the same but from the point of view of appearance and quality, they are different. Seed has become a tree and there is seed in the tree. Tree bears all powers to contain seed. In some situations, a seed again develops into a tree. Seed is different from the tree from the point of view of shape, quality etc. Seed becomes a tree and assumes a different form. Where from the tree has come? Answer is from the seed. The seed is the tree. Thus, Brahman has become a jiva and jiva is none other than Brahman. Water has become ice. Ice is nothing but water.

Wherefrom jiva has come? The answer is- Brahman has become jiva. The scenario is different from that of seed and tree in the sense that Brahman remains both as Brahman and Jiva simultaneously. From appearance point of view Brahman is different and Jiva is different. The greatness of Brahman

---

26 Oriya Divya Dhara Vol 8 Page 7

is that even if He remains eternally as Brahman in His True Self, He has the potency to become many.

Example: Ice has become water. Ice also remains as ice elsewhere. All ice has not become water at once. All water has not become ice also. For the tree, in order to become seed, some situations are necessary. The situations depend upon external factors. When we speak of Brahman, Brahman Himself manifests as the environments and circumstances also. The Truth is also involved in situations and circumstances. Brahman manifests as many. We call those by different names just to differentiate and identify them.

Brahman is all-pervasive. What else the manifested objects can be? Hence everything is Brahman. The gross world is made of five gross elements. Brahman manifests as all. They are named differently only.

When that level of consciousness dawns upon a person, at that time he would realise, "I am Brahman; now I am in jiva form". Because of jiva bhava, sufferings and fear come on his way. When one will be overwhelmed with Brahman bhava, these feelings would not affect him. He would say, "Since I am in this form, people talk so many things. He, who is commenting on me or criticizing me, is also Brahman."

Example: In a drama, if a master plays the role of a servant, he may be insulted while playing his role. He will not feel insulted since he is aware that he is actually not a servant but is only playing a role. Rather he will laugh only. When man realises his Brahman state, he would not be affected by jiva feelings. He is Brahman only and is eternally Brahman; nothing other than that.

છ⋆છ

[27]Scriptures reiterate that Jiva and Brahman are one and the same. But generally, people disbelieve this statement. But those, who are on knowledge path, can understand and appreciate the essence and intricacy of this truth asserted by the sages of good olden days. They had realised this truth, but

---

27 Oriya Divya Dhara Vol 4 Page 38

the common men bereft of spiritual knowledge cannot understand this statement. Realisation of this is Siddhi. The advanced mendicants can realise this. But to explain the spiritual subject to the common men, it would suffice to say that God is Peace-Absolute and Bliss-Absolute. He, who knows Brahman as Bliss-Absolute, would get bliss and live in bliss. This bliss arising out of God-realisation is unique and therefore cannot be compared with the worldly pleasure. God is all-pervasive; His grace can also be experienced everywhere. Therefore, the relevant knowledge has to be acquired to realise the highest truth. Divya Darshan explains in very simple words how a man can get happiness, peace and bliss.

While explaining the subject to the people, happiness, peace and bliss must be given greater importance. There is bliss in happiness. Happiness, peace and bliss are of one category. But while explaining the same, they are put under separate classification. To get rid of all sufferings is liberation. Suffering does not come only from the material world. Doubts, despair, fear and anxieties also make us suffer. He, who is free from all these, is liberated. Divya Darshan says that man must know the laws of God which are ever operative, to get rid of sufferings. Truth is ever present in everything and expresses itself according to the Law of Eternity.

Fragrance of flower and sweetness of sugar are governed by some laws. For preparation of cake, certain set of principles, processes or laws are involved. When the laws are operative, automatically the latent truth expresses itself. Survival of man is also truth. There are some laws to be followed for survival. If there are deviations, man cannot survive. Man, in order to live in peace, must observe some principles. Unless the laws are followed the latent truth would not express itself. These ever-operative laws are called the Law of Eternity. This Law is operative in the kingdom of nature, commonly known as natural laws. By observing the natural laws, man can get peace, bliss and liberation. Divya Darshan explains the importance and indispensability of the Law of Eternity. The sages of yesteryears had realised the Law of Eternity well and explained the same to mankind. Divya Darshan, while explaining Law of Eternity, also explains how to observe the same. Observance of this Law of Eternity is the Dharma of mankind.

"With dispassion and without attachment or obsession, you must take up your duty as your Dharma." This is what Lord Krishna exhorts Arjun in Shrimad Bhagavad-Gita. "Give up your sense of 'I'-ness; proceed with your duty and observe Dharma; even plunge yourself into war for establishment of Dharma." If man knows the Law of Eternity and observes the same, he can enjoy bliss. On the one hand, ignorance about Law of Eternity would bring in sufferings. The man, who can understand the operative laws in the kingdom of nature, would not grieve any more. All the natural laws are for the good of all. Man cannot know them with his limited or fragmented knowledge. God is Truth-Absolute, Bliss-absolute, Peace-Absolute, Energy-Absolute and Knowledge-Absolute. He, who knows 'That', becomes 'That'. In order to get peace and bliss, one must know the basis of it. This kingdom of nature contains all knowledge. He, who makes sincere attempts to know, can know anything he likes or chooses to know. Divya Darshan teaches this divine knowledge, by which man can acquire the knowledge in the kingdom of nature and be enriched with *bhava* to reach his goal.

Man is not able to know what his Dharma is. Hence man suffers as he is not able to practise Dharma. Divya Darshan explains how man can ensure his individual living and harmonious social living with peace and happiness. Divya Darshan has been imparting all-inclusive subject matter of the Law of Eternity by knowing which man can lead a happy and peaceful life. If man would know the Law of Eternity, he would not get afflicted by any superstition. Divya Darshan is God's Will. Everyone should understand and appreciate the Law of Eternity and spread this knowledge among others so that happiness, peace and bliss shall prevail in the society.

❧ ✦ ❧

[28]It is particularly important to know what Sanatan Dharma is. If man does not want to know what Dharma is, how can he observe Dharma? Unless there is a proper understanding of Dharma, mistakes are bound to happen

---

28 Oriya Divya Dhara Vol 16 Page 48

even though occasional rituals are performed sincerely. Due to lack of knowledge, sometimes adharma is misconstrued for Dharma because of which the desired results do not come forth. Now I am telling you something about Dharma. The law that rules everywhere in this Creation is the Law of Eternity. Knowing this law is knowledge. When we talk about the Creation, we must include nature, jiva and Brahman. Observing the Law of Eternity means practice of Dharma. It is essential to know the Law of Eternity in order to perform Dharma properly. Now in Kali Yug, very few people know and talk about the Law of Eternity that has been governing the whole Creation since its inception. Now Divya Darshan imparts this knowledge to the whole of humanity. By acquiring this knowledge and understanding what Dharma is, one can realise True Self. He is truly Dharmic who possesses divine qualities. There are many people who possess demoniac qualities, perform different kinds of rituals and claim that they are doing Dharma. Such persons cannot serve others. They cannot renounce for others' sake. Divya Darshan says that possessing divine qualities is Dharma. It must be remembered that virtues take us on the path of self-development. Divine qualities and virtues (Punya) are one and the same.

Therefore, Divya Darshan lays emphasis on true knowledge and divine qualities that bring peace and bliss to ultimately lead the aspirant to the goal. Without knowing about God and the Law of Eternity, how can anybody observe Dharma? Therefore, Divya Darshan is a complete philosophy of life. Sufferings are on the rise because most of the people are deviating from the Law of Eternity without knowing what it is.

Hence Divya Darshan explains the true knowledge in an amazingly simple manner and shows the way to peace, bliss and freedom. Dharma protects us. He, who preaches about Dharma, is great because the entire mankind gets benefited. True knowledge must reach everyone irrespective of caste or community.

ᘓ✶ᘓ

[29]Brahman is described as formless and also with forms, with attributes and without attributes. Some philosophies preach about Brahman who is without attributes, while some others ascribe attributes to Brahman. Some people lay stress on bhakti and some on jnana; Some follow dualism while others follow non-dualism. There are some sages who emphasise on loving God with attributes while some others emphasise on loving God without attributes. Thus, there are different views prevailing.

Divya Darshan synchronizes between the two apparent diversities. According to it, Brahman is with attributes as well as without attributes. True knowledge is essential to sort out the apparent diversities to realise the Unity.

All attributes have emanated from Brahman who is attributeless. All attributes ultimately merge with the attributeless. Due to the greatness or potency of the attributeless Brahman, all attributes are manifested. Further, the attributes are all changeable.

Divya Darshan says that there is a causal factor behind forms and attributes. The causal factor is itself uncaused and unconditioned, also attributeless and formless.

One must know the Creation with attributes to reach the Creator without attributes. The attributes are befitting outcome of incessant flow and transformation of energy. Consciousness remains in everything which is energetic. Hence both the Creation with attributes and the attributeless Creator are one and the same. One is 'shaktiman' and the other is 'shakti'.

We know the role of energy to some extent. But we are not able to know the energetic Consciousness. There is infinite Consciousness who is the reservoir of all energies. He is the undivided whole, i.e. Unity, Eternity and Infinity. Divya Darshan resolves the anomaly between God with form and God without form, God with attributes and without attributes. Divya Darshan holds on to the middle path and synchronizes the two by establishing unity between the two aspects of the One Existence.

---

29 Oriya Divya Dhara Vol 2 Page 31

Generation, sustenance and dissolution take place in this Creation which is full of forms and qualities. A spiritual mendicant has to know the manifestations of Brahman in saguna forms and thereafter has to transcend all these to realise Brahman who is without forms and qualities. Behind the changeable Creation, there is a basis (underlying support) who is none other than the eternal Brahman, just as a wheel in order to move has to rest upon an axle.

One must try to know more and move still higher. Beyond this world of forms and qualities, there is a Supreme Existence. That Supreme Existence must be realised for completing the grand cycle.

The sages and seers on realising Brahman teach others. At that time, we see in them the qualities of love, respect, affection, magnanimity, humbleness etc. These are the symptoms of true devotion.

Bhakti is of two types; with desires and without desires.

Desireless devotion comes after realising the Supreme Brahman. That is expressed in the conduct of the devotee. Love rules supreme. It is perfect love that comes only after realising the Supreme Brahman. In other words, after realising the Truth, pure love overwhelms the realiser.

All six systems of philosophy mainly speak about how to get rid of sufferings. They preach about self-surrender and knowing the Supreme Brahman in order to get rid of sufferings.

Divya Darshan while concurring with the knowledge and experience of the ancient sages and seers, explains lucidly how to attain the stage of self-surrender. What knowledge must be acquired and what type of spiritual practices are to be undertaken in order to get elevated to that stage of self-surrender? Divya Darshan dilates in detail about the greatness of Brahman, His lila and manifestations etc. after knowing which one would be inclined for self-surrender.

Some try to propitiate God for getting rid of sufferings. Some try to get rid of sufferings by refuting and ignoring the existence of God. In the six systems of philosophy such as Samkhya, Yoga, Nyaya, Vaiseshik, Purva Mimamsa, and Uttar Mimamsa (Vedanta Darshan) various instructions are laid down to get rid of sufferings. But the importance of such instructions remains hazy and incomprehensible for most of the people. Hence little benefit is reaped from out of them. Scriptures teach that we are gifted with senses, mind and intellect in order to enquire about the Creator and ultimately attain the Supreme Truth. He, who believs and surrenders to the Supreme Truth follows the Sanatan Dharma that pervades and regulates the whole Creation.

✧

[30]Only knowledgeable or wise men can know about Dharma and observe actual Dharma. Whatever laws are operative in the kingdom of nature for maintenance of the body, harmonious social living with peace and happiness, and self-realisation are nothing but Sanatan Dharma. Due to ignorance about scriptural instructions we are not able to understand what exactly Dharma is.

Everything has been created from Brahman and gets merged with Brahman. In between the Creation and ultimate immergence with Brahman we come across various stages along with names, forms and attributes. In other words, God's manifestation is termed as the Creation full of names, forms and qualities. We see the Sun, the Moon, birds and animals, man etc. Aggregation of all these is the Creation. Different things have been assigned with different names. When the sages realised the presence of different personal godheads, they named them. When they realised the existence of Ishwar, they named Him as such. Similarly, after experiencing the creation of birds, animals, planets and humans, they were named as such. Every moment the process of creation and dissolution is going on. Some examples are cited below.

The water from the ocean goes up as vapour and rains as water drops. The water flows through the streams and rivers and go back to the ocean. Likewise, a seed becomes a seedling, a plant which bears flowers and fruits, and again becomes a seed. From a seed it starts its journey and grows till it becomes a seed again. Like these, innumerable cycles are

---

30 Oriya Divya Dhara Vol 4 Page 27

incessantly operative in the Creation. Similarly, a grand cycle is also operative which is all-inclusive. Everything is emerging out of Brahman and ultimately getting merged with Brahman. This is the all-inclusive eternal cycle. It includes all names, forms and attributes in this Creation. Corresponding to the forms, attributes are embedded in them. Corresponding to the qualities also the forms are made. In different forms different qualities are embedded. Like forms like qualities. Some laws are there in the background for the creation and existence of the forms. For the plant to be created and to exist, some laws are there. Likewise, in order that man will be created and would live for certain years, some laws are operative in the background. Different forms are endowed with some specific qualities relevant and need-based. Whatever laws are operative for creation and sustenance ultimately impel everyone to merge with Brahman. In other words, whatever laws are operative from creation to dissolution are called Sanatan Dharma. These laws are eternally operative. Hence this is also known as Law of Eternity that works unerringly or without aberrations.

Breaking the Law of Eternity results in a backslide which consequently distances oneself from the goal.

Everyone is getting regulated by the Law of Eternity. The movement of the heavenly bodies, the mineral kingdom, plant kingdom and animal kingdom are all governed by the Law of Eternity. The sages had known the Law of Eternity perfectly well whereas the ordinary men neither know the Law of Eternity nor the Creation.

I (Sadguru Sri Sri Arjun) am giving some hints about the Creation. Everyone should know about the Creation to appreciate this knowledge better. There are innumerable things, but I am giving a few hints starting from a specific stage of Creation.

For the journey from origin to one's destination, certain laws are at work. These Laws are called the Law of Eternity. It is equally applicable to everyone in the Creation irrespective of caste, creed or belief. A man should follow the laws which are meant to be followed by him. That is called the Manav Dharma. Here there is no question of groupism, casteism or sectarianism. But due to ignorance you do not know the Law of Eternity. You do not know what the Manav Dharma is, as a result of which there are distortions in your behaviour and conduct.

The sages and seers knew Dharma perfectly well. If we do not come in contact with such wise men, how can we know our mistakes, dispel ignorance and tread on the righteous path? We are not approaching wise persons for knowledge nor are we interested to be in touch with them. We do not even pay respect to them. How then shall we know what Dharma is? He, who will know Dharma, shall surrender to Dharma. For this, it is essential to be in regular touch with sages, Gurus and scriptures.

When we are interested to know what Dharma is, it means, we are observing Dharma from the beginning. He is a sinner who does not want to know what Dharma is. He, who shall try to know, will know Dharma and will ultimately get rid of sufferings.

If man observes the Law of Eternity, he can get peace and bliss and ultimately liberation. This Law of Eternity is also operative in the kingdom of nature indicating its universal application. Realisation of Self means immergence with Brahman. That is our True Self. Observance of Laws for attainment of our goal is our first and foremost duty and Dharma. Dharma means realisation of True Self. Now the question is whether whatever we are doing are for realising our True Self? Yes, you are born for realisation of Self. You are taking food and maintaining body only for realisation of True Self. But ordinary men do not have this idea. Without knowing this how can anybody observe Dharma? By blind observance of certain rituals, some people call themselves dharmic. It shall lead them nowhere. Therefore, the laws are to be known first and then observed for attainment of the goal. We boast of our religions but rarely evince interest to know what Dharma is. Spiritual practice for self-realisation is true Dharma. Everyone must approach wise persons or Sadguru to know about Dharma and the laws to be followed for self-realisation.

The people of Satya Yug were observing the Laws and they were peacefully leading long life. The sages were living for thousands of years. Maharshi Vashistha was the Guru of King Dasarath and his predecessors also. He was also Guru of Lord Ramachandra. A sage named Changadev of Maharashtra who was a hatha yogi lived for hundreds of years. They were observing the natural laws very meticulously and that is why, they were living happily and peacefully for hundreds of years. People of Satya Yug were leading honest life. There was no need of lock and key to preserve their personal wealth. But at present, there is depletion of knowledge about Dharma. Out of ignorance, people are thinking that they are doing Dharma. They are actually doing adharma. There is degeneration of ethical standards now-a-days.

Divya Darshan says, "He, who does not evince interest to know what Dharma is, is doing adharma." Many people undertake charitable activities like serving others, donating, digging wells, and building temples etc. without knowing what Dharma means.

Due to ignorance man attaches more significance to smaller things. The above activities are not true Dharma. The basic purpose of observing Dharma is realisation of True Self. Whatever spiritual practices are undertaken for realisation of True Self is Dharma. For self-realisation there are many auxiliary points of Dharma. But we misconstrue one or two auxiliary points for Dharma. One hand, people cheat others and on the other hand they give donations quite liberally and build temples also. No virtue shall accrue from out of such activities undertaken from ill-gotten money.

Happiness, peace, bliss and freedom will also be there where there is Dharma, because that is our true nature. Sanatana Dharma is an infinite subject. We have in the above paragraphs discussed about some specific dimensions of fundamental issues only. Once we take keen interest to know about Dharma, we shall be able to know about Dharma more and more.

⁊

[31]Whether yoga is relevant for any spiritual practice? The answer is an emphatic 'Yes'. If one knows what yoga is and accordingly carries on the spiritual practice, one will attain the goal.

---

31 Oriya Divya Dhara Vol 2 Page 34

Yoga means union; union between two. If we are connected to somebody, we come to know more and more details about him. Likewise, if we maintain regular contact with God we come to know more and more about God or Brahman. Yoga is union with Truth, i.e. union with God. This knowledge is self-knowledge.

Whether yoga is necessary for acquisition of knowledge? Answer- Yoga has intimate relationship with knowledge. In the foregoing paragraph, it is already stated that relationship with God is yoga. Chanting the name of God is also yoga. Since man wants peace and happiness, he craves for good. Only God is good and perfect. The divine thoughts are all good. Good means divine and pure. Good denotes happiness, peace and bliss. Hence contact (union) with good is yoga.

Who is God? Where is He? What is His importance or role? Whoever contemplates in this line of thought is in yoga with God. Many people advocate for meditation but that is not easy. If a person does not know anything about God how shall he meditate? To make efforts to know God or about God is yoga. Many ask the question, "Why God is not realised even after chanting God's name and offering prayers for years together?"

Even evincing interest to know about God is yoga. If a man always contemplates on God, his mind gradually gets more and more inclined towards God. Hence Divya Darshan does not advocate for singing God's praise just to propitiate Him. Divya Darshan exhorts mankind to evince interest in knowing Him.

"By trying to know Him and His greatness, you would meet with one truth after another. In this way you would acquire knowledge and realise the Supreme Truth." This is the relation between yoga and jnana. When we operate some machine we gradually come to know about the machine and its different components one by one. Likewise, if we are in yoga (union) with God and if we have intense desire to know God, very quickly we can get the result. Strong inquisitiveness is essential to know God.

Mechanically chanting mantra or counting beads while repeating God's name is not that much effective because without knowing the importance of God, many people are seen to be chanting His name without much concentration or inquisitiveness. One should move to *bhava* stage so intensely that tears should come out while uttering the name of God. The concentration may get disturbed while focusing on the number of beads counted.

The path of Divya Darshan is knowledge path which includes listening or reading (sravana), meditating (manana) and repeatedly contemplating (nididhyasana).

In the Laya Yoga, the outside and inside become one. Whatever is outside is there inside. Whatever is inside is there outside also. In other words, one's own *bhava* takes the form of energy that manifests as many, as the outside world of names, forms and qualities. Laya Yoga is an advanced stage of meditation (Dhyana). Hence Divya Darshan starts from Dhyana Yoga.

ରେ✦ର

[32]Brahman and Jiva are one and the same. The Advaita philosophy upholds this truth. The common people without adequate knowledge on spirituality do not accept this. They think it to be impossible or unrealistic. Some argue, "How can we be one with our Creator?" Divya Darshan explains the difference between the two and then establishes the unity between the two.

God is Bliss-Absolute. This is what the sages and seers have realised. If someone knows God as Bliss-Absolute, he will get bliss. This bliss is different from the worldly pleasure. Worldly pleasure is blended with sufferings. Worldly pleasure is transient and therefore it may vanish next moment or after some time. But God is eternally blissful. In other words, bliss is ever present. God is the basis of infinite and unbroken bliss. He, who attains God, enjoys infinite bliss.

To get happiness, peace and bliss, one must take shelter of God who is the source of infinite bliss. Where there is fear, illusion and doubts there shall

---

32 Oriya Divya Dhara Vol 2 Page 36

be sufferings. All these impede liberation. Liberation would be there once all these are dispelled totally.

There is truth in everything. In consonance with certain laws, truth expresses itself or manifests. Every man wants to live. For living, he must observe some laws. To live in peace and happiness, he must observe certain laws. To live in society also, he has to observe certain laws. Peace is not any object to be acquired. Peace is only to be experienced. The laws which are operative in the kingdom of nature come under the ambit of the Law of Eternity. Divya Darshan therefore lays stress on the Law of Eternity, its greatness and implications. Observance of those laws is Dharma. Going against this law means adharma which would cause sufferings. While the Law of Eternity rules everywhere and acts upon everything, it is essential for the human beings to observe it.

Shrimad Bhagavad-Gita preaches observance of swadharma. Divya Darshan lays emphasis on how a person should conduct himself to accomplish the goal of life. Animals are bound by their instincts. Man is bestowed with intelligence and can ask questions to know about his duty, righteousness and about the appropriate path to reach his goal. The sages are also called seers because they were able to experience the laws in operation everywhere in the kingdom of nature. This Law of Eternity is the spontaneous expression of chit shakti. The human beings who observe the Law get happiness, peace, bliss and freedom. Everything in the kingdom of God is for bliss and happiness. The priority of Divya Darshan is to spread the importance and greatness of the Law of Eternity and impart true knowledge to the mankind. Divya Darshan explains the Law of Eternity and its rules of observance. Divya Darshan does not support any blind belief. It lays emphasis on

❖ Survival i.e. maintenance of physical body

❖ Living harmoniously in the society with peace and happiness

❖ Self knowledge to get freedom ultimately

The Law of nature is such that after taking birth, everyone would try to live; he would like to live in a society harmoniously with peace and happiness; he would acquire self-knowledge for liberation.

But we remain stuck up at the first stage i.e. somehow to survive by maintaining the physical body.

Second stage is living in a society in peace and happiness. We do not acquire adequate knowledge for this. Discipline, courtesy, ethics etc. are required for a harmonious living in the society. Without these qualities, we cannot live properly. In other words, divine virtues are essential for a good living.

By acquiring divine virtues, one can ultimately realise the Supreme. That is the source of all peace and bliss. Realisation of True Self is liberation. For self-realisation, the role of Sadguru is essential. On realisation of True Self, the individuality shall be lost to the total, unitary and infinite Self-Awareness. This is non-dualism. All fears, doubts and sufferings shall vanish forthwith. All bondages would be cut asunder. That life is called truly a divine life. Self-efforts together with Sadguru's Grace bring the much sought-after liberation. Jiva bhava vanishes. Jiva realises that he is none other than Brahman.

❧ ★ ❧

[33]There are many spiritual organizations, which are carrying out and promoting spiritual activities. Despite so much of efforts, people are not getting peace and happiness. People are not still aware of the basis of peace and happiness. Although people try out different kinds of practices and rituals, still they do not get the desired result because of not knowing about the basic principles. For example, the basis of love is knowledge, and the basis of bliss is love. Without possessing love, bliss cannot be attained by merely performing rituals or worshipping some gods and goddesses.

That is why, the sages always emphasized on divine virtues such as truth, love, and service. The Vedas and the Vedanta also lay stress on all these

---

33   Oriya Divya Dhara Vol 20 Page 46

divine qualities. When people will learn the essence of all these scriptures, they can live peacefully and reach the goal of self-realisation. Now in our society, the scriptural essence is not understood and appreciated. Modern man's priorities are different. The scriptures are relegated to the background. Divya Darshan therefore preaches the essence of the scriptures in a novel and simplified way that can easily be comprehended. Many temples, mosques and churches are there and more and more are being built. But man is not getting peace despite all religious practices. Rather there is increase in chaos or indiscipline. But the truth is that no rituals or practices with religious fervor can help man earn peace and happiness. Man must acquire true knowledge without which peace and happiness is impossible to attain. By acquiring true knowledge, man can be pure and perfect. In the *ashrams*, true knowledge is imparted to the devotees and followers. He, who does not possess true knowledge, gets saddled with more desires. At the end, he gets sufferings only. Most of the people visit religious places for fulfilment of their long list of desires. Some priests also encourage them to go for different kinds of rituals. As a result, true knowledge remains far away.

In the olden days, there were Gurukuls (residential schools which used to teach holistically) managed by the rishis who were proficient in the scriptural knowledge. Divya Darshan therefore aims at opening Gurukuls in large numbers. Although there are discourses on the scriptures at different places, people are not able to focus their attention on the same because of which they understand little about the essence of the scriptures. *Ashrams* and Gurukuls can contribute a lot towards dissemination of true knowledge as laid down in the scriptures.

While this is the importance of the *ashrams*, it is observed that people come forward to give heavy donations for construction of temples, but they hesitate to help the *ashrams*. If there will be more and more *ashrams*, there will be more opportunities to spread true knowledge among the people and more benefits shall accrue to the society.

Although there are many religious institutions at different places, true knowledge is being imparted at few places only. Most of them celebrate religious festivals and perform different kinds of rituals instead of teaching about the Almighty as pointed out by the Vedas and Upanishads.

Divya Darshan lays emphasis on true knowledge by which divine thoughts will come. Divya Darshan preaches about right thought, right expression, and right action. Human life is characterized by the above three principles, the observance of which will bring peace and happiness. These three principles stated above are akin to karma, bhakti and jnana as taught in the Shrimad Bhagavad-Gita. Although there are nectar-like knowledge stored in the scriptures, due to lack of adequate knowledge, many people do not understand and appreciate the significance of the scriptures.

First, we all must know the importance of karma. What type of karma is to be undertaken and what not? Which karma comes under the purview of karttavya and Dharma? Therefore, we must undertake such karma that is aligned with karttavya and Dharma. Purposeless toiling will lead us nowhere. The whole subject is taught to the spiritual seekers on a stage to stage basis keeping in view their ability to assimilate the knowledge. In the next stage, God's greatness and His indispensability is explained which arouses love and devotion in them. Finally, true knowledge is imparted that leads to self-realisation.

All the above three steps form the core of Sanatan Dharma or the Law of Eternity. Hence Divya Darshan says, "Knowing the Law of Eternity is knowledge and observing the same is Dharma." This knowledge is imparted in an amazingly simple and unequivocal way without using difficult jargons but citing examples from the day to day life. He, who will know and observe the Law of Eternity, is truly Dharmic and he will attain divinity. He, who accepts and adores truth will acquire true knowledge and can confidently impart knowledge to others.

જી✴જી

[34]Although all the six systems of philosophy have stressed upon the alleviation of sufferings, in the last Darshan i.e. Vedanta Darshan,

---

34 Oriya Divya Dhara Vol 2 Page 38

Vyasadev has clearly pointed out that if Self remains unknown, man cannot get rid of sufferings. Once Atman or Brahman, who is the basis of everything, is realised what else is to be known? There is nothing else beyond Atman or Brahman. It is the unchangeable eternal essence i.e. the Supreme after knowing whom nothing else remains to be known.

In the six systems of philosophy Vedanta Darshan is the latest Darshan that imparts complete knowledge. Divya Darshan is in line with the essence of Vedanta Darshan but with some difference in the style of presentation. Since everything in this Creation has come forth from Atman, how is it possible to know Atman, the basis of all? To Know about Atman is to know about the greatness of the Creator. Once the Creator is known the Creation can be known. Knowing Him means following truth and realising truth. When we know Him and His manifestations, it is complete knowledge. He, who possesses complete knowledge, would be free from all doubts and despairs, anxieties and agonies.

In arithmetic, if we do not know 1 (one), we cannot correctly know other numbers because 1 (one) is the common constituent of all numbers. Hence Divya Darshan says, "Once we know the Creator, we can know everything and get rid of sufferings. His manifestations are based on certain Law called the Law of Eternity."

After experiencing the Supreme truth, the realisers impart true knowledge to the aspirants. After self realisation dualism vanishes and there is no scope for any argument at this stage. Here there is no question of any blind belief. The Truth having been experienced is now presented in the form of Divya Darshan. Unless man knows Self, he cannot be simple. Only Self is ever simple. It is never attached to anything else. Hence it cannot be complex although it appears to be so. Divya Darshan expounds the secrets of spirituality in quite a simple manner so that it can reach one and all.

Naming of Divya Darshan: Darshan means 'seeing'. By what one can see? The answer is – By eyes, by intellect or by intuition. What is experienced is Darshan. Man always wants happiness, peace and bliss. All other five Darshans in the six systems of philosophy preach about mitigation of sufferings. The sixth and last Darshan, which is Vedanta Darshan, speaks about total elimination of sufferings. It shows the way to self-realisation. Complete peace and bliss would not come until one attains Self-Knowledge.

The following are the six systems of philosophy.

- ❖ Samkhya Darshan-   By Maharshi Kapila
- ❖ Yoga Darshan-   By Maharshi Patanjali
- ❖ Nyaya Darshan-   By Maharshi Gautam
- ❖ Vaiseshik Darshan-   By Maharshi Kanad
- ❖ Purva Mimamsa Darshan-   By Maharshi Jaimini
- ❖ Vedanta Darshan-   By Maharshi Vyasadev

Divya Darshan is all comprehensive and lays stress on knowledge and divine virtues. It starts from the very survival of the individual to the goal of self-realisation which amounts to total liberation.

Divya Darshan presents Jnana in three stages.

- ❖ Lila (Play of Brahman) - Lila relates to Maya through which all forms and qualities are assumed by Brahman through the process of manifestation.

- ❖ Greatness (Glory of Brahman) – The Eternal Law, by which the Conscious Energy manifests as many through an intelligent, integrated and ingenious process of evolution to appear as the ever-changing Creation full of truth and knowledge, forms and qualities, is but the glory and greatness of Brahman. Fire burns everything due to its burning power. Since Brahman has great powers in Him, He can effortlessly and spontaneously manifest as many. Manifestation constitutes His lila. Through lila, His Greatness comes to light. Water, fire, Sunrise, dawn and dusk which we come across are all due to His greatness. Wherever His greatness is there, His lila is there. In other words, His lila takes place due to His greatness.

❖ Realisation of True Self - Whose greatness are all these? Who is doing the lila? He is Brahman. Realisation of Brahman is realisation of True Self. To know Him we must know about His greatness and consequent lila. Lila indicates His greatness. If we understand His lila, we come to know about His greatness. If we know about various forms and their inherent qualities, we can well appreciate and understand His lila as well as His greatness. Knowledge on lila and greatness would ultimately lead to Self-Knowledge. But those who confine themselves to forms only, they cannot realise the formlessness of Brahman. Similarly those, who know only formlessness of Brahman, cannot realise Brahman in totality. Those, who know forms of Brahman as well as His formlessness, His attributes and attributelessness, know Brahman. They can say that everything is filled with Brahman. Brahman pervades one and all and is everywhere as the Supreme Truth.

ര‌ാ∗ര‌ാ

[35] *["Varieties in lila create the ideas of dualities but on knowing the maker of lila, all such dualities disappear, yielding place to monism (Advaita)."*

(Amritbindu -66)]

It is the gist of Divya Darshan. In this quote, three basic aspects of spirituality are mentioned. Those are -

❖ Lila

❖ Maker (Producer, Director and Actor) of lila

❖ Maya.

It is stated in the above quote that if you can know the maker of lila, you shall get rid of Maya (all illusions). Not knowing the above is ignorance. Ignorance is a great sin. Thus, said the great Greek Philosopher Socrates. I

---

35 Oriya Divya Dhara Vol 19 Page 33

(Sadguru Sri Sri Arjun) had drawn inspiration from this great quote and heartily accepted him as my Guru. I deeply contemplated on this great statement and repeated it several times. I whole-heartedly endorsed this statement which had a magical effect of *Mantra Shakti* on me. That brought about great transformation in me. I pursued true knowledge with my intense inquisitiveness consequent to which I received God's grace. Whoever pursues knowledge and walks on the path of Dharma shall attain bliss and freedom.

Take the example of a man. He lives in the society with his family. He fully depends upon the kingdom of nature for his survival. Family, society and nature are the pre-requisites for lila. Man gets attached to certain things and develops dispassion for something. This is lila. God does this lila. We are all born in the ambit of lila. For our survival, we require so many things; we collect those things. God has made this Creation to take care of our total needs.

Why this Creation is there? Who has created all these? Not knowing the answers to these questions is ignorance or Maya. Had there been no Creation, we would not have been there at all. There would have been none to raise a question or give an answer.

Not knowing the maker of lila or truth is Maya. Even if truth remains unknown, we come across truth always but we misconstrue something for the other. It is Maya. Without knowing the purpose, doing something in a whimsical manner is also Maya. Maya creates misunderstandings even between husband and wife. In other words, it is ignorance that creates all such situations. Wherever there Is Maya, there is suffering. With the acquisition of right knowledge, we will understand that God has created everything including tree, forest, rivers and rivulets, mountains, food grains, animal kingdom and plant kingdom etc. But due to ignorance we misuse things. For example, if we consume more than we actually need, we will suffer. This suffering is due to ignorance or Maya.

Maya surrounds us everywhere. If there is Maya, it means there is lila going on. The maker of lila is also present there. Since we do not know Him and

His lila, we suffer. In other words, due to want of true knowledge we misconstrue something for the other. This is called Maya.

Lila is eternally on. The maker of lila is also eternal. If the maker of lila is realised, one can understand His lila. While trapped in Maya, the man cannot know that he is in Maya. When one will come to know that everything in the Creation is done by Him, one's suffering will go away. By knowing God's greatness, a seer can know God's Will also. He can know that God has created him; God has made all provisions for him for his peaceful living. Whenever God so wills, He can do anything according to situations. He can change the situations also. After our death also, He will take care and create more opportunities for us depending on our samskara (impulses).

Although man is committing sins due to ignorance, he is not trying to know what vice is and what virtue is. If you acquire true knowledge and know more and more about God, you can know His lila and His Will. You will not be affected any more. Your sufferings shall vanish. A magician mesmerizes the audience by his tricks. But once you know his magic tricks, he cannot surprise you anymore.

Due to ignorance, man is not able to know the maker of lila. Hence he is in Maya. He suffers a lot. God or Brahman is there in you all. He is your Atman or Self. He remains veiled by ignorance. He, who realises Him, can get rid of Maya and consequently all sufferings.

಄⋆಄

[36]The different powers of Atman are called personal godheads. In other words, Atman manifests as such. Whatever we see, or experience, are nothing but His manifestations. Fire remains everywhere but according to the circumstances, it manifests. Energy is all-pervasive. Energy has manifested as everything according to circumstances. Atman or Truth remains as it is, without undergoing any change. It is everywhere and manifests as everything. We are not able to realise this. To experience Him, situations and circumstances are required. Sorrows and sufferings

---

36 Oriya Divya Dhara Vol 2 Page 42

come under certain specific circumstances. Bliss is also like that. To realise Him, there is need for circumstances and situations. The sages and seers who have already attained self-realisation do not depend upon any situation. Whenever they remember Him or be in contact with Him, they are with Him. Guru has realised Brahman. The disciple may innocently ask, "Please show me Brahman." Guru cannot show. How can he? Brahman is not like any object that He would show. Guru only creates favourable situations and circumstances for the disciple to realise Brahman or Atman.

How is Atman realised? In course of interactions with Guru, a favourable climate is created. Questions and answers come under the ambit of knowledge. In the process of interactions, a stage is reached where knowledge cannot reach. That gets transformed to '*bhava*'. The '*bhava*' of the Guru (master) and that of the disciple shall tend to mingle. Until the *bhava* of the disciple has been unified with the *bhava* of the master, Brahman cannot be experienced by the disciple.

Guru has already reached that stage. So, it is imperative for the disciple also to reach that stage of *bhava* to realise Brahman. When Guru's *bhava* and disciple's *bhava* become one, then only Brahman will be experienced. That state is called Mahabhava.

For example- A person loves another person. Their love reaches such a stage that one will be ready to sacrifice himself for the other. Similarly, the *bhava* of the master and the *bhava* of the disciple should be such that there would be union between the two i.e. Atman of the master and the Atman of the disciple. Then only the disciple shall realise Brahman. The light of Brahman which is ablaze in the master will also ignite the flame in the disciple. The disciple no longer remains as the disciple. Atman realises Atman. Atman is not any material object that the master would hand over to the disciple. Experience or realisation depends upon the intensity of *bhava*. It is essential to possess unstinted faith, devotion and love towards Guru. Guru has spontaneous love towards the disciple by which *bhava* arises in the disciple. Thereafter only Mahabhava overwhelms him. The basis of all this is faith, devotion and love.

When the thirst for self-realisation becomes acute, thereafter comes love for God i.e. *bhava*. When *bhava* gets saturated it becomes Mahabhava. There are many who have not approached any Guru. Those who possess good impulses (samskara) may not need a spiritual guide or Guru. He, who has faith, devotion and love for God or Brahman, cries for Him. The relationship between disciple and master becomes such that love predominates there; that is *bhava* i.e. love for God-realisation. There the *bhava* that emanates from inside, merges with the outer and thus there is a total Brahma-bhava. That is union or Mahabhava, complete fusion; one becomes one with Brahman. That is divine experience as the Undivided Whole. By studying scriptures, one may not attain God-realisation. Brahman is beyond all knowledge. According to Socrates, knowledge is the path only. He, who realises Guru, realises God also.

⁊*⁊

[37]Everything is truth in this Creation, according to Divya Darshan. One truth has come out of some other truth. Every truth is linked with the Supreme Truth. Now the question is- If everything is truth, from where untruth has come? The answer is- every untruth is also truth. The horse has horns. It is true that it is an untruth. True, it is false or wrong. Divya Darshan says, "Everything is truth". Truth is truth. Falsehood is also truth. Scriptures explain that untruth is an attribute of truth. Truth manifests in many forms. Untruth is one of such forms. Falsehood or untruth is a form. Whose form is this? It is a form of truth. There is nothing like untruth. Untruth is a derivative of truth. All derivatives or attributes have come from truth. Likewise, Jagat is a form of Brahman. In other words, Brahman has taken the form of Jagat. Jagat has emanated from Brahman. Maya has no form. But Maya always remains. To identify or explain something we assign a name to something or other. Name is false. On the other side, Brahman is true. Scriptures say everything is Brahman. Divya Darshan also says that everything is Brahman. Then where is untruth?

---

37 Oriya Divya Dhara Vol 2 Page 44

Everything is truth. Jagat is untrue or unreal. Are these two statements not contradictory? When man will come to know the true meaning of the above two statements, it is to be understood that he has acquired complete knowledge.

Jiva is different. Brahman is different. Again, scriptures say that there is no difference between Jiva and Brahman. There is diversity in unity and unity in diversity. He, who knows this completely, really knows Brahman (The Supreme Truth). When his knowledge will be complete, he can understand that this Jagat is pervaded by Brahman. He can understand that this Jagat is a manifestation of Brahman. When we say that Jagat is unreal, this is only a particular aspect. On knowing a specific form or part only, we cannot say that Jagat is full of Brahman. Knowledge about a specific form is not knowledge about the total form.

Upanishads say- Brahman has no form, no quality. Yajnavalkya's final answer was, "Neti, Neti" which sounds inconclusive. It means, "Not this much, not like this." This means He is indescribable. To realise Him, who has no forms or qualities, is Param Siddhi.

❧✦❧

[38]What is the uniqueness of Divya Darshan?

Divya Darshan is not a community, dogma or any sect of religiosity. Divya Darshan explains Sanatan Dharma in a unique way. The essence of the scriptures such as the Upanishads and the Vedanta Darshan is Atman or Brahman. Divya Darshan explains the same very lucidly without any incomprehensible jargons. The idea is that it should reach one and all. Everyone should understand it. The Law of Eternity is unchangeable. Divya Darshan expresses the Law of Eternity in a very simple language intelligible to the common men. Divya Darshan is always there and shall never fade into oblivion since it speaks about the Eternal Supreme Truth.

In the Vedas, the Law of Eternity is an essential topic of discussion. The sages had perceived in the *Samadhi* state the operative law that governs the

---

38 Oriya Divya Dhara Vol 2 Page 45

Creation in its entirety. Divya Darshan dilates upon the Law of Eternity which, being ever functional, regulates everything. Divya Darshan is an offshoot of the Law of Eternity. Hence Divya Darshan is also eternal. There shall be no decay or death of Divya Darshan. Divya Darshan does not belong to anybody. It belongs to everybody. This is not just another sect or community, class, creed or category. Everyone belongs to Divya Darshan, for it is total and all-inclusive, and applicable to everyone. Everyone is on their journey to reach a common goal. Everything is in its passing phase. Hence Divya Darshan should not be categorised under any system of philosophy. It is unique; embraces all and includes all irrespective of their gradations or classifications. It is not just another philosophy limited by any specificity or boundary.

To know the Law of Eternity is Knowledge. The uniqueness of Divya Darshan lies in its uniqueness of presentation of the Law of Eternity and Brahman Tattva. It is new for the present age. It existed millions of years ago. It has surfaced again to suit the present day requirement. Divya Darshan belongs to eternity. The expounder of Divya Darshan is also eternal. Man owes his very existence to the Law of Eternity. Therefore, any disregard to the Law of Eternity amounts to self-negation and disregard to true knowledge.

ೞ★ೞ

[39]Everything has come out from Brahman and goes back to get merged with Brahman. In the process, we come across innumerable happenings, multiple stages of the grand Creation composed of many forms and many qualities. We see around us stars and planets, different animals and plants. We see a seed becoming a seedling that gradually spreads out with trunk, branches, leaves, flowers and fruits, and finally of course seeds again. Thus, a cycle is completed. Similarly, a grand cycle is on. All have come from Brahman and ultimately would go back to Brahman traversing long distance and passing through innumerable stages with differentiated forms and qualities. For anything to happen, many laws and causalities are there.

---

39 Oriya Divya Dhara Vol 8 Page 1

These ever-operative laws take forward everything ultimately to get it merged with the source i.e. the Supreme Brahman. This is called the Law of Eternity. At different stages, different qualities find expression. Just as during youth, there comes sexual urge which was not there during childhood. Sperms are created in the body which were not there before. With the change in stages, different types of thoughts overwhelm us, and we proceed to act or behave accordingly. According to the Law of Eternity, inquisitiveness is also seen in us at different stages of life. We develop ourselves accordingly. This Law is called the Law of Eternity. This law of Eternity is operative in the kingdom of nature i.e. in the plants, animals, humans, Devas etc. it is different for water. Water has different property. It is different for plant. The plant bears fruits and flowers. It is different for humans. Different types of thoughts come to humans and they undertake different activities with their calibres and competencies. Thus, man would develop the inquisitiveness to find ways to go back to the source point from which he has descended. The sages and seers knew this law of Eternity and accordingly they were conducting themselves. Thus, they were getting happiness and peace. Sufferings remained far away from them. But since we do not know this Law, we are suffering, and we do not also live as long as the sages of yesteryears were living. To love all is the basic tenet of the Law of Eternity. But we find that many of us are jealous of others and give pains to others. In Satya Yug, people were conscious of the Law of Eternity and were respecting the Law of Eternity.

We talk of Law of Eternity but very few are aware of what it is. Sages descend at periodic interval to make the people aware of the Law of Eternity. For example, while Lord Buddha emphasised on truth & non-injury, Lord Jesus laid stress on love and forgiveness. Sri Chaitanya Dev stressed on devotion and love. Whatever the sages and great souls preach are all based on the Law of Eternity. But at a subsequent stage, followers have given different names to such preaching, and divided themselves into different groups. Another example may be cited here. The various powers of the Supreme Brahman are called Devas. Divya Darshan reiterates that knowing the Law of Eternity is knowledge. True knowledge is expressed in the scriptures. The Vedas and Vedanta preach about the

Law of Eternity. When we are not reading scriptures or not trying to understand the scriptures, it means that we are overlooking the Law of Eternity. This also means we are ignoring true knowledge. To preach Sanatan Dharma in the society, it is the Sanatan Dharma that is at work. Divya Darshan lays emphasis on the Law of Eternity. Divya Darshan comprehensively covers all points of the Law of Eternity. Keeping in view the present society which has distanced itself from true knowledge over a period, Divya Darshan very carefully and systematically teaches all facets of the Law of Eternity. Divya Darshan covers all aspects such as proper living, living harmoniously in the society with peace and happiness, and realising the Self. Hence Divya Darshan is not a new religion or any new sect. In Divya Darshan, the approach may be found to be new and the style of teaching may be new but it only reiterates the Law of Eternity in totality i.e. from survival to harmonious social living and ultimately to self-realisation.

Divya Darshan lays stress on karma, bhakti and jnana simultaneously and not in a compartmentalised manner. Divya Darshan revives our forgotten knowledge by revealing the Law of Eternity thoroughly. We all are observing the Law of Eternity. We all are in the ambit of the Law of Eternity. But because we are not aware of the same, we are bound to commit mistakes in its observance. Proper observance of the Law of Eternity would lead to Dharma and divine knowledge.

What language can be used to describe the exponent of Divya Darshan? The preacher of Sanatan Dharma is Vyasadev. Whatever he has spoken are all subject matters of Sanatan Dharma. At present also Vyasadev is taking all steps to reveal the Sanatan Dharma by way of Divya Darshan. At present there are few takers to really appreciate what Divya Darshan speaks all about. Those, who denigrate Divya Darshan or are not able to understand and appreciate Divya Darshan, would take more time to understand i.e. only after they acquire some more spiritual knowledge. If somebody criticizes the Law of Eternity, what can be spoken of him?

ఴ★ఴ

[40]Uniqueness of Divya Darshan: What is new in Divya Darshan? This type of question is inappropriate so far as spiritual knowledge is concerned. Divya Darshan is not a particular group or community. Divya Darshan preaches about Sanatan Dharma which is eternal and applicable to one and all. Divya Darshan explains Sanatan Dharma and the unitary concept of Brahman with a different style or approach. It is a new presentation under the name of Divya Darshan. The subject of Sanatan Dharma has been explained in the Vedas and Vedanta. Such knowledge of Truth, being eternal, was there in the past, continues now and shall be there in future also. That is why it is called the Law of Eternity. The Vedas and the Vedantic texts were written in Sanskrit. Today's man is not able to clearly understand the intricacies as explained in the scriptures. Divya Darshan explains the same Truth in an easy-to-understand manner to suit the present generation of seekers and common men.

In the Vedas, true knowledge has been presented. In other words, the Law of Eternity or Sanatan Dharma has been well-explained. Divya Darshan presents the same Truth that the sages had experienced. Sanatan Dharma is eternal. Therefore it has no beginning and no end. Divya Darshan is also eternal. It is for all irrespective of caste, creed and colour. Divya Darshan belongs to everybody. At the same time, it belongs to none. Whoever realises it, it is his.

Knowing the Law of Eternity is knowledge and observing the same is Dharma. Divya Darshan is not an organization or establishment. If it is asked what is there in the Vedas, the answer would be- there is true knowledge in the Vedas. Veda literally means knowledge. It has come subsequent to realisation of Truth or the Law of Eternity by the sages. Now the same eternal knowledge under the name and style of Divya Darshan is presented with a scientific approach which is more suitable for the scientific mind of the present generation. This approach was also there thousands of years back. It has re-appeared now to address the present need. Sanatan Dharma is eternal. The expounder who now preaches Divya Darshan was also there in the past. He has now descended in another form. He is eternal.

---

40   Oriya Divya Dhara Vol 15 Page 50

He is a divine descend of the Divine Consciousness. This changeful Creation is a passing phase of the unchangeable Pure Consciousness. Pure Consciousness is attributeless and formless. Sadguru had further said, "I am always there. I am always with you all. I am watching your courage, determination and activities. I am speaking about the Law of Eternity that governs the Creation. I am speaking about Atman or Brahman who is the eternal essence of the Creation. This Creation itself is manifestation of Brahman. You should be happy that through Divya Darshan you are able to know the essence of the Vedas and other scriptures. Divya Darshan is complete knowledge. He who realises Divya Darshan realises his True Self that amounts to attainment of Supreme Bliss. He, who disowns or shuns Divya Darshan shuns the Vedas and the Law of Eternity. We all owe our existence to the Law of Eternity. I (Sadguru Sri Sri Arjun) expect that the disciples will vigorously try to grasp the essence of Divya Darshan and move forward to their destination."

CS★CS

[41]It is necessary to know what Darshan stands for. Darshan means to see and know. Now the question may be- what is seen and what is known? The answer may not be clearly known to everybody. The great sages have presented Truth through the six systems of philosophy with different approaches.

Man wants to live in happiness, peace and bliss. It is the basic tendency of every one. But although he wants to always enjoy happiness, he suffers throughout. There are some ways to fulfil all daily needs and live happily. This is called Darshan. The sages had contemplated on it and discovered different truths that are essential for everybody to live in peace and happiness. The philosophical works of different Rishis have been named as different Darshans. In Goutam's Nyaya Darshan it has been stated that if one lives righteously, one will get peace and happiness. Similarly there are other Darshans such as Sankhya, Vaisheshika, Yoga, Purva Mimansa. The sixth and the last Darshan is known as Vedanta Darshan or Uttar Mimansa.

---

41 Oriya Divya Dhara Vol 17 Page 63

The last Darshan i.e. Vedanta Darshan by sage Vyasadev has fulfilled all deficiencies by synthesizing and synchronizing complete knowledge and has been presented in an integrated manner that continues to be accepted as a valid document. It boldly presents the unitary existence called Brahman who is Supreme. The jiva who has come from Brahman shall go back to Brahman. It is clear from the above that realisation of True Self is the ultimate goal. The jiva will get rid of all sufferings only after attaining his true nature. In those days, people were able to understand the Vedic texts as well as the Darshans including Vedanta Darshan. But in the present time, it is not at all easy to grasp and interpret Vedanta Darshan correctly. For the present mankind, Divya Darshan is the simplest presentation of the true knowledge which is Advaita Philosophy (Theory of monism).

Divya Darshan has not been named as such by Gurudev. It has been named during a satsanga programme, by a Telugu lady disciple. She said, "Since this Darshan gives us divine knowledge of Brahman and takes us towards divinity by unfolding divinity in us, it should be named as Divya Darshan." Her proposal was accepted then and there at the satsang in the year 1977.

Divya Darshan teaches how a man can become divine. To become divine means moving Godward. It is the basic approach of Divya Darshan to impart such knowledge that can arouse divine feelings in the mind of the recipients. Those who acquire divine knowledge can definitely become divine. Everyone is capable of receiving and assimilating this knowledge in whatever state one may be. Everyone can learn and spread this knowledge of goodness and can become a small link of a big chain. This will definitely do good to the people at large.

❀

Sadguru's Teachings

(We have compiled a few selected sayings of Sadguru Sri Sri Arjun during various discourses. These short sentences are thought provoking and carry deep meaning)

- Living in peace and happiness for the purpose of realising true nature is Sanatan Dharma. This is Divya Darshan. It speaks about Brahman and also teaches how to realise Brahman. Divya Darshan lays emphasis on inculcating divine virtues by which peace can prevail in the world.

- Divya Darshan does not preach only about God or Brahman. It also speaks about how the illusory self-identity with body would be dispelled. Divya Darshan teaches how to become self-dependent by properly discharging duties while aiming at the goal of life. For this, knowledge has to be acquired and the latent divine qualities have to be developed.

- Divya Darshan imparts spiritual knowledge in three stages, such as lila (play), greatness, and true nature.

- Who has provided the food materials? Who is the enabler of our sight power or hearing power etc.? Who enables our breathing while we are asleep? It is all by Brahman.

- On getting some money, you become ecstatic. Who is the provider of the basic materials for manufacturing money? He is the Bliss of bliss.

- Why should a man live in this world for such a long time? It is his first and foremost duty to learn what his life's purpose is. Then only his life would be worth living and meaningful.

❖ We are not aware that our senses do always control us. We do not know much about our senses. We have never stopped and pondered over how they have been drifting us away from our highest goal. He, who is conscious of the mesmerizing spell of the senses, will remain protected from their injurious influences. He, who knows the machinations of Maya, gets released from the clutches of Maya. For him, Maya, that is said to create all illusions, itself becomes an illusion. In other words, Maya ends there.

❖ Man has been suffering because he does not know as much as he should know to get rid of sufferings. If he knows more, his jiva feelings shall be dispelled. He will know the Devas and thereafter he will realise Brahman.

❖ Not knowing the self is the biggest ignorance.

❖ Whatever occurs, happens or manifests every second is only Brahman's manifestation. Shakti is called consciousness when it is in action. In the waking state of consciousness, mind and senses are active. In the dream consciousness, intellect is active. In the sleep state, vivek is functional. Beyond vivek, there remains Turiya consciousness.

❖ Plants behave in a certain manner due to Consciousness and a man behaves differently due to knowledge. In other words, Consciousness in man expresses itself as knowledge.

❖ Everything in this Creation is well-disciplined and well-organized. But man is unable to know this. He, who knows this, shall get Bliss.

❖ We are Happiness-Absolute, Peace-Absolute and Bliss-Absolute. That is why we all instinctively seek happiness, peace and bliss. This means, we are seeking 'True Self'.

❖ Jiva and Brahman are one and the same. Due to want of true knowledge, we are not able to realise this. With increase in knowledge one will come to know the difference between the two, and thereafter about their unity. Brahman is Bliss-Absolute.

The more one experiences it, the more one will get it. Self-Absolute only remains at the end. That is True Self.

❖ Brahman became jiva but jiva cannot know that he is Brahman. In his jiva form only the qualities pertaining to a jiva will appear. As forms differ, the corresponding qualities also differ.

❖ Brahman manifests as the Jagat. This entire Creation appears due to His greatness.

❖ This Creation, that we come across, came out of His self-glory. The Creation is manifestation of *Apara Shakti*.

❖ He is both Para and Apara. He is transcendental or Turiya consciousness, also called *Atma-Chetana* that appears as sleep consciousness, dream consciousness and waking consciousness.

❖ Mind cannot know the intellect (buddhi). Intellect cannot know the conscience (Vivek). Vivek cannot know the Atman. Mind can know mind; buddhi can know buddhi and Atman can know Atman.

❖ What cannot be perceived by the senses, can be perceived by knowledge. With enhanced knowledge man can also know God.

❖ The knowledge by which one can know Brahman's Ahladini Shakti or greatness and finally surrenders to Him is the real or true knowledge. How can you believe someone whom you do not know?

❖ Acquiring knowledge about God every moment is meditation.

❖ Knowledge sustains us; protects us; gives us happiness, peace and freedom.

❖ By knowledge we know clay as well as diamond. How can one know Brahman without right knowledge?

❖ You have power to understand things. By the same knowledge when you know some truth about the other, you start believing him.

❖ One cannot attain what one does not know. Even after attainment also, it remains unreached and unknown. Even if something is near your hands, you cannot get it unless you know about it.

❖ Some people wish to see God in physical form. But the crux of the problem is that they do not know who God is and how He looks like. Even if they happen to see, will they be able to recognize Him?

❖ He generates and activates all our imaginations. How can He be realised by mere imaginations?

❖ Those, who claim having received some boons from God, are in either waking or dream state. The Reality is far away.

❖ Without knowledge, there is no faith, no devotion and no love. Real Bhakti is there at the stage of love.

❖ Evincing interest in knowledge amounts to taking shelter of Satya (Truth); getting inclined towards divine virtues amounts to taking shelter of Dharma.

❖ Man is bestowed with the power to realise truth. He can also imagine remote things and experience happiness and pain. Reality and appearance, light (object) and reflection happen in Brahman's manifestation.

❖ Truth is peace, Truth is bliss. Truth can be attained by Truth.

❖ By which truth, you can know the Supreme Truth?

❖ In the state of *Samadhi*, the mendicant goes to Satya-Loka. When he attains nirvikalpa *Samadhi*, he goes to Nitya-Loka.

❖ Sat (Truth or Existence) is attributeless Brahman; Chit is Brahman; Ananda (Bliss) is 'Om'.

❖ Everything movable or immovable, visible or invisible is contained in 'Om'. 'Om' represents the Whole Creation. 'Om' represents His true nature, greatness and the lila due to His greatness.

❖ 'Om' representing infinite thoughts, is a Mahabhava (a thoughtless state). Where there is no thought, there cannot be any speech or expression; nothing but silence!

❖ Regarding Chandra Bindu of 'Om' (ॐ) -The crescent moon is naada or consciousness. The dot on the moon sign is Brahman.

The sound waves come out of naada. 'Om' is Brahman with attributes and without attributes. (Saguna Brahman and Nirguna Brahman).

❖ What we call the Law of Eternity is Dharma. What we call Dharma is the Law of Eternity.

❖ By certain Laws, a seed comes up as a plant. It is Dharma. For realisation of true nature whatever laws or processes are to be practiced are nothing but Dharma.

❖ Different attributes are there in different forms. (A dog has characteristics different from those of a cow. A monkey has different form with different characteristics. Be it a stove or a cooking pot, the forms are different; so are the attributes. Similarly water and air shall behave differently because of their inherent qualities. A human being is different from other animals. A human being is special as he has so much knowledge and power.)

❖ Different attributes and forms come out depending upon situations and circumstances.

❖ Instinct for survival comes from the very birth. It is not learnt from anywhere. This is nature-given instinct. A plant sucks the required substances from the soil. None has taught this to the plant.

❖ Divine virtues and noble actions are the characteristic qualities of the great souls.

❖ Consciousness has different states. The highest state, which is Pure Consciousness, is Sadguru.

❖ When Sadguru imparts knowledge to the disciples, He descends to saguna state from His nirguna state. Therefore Sadguru is both nirguna (Attributeless) and saguna (With attributes).

❖ People cannot know me (Sadguru Sri Sri Arjun) while I am alive. After I shed my body, people will know me. I am teaching about subtle things which cannot be comprehended so easily. It will take time, may be thousand years.

৩✦৩

Spiritual Practice (Sadhana)

[42]Why do we do spiritual practices? The answer would be –"Realisation of True Self." He, who does not set this goal, all his practices go aimless. It is not necessary at all to make any physical penance by entering some fire or going inside water. It should be remembered that whatever is done for self-development is a spiritual practice. Therefore, Divya Darshan lays stress on Jnana Yoga.

Listening, meditating and repeatedly contemplating are the essential requirement under Jnana Yoga practice.

By repeated contemplation on the same subject, knowledge gets set. One will not forget easily. One assimilates the essence and junks the unwanted information. This world is a laboratory. We receive knowledge by seeing, listening and experiencing. By repeated remembrance, we are in regular contact with the Truth. The aim is to realise Brahman. For this only, everyone should carry on spiritual practices. Many people say that they are doing spiritual practices, but they are not getting any result. Many persons belonging to different sects are engaged in spiritual practices but since many of them do not know the goal of life, they are not getting success. The question is how the success rate would increase? Unless we know clearly for what purpose we do spiritual practices and what the goal of this human life is, our practices will not be meaningful or effective. We must take adequate interest in all our endeavours or spiritual practices. We must have adequate inquisitiveness to know things well and thereafter proceed. All

---

these deficiencies are well addressed by Divya Darshan. Hence the success rate would be higher.

"Surrender to God; have devotion towards God." These advices are given by many spiritual leaders. But since people do not have adequate knowledge about God, they carry selfish desires and try to appease God for fulfilment. "Who is God? How is He? Where does He exist?" Unless the answers to these questions are known, how can one reach and recognize Him? The devotees with bundle of desires keep on asking for something or other from God. Hence there remain many loopholes and drawbacks in their spiritual practices. The reason is ignorance. Devotees of knowledge path on the other hand know the importance and indispensability of God. That is why, their devotion as well as love towards God becomes desireless and unconditional.

Divya Darshan explains lucidly about God's existence and His active role in creating and governing this universe. After believing firmly in the existence of God, a seeker would get some idea about the true nature of God. The seeker comes to know more and more about God's existence, the important role He plays, His greatness and true nature. He would come to know how the unitary existence manifests as this heterogeneous Creation. He would also know how He is the Supreme ruler. God is all powerful and all pervasive. He is the conscious energy. All emanate from One. One remains in all. All remain in one. One remains eternally as one without any division or fragmentation. Although someone tries to meditate on God, his mind does not remain fixed. The more a man knows the value of something the more his mind would be attached to that. When we know the value of gold, our mind gets attracted towards gold. When our mind knows the value of diamond, it moves on to diamond leaving all other things.

When mind would come to know that God is the most valuable eternal existence, it would crave for God. The sages know the value and indispensability of God. But the ignorant do not. It is not necessary to force the mind to get attached to God. In such a case, mind may get attached and after some time it will get detached. While meditating some people feel sleepy. One must acquire knowledge about God and His greatness so that mind will be automatically and instinctively attracted towards God. At the time of adversities some people remember God and thereafter they forget. If positive result comes, they believe in God but if things do not happen as they desire, they disbelieve. This is due to inadequate or incomplete knowledge about God.

How to know about the True Self? A lot of things must be learnt about God. To know somebody, we need to learn about his complexion, height, appearance, his nature, or qualities etc. The more we know about something, the more quickly we get it. The more we know the properties of any matter, the more we can be benefited from out of it and put the same into different uses. If we do not know anything about gold, we cannot get it or possess it. Not only gold, but it is also equally applicable for any herbal leaf or root even. Knowing about God, His greatness and true nature is spiritual practice. Any aimless or stray pursuits are meaningless. In such a case how can one expect to get rid of sufferings?

Sadguru Sri Sri Arjun says, "You must remember that you are Brahman. From that state you have come down and are suffering as jiva. You will have to regain your position. For this you are in spiritual practices."

"I shall know God who resides in me as my 'Self'." This should be your determination. Due to lack of adequate efforts, many people swerve from the spiritual path and become unsuccessful. After a lot of contemplations on this, I (Sadguru Sri Sri Arjun) have explained about success and failure in spiritual practices. I trust the disciples would proceed faster. Intense spiritual practices must be carried out. You must be mentally and physically fit. Slowly you will have new thoughts. At the time of initiation, I have advised you to be stronger by sincerely doing spiritual practices. I have told you to cross all hurdles that may come on your way and move firmly towards the goal. I wish to give you my total knowledge, but I find little enthusiasm in you to receive that. Many of you turn your faces away. Many are still in the clutches of samsaric (worldly) thoughts and Maya. They are sleeping like the mythological Kumbhakarna. They are not conscious of their spiritual journey and the requisite tasks. I shall break your slumber. I have been trying a lot but you are not able to know. Since you are all living in the physical world, always wish for the good of the world. The world shall be good, and you would be a part of it. You should have unstinted devotion towards God without any desire. Those who have participated in this spiritual congregation will grow from strength to strength. You are going to attain the most powerful Existence called God. You will have to increase your power by getting more and more knowledge. Everyone must remember this spiritual congregation. You should have good thoughts and feelings towards each other. Every year try to organize such congregation. Take care of the *ashrams*. Try to make the centre strong so that the branches can be ultimately benefited.

"Even at the cost of my sleep, I must work for breaking your slumber. You will one day know that Guru has come to break your slumber, indolence and inertia. I have completely dedicated myself for your self-development. I have descended with that purpose. My sincere wish is that during my lifetime at least one Guru like me should come up."

಼⋆಼

[43]Spiritual efforts are of many types. Any effort can be made in various ways. Spiritual efforts are discussed in various scriptures in various ways. It is not proper to conclude that only one technique is correct and the others are wrong. According to our level of intelligence we find various alternative methods and choose one of those, which is most suitable to us. There are also different strenuous practices but man being intelligent should think if there is any other simpler method. Rising from the lower truth to higher truth is sadhana (spiritual practice). Doing tapas is also sadhana. According to Ashtanga Yoga practices, Yama, Niyam, Asana, Pranayam, Pratyahar, Dharana, Dhyana and *Samadhi* are the stages. God can be realised through this route. But after *samadhi* is over or during breaks in the *samadhi*, God realisation will not be there. Is there any technique to be with God always? Vedanta Darshan was the last Darshan of the six systems of philosophy. Vyasadev concluded, "I am verily the Atman or Brahman." When one realises this, one is ever free. But without understanding the essence of

---

43 Oriya Divya Dhara Vol 3 Page 54

Vedanta Darshan, we talk of seeing God. Atman is to be experienced from within. When God is seen in the forms of Brahma, Vishnu or Maheswar, it is all due to Maya. We see different roles in a drama on the stage. We come across different characters. But we cannot know who is playing such roles. Seeing any particular form is not real God experience. His Maya form comes out of our imaginations. Therefore, it is not real.

According to the Vedanta Darshan if man has not realised, "I am Brahman", he cannot get rid of sufferings. After seeing some Maya forms at times, we think that we have been successful in our sadhana. These forms are but temporary. When we do practices for attaining lower truths, those cannot be called the right type of sadhana. Because the results that accrue are not permanent. True spiritual practice (sadhana) helps in our self-development. Mere worshipping or chanting without *bhava* becomes a mechanical practice. Many worshippers in temples and holy places worship throughout the life but no one is credited with God realisation. Through the jnana marga or knowledge path, one can attain God realisation. Knowledge path has three steps.

The first step includes listening to the wise, learning from spiritual masters and reading the scriptures.

Second, whatever is learnt, if we think over or repeatedly remember it, knowledge would get clarified, and we can understand the deeper meaning of it.

The third is continued contemplation. Repeated remembrance and reasoning out the same help us to still go deeper for proper assimilation and appreciation of the truth in it. One should always remain alert while listening about God and meditating on God.

God is there everywhere in all forms and qualities. The world is a laboratory for the spiritualists of knowledge path (jnana marg). If someone minutely observes this laboratory, he can gather knowledge quickly. Like this if he proceeds, he can attain the Supreme Truth. He, who tries to know, can know and get. He, who does not evince interest to know, can never know. From the knowledge point of view, it is necessary to have learning attitude always. "How shall I attain God?" He, who possesses this attitude, always, is a true seeker. All other efforts may be auxiliary.

By spiritual efforts, one's capacity gets enhanced. Knowledge path leads us faster to our goal. We always talk of God but who is God we do not know.

Knowing more about something means getting more benefits from out of that knowledge. If we know more and more about God, we can come closer to Him gradually and get good results. The more we know about God, the more we shall have faith and devotion towards Him. The best spiritual practice is to try to know God. In the spiritual practice under knowledge path, success rate is remarkably high. Evincing interest to know God is Dharma. He, who is not trying to know God, is doing adharma only.

Spiritual pursuits start from belief. Belief would be developed into faith and thereafter to devotion. This devotion gradually gets transformed into love. At that time, he will think that God is his life; God is his consciousness

Since I (Sadguru Sri Sri Arjun) had a constant inquisitiveness to know, I could come to this stage. Hence, inquisitiveness alone will take a person to higher stage. I am ready to impart true knowledge to you all. But you do not have curiosity to know. When I give it to you, you are throwing the same in some dark corner. I have detached myself from everything to impart knowledge, but you do not have longing for the same.

❧✶❧

[44]Making necessary efforts or arrangements for attainment of certain goal is called sadhana or spiritual practice. Man has got this rare form which is even craved for by Devas. First, man wants to survive. Second, he wants to live in peace and happiness. Third, he wants to attain eternal liberation. In other words, the instinct to realise True Self is present in every man. We are working day and night for our survival. But we attach lesser importance to our harmonious social living with peace and happiness. We have almost forgotten about self-realisation. In other words, we do not prioritize the

---

44 Oriya Divya Dhara Vol 6 Page 28

last two things. Due to ignorance not only we suffer, we also make others suffer. We do not know why should we eat and survive. Why should we live in the society with peace and happiness? We do not think about the goal of life. We suffer because our life turns out to be an aimless wandering.

The supreme goal of every human being is to realise the Self or realise Brahman. Since our life moves on, unmindful of this goal, there are lots of disturbances and distortions in our life. Man does not know even what type of food he should take to maintain a healthy body. Due to want of proper knowledge he suffers from different diseases. These are obstacles to his self-development. Those who have a set goal of self-realisation they conquer their six enemies such as – Desire, anger, greed, infatuation, arrogance and jealousy.

Since we have never attached importance to realising Brahman, we are not able to attain that state. Every spiritual mendicant should have determination to realise Brahman. We are thoroughly engrossed in worldly matters and just think that by performing some rituals we can get God's blessings.

First, we should have purity to be eligible to attain God. We cannot reach that state unless there is purity in us. We must muster up power to realise the Almighty. We are all reading books to enhance our knowledge, but we are not strong enough to progress on the right path. After acquiring some knowledge, we must try to reach the essence of it. A schoolboy may get by heart the entire Shrimad Bhagavad-Gita, but he cannot know the essence of it nor can he explain it.

Without understanding the implications and essence, whatever we read and remember is just like a shadow without any substance. We have to go to '*bhava*' stage to understand the essence of any subject matter. Once we do that, we can also easily understand the theme and substance of the related subjects. It should be remembered that if we really know, the related power should be seen in us. If it is not, then it is to be understood that we have not mastered the subject properly. In the spiritual subjects, divine powers are involved. A person with self-confidence would have more of self-power. For this power to come one must understand the subtle things.

When we learn about Atman from Sadguru, acquire true knowledge and contemplate on the subject, we will have more self-power.

With our disorderly way of living and improper food habits, how can we develop self-power? Many people have got by heart some scriptures and consider themselves to be truly knowledgeable, but they have not controlled their food habits even. They also possess many negative qualities such as infatuation, anger, greed, ego and jealousy etc. In such a case, how can they know God and how can they understand or appreciate the subject matters of the subtle kingdom? When man will have purity in his food habits, purity in speech, purity in conduct then only the self-power in him would get activated.

Man is not aware of the fact that he has been rewarded with this human body in order to attain God. He is ignorant about the purpose of his birth even after reading so many scriptures. He, who would know that his goal is to attain self-realisation, would attain his goal one day.

People in the Bhakti Marg perform many rituals and conduct themselves according to practices and traditions. But many of them do not evince interest in acquiring knowledge because of which their progress gets halted. Where is God and how is He? How does He express Himself? What are His Laws? Unless one has clear answers to these questions one cannot attain God. How can someone identify and experience Him unless he knows who God is?

One may at best attain a God of one's own imagination. Some drawbacks remain with the aspirants. That is why even though many aspirants do spiritual practices, the success rate is extremely low, almost negligible. Truth remains far away. He, who would have devotion as well as knowledge, is more likely to attain God.

By Bhakti, his conduct shall be restrained and refined. By jnana he would have clear idea about God. Therefore, he is sure to progress faster. His inherent power would wake up and he would be able to cross all obstacles that may come on his spiritual path.

If someone sees Brahma, Vishnu or Maheswar in gross form, will he be benefited by that? God or Brahman is formless. Gross form is only an outer garb. Irrespective of caste, creed, culture and religiosity, God is one and the same for all. Scriptures describe him as Consciousness-Absolute. Therefore Consciousness-Absolute can be realised by knowledge. The Atmic Power is to rise in order to realise the Consciousness-Absolute. One must have strong conviction about God and carry on his spiritual practices with determination to realise Him. Such a mendicant would realise early and for this whatever qualification is required will develop in him.

By spiritual practices Atmic Power increases. Unless one knows the greatness and true nature of God one cannot realise Him. Sense of surrender shall not come unless someone knows about His greatness. Only chanting His name day and night would not help much. One must know the reality behind all names. The name and the named are one and the same. There is no meaning in just parroting God's name.

God has no names, forms or qualities. To realise him lot of Atmic Power is essential.

Hence, I (Sadguru Sri Sri Arjun) am advising you all to acquire knowledge and meditate upon Him once or twice in a day. Try to purify yourself more and more. Without purity He cannot be realised. Brahman eternally expresses Himself as Sat, Chit and Anand and the Law of Eternity. It is to be understood that the Supreme Truth manifests as various truths. Example-seed becomes a plant. Branches, leaves, flowers and fruits also come one after another in stages. Individually everything is truth. It is not just enough to know a branch or a flower. We must know the whole tree. Seed becoming a plant or the plant getting transformed to a seed is the Law of Eternity. A tree must be taken care of well to get fruits and flowers. It must be regularly watered for proper growth. It should be remembered that purity, humbleness and submissiveness strengthen spiritual practices. Unless we do away with the negative qualities in us, we cannot progress on the path of spirituality. Old leaves wither away, and new leaves grow by true sadhana. There are many deficiencies in us. All those are to be eradicated. In other words, bad qualities should be replaced by good qualities; vices should be replaced by virtues.

During the period of sadhana, many supernatural powers may be seen in the spiritual seeker. He gets blessings from Devas as he progresses on the path of sadhana. This becomes helpful for self-realisation.

You are unfortunate if you are not able to understand and appreciate my teachings so clear and simple. Have strong determination to realise God. Guru is always with you. You should change your mind (worldly attitude) as well as your conduct and speech. Have strong faith on Ishta Mantra. All your wishes shall be fulfilled, and you would move forward. Get blessings of Ishwar.

৩~৩

[45] Keeping the body neat and clean and wearing good cloth come under outer cleanliness. But along with body, mind should also be strong and healthy. We must do certain practices for good upkeep of our mind also. The health conditions of the physical body impact the mind also. Mental health also impacts the body. Mind wavers in between good thoughts and bad thoughts, hope and anxieties. The body slowly undergoes growth and decay. It is necessary to take care of the body for the accomplishment of life's goal.

Normally all the daily routine works we undertake come under outer cleanliness. But along with the outer cleanliness of the body, the inner cleanliness is also essential. If mind is not kept clean and stable our duties will get affected and proper results would not accrue. When mind gets stirred by distorted thoughts, there shall be distortions in our work also. For example, I want to reach a specific destination. I start my journey but, on my way, if I quarrel with others, I would be stuck up there and shall not be able to reach my destination in time. Likewise, man's goal is to attain liberation. For achievement of the goal, purity of the mind is an essential pre-requisite. If we are not conscious of the purpose of journey, we may move in the opposite direction and it would take much longer

---

45 Oriya Divya Dhara Vol 7 Page 19

time to reach our goal. Only outer purity or cleanliness is not enough. Outward worship also will not help much to attain God. Many such worshippers are there who have been worshipping like this, but they are not getting the results. Liberation remains far away. He, who has not achieved inner purity, cannot attain God. Therefore, outer purity as well as inner purity is so important for God-realisation. A quite simple way to achieve inner purity is to observe or follow Guru's instructions sincerely so as to improve or bring about refinement of the conduct. Mind also gets purified in the process of observance of Guru's instructions. If one carries on spiritual practice with internal purity, he becomes eligible to attain God. Whoever remembers God always and follows His laws will be heard by God. God is all-powerful. One must become powerful to attain Him. Hence, we must make ourselves powerful. That should be our goal. Both outer and inner purity is essential for this purpose. Once inner purity is attained outer purity becomes secondary. First mind should be purified; body comes next in priority. Diseases will go away from a man who remains in a blissful state.

Bliss is always there. He, whose heart is enriched with a feeling of love, can experience bliss. Love is the basis of bliss. He, who loves all, would remain in bliss. By thinking ill of others, one cannot get peace or bliss. Where is peace for a crooked or deceitful person? Inner nature expresses itself as outward conduct. Those, who think good of the society and who constantly remember God, live a healthy life. By repeated contemplation on God, mind becomes calm and pacified. For this one should approach Sadguru and take initiation and join satsang. Those, who are not able to meet Sadguru frequently or not able to attend satsang, should chant Ishta Mantra regularly. While chanting Ishta Mantra, one should contemplate on the greatness and contribution of Ishta. Everyone can practice this. By that, mind will get purified and one can easily attain peace and bliss.

The sages say that Atman can be attained by Atman only. This means Paramatman is present in everybody as Atman. He, who thinks that Paramatman is inside as Atman and meditates accordingly, attains Atman easily. But due to ignorance man wanders here and there, not knowing that Paramatman is very much inside.

When Paramatman is there inside us as Atman, He knows everything about us like our attitude, approach and thoughts. That is why, He is called Antaryami. Hence the spiritual mendicant should always contemplate on Atman. By this process, Atman can be attained easily. Those, who realise Paramatman inside, attain Supreme Bliss. By outward rituals, sacrifices, worship and fasting, Paramatman cannot be realised. The sages and realised souls have spoken thus. Heart must be cleansed first. By divine thoughts, it becomes possible. Hence along with physical cleanliness, heart must be purified. Once heart becomes divinised, Paramatman would be reflected on it. All impurities must be removed from the mind. If impurities and ill feelings are there in the mind, those would be reflected in our conduct also. If we entertain divine thoughts in our heart, we can experience God. God is reflected only on a pure and clean heart and not otherwise.

༺✷༻

[46]In the scriptures it is mentioned that through yoga, God can be realised. Yoga means union, i.e. union with God. We resort to various kinds of worship, chant mantra, make different offerings etc. as a part of our sadhana. We undertake different kinds of tapas. Making contact or creating relationship with God is yoga. Even if there are various ways, some give faster results, and some are time taking. Depending upon our situations and circumstances we must adopt the most suitable way for us. It is wrong to believe that only a specific path would lead us to the destination. It is necessary for us to adopt a suitable practice to maintain relationship with God. Every moment we should try to learn about something or other. The more we learn about God, the more we come nearer to Him. Without knowing about God how can we attain Him? Who is God? No blind approach would help us. We must know about Him, whom we are trying to attain. Divya Darshan says, "Try to know Truth". Truth is God. Knowing the Truth is knowledge. Without knowing Him and His manifestations, if

---

46 Oriya Divya Dhara Vol 8 Page 21

we try to attain God, our efforts may not bear the desired fruits. Divya Darshan teaches how to keep contact with God even if one has not fully realised God.

To get means knowing something perfectly well. The scientists similarly realise the truths of matters. Knowing the truth means attaining the same. If we do not know about God, we cannot attain Him. Even if you get something you cannot know what it is. In that case it is like not getting the same. According to Divya Darshan the more we know, the more we get. Getting knowledge means getting Him. Getting Him means getting knowledge. In the process of knowing, when you know complete Truth perfectly well, it amounts to realising God. For knowing Him, one need not quit one's home. There is no need for offering anything to God. He, who always has the inquisitiveness to know God, does spiritual practice for 24 hours. With this aim, whatever work we do becomes spiritual practice. We are learning something or other every day. That means we are going nearer to God every day. Only problem is that we are not able to get Him fully. He, who believes, gets Him. He, who knows and believes, gets more. Blind belief may not yield anything.

We can take the example of a machine. He, who possesses intense and continuous inquisitiveness to know about the machine, is really learning about each part of the machine one after another which means, he is knowing about the machine more and more. When he will know the whole of it which includes all parts, it means, he knows the whole machine now. He has realised Brahman.

೨೦✶೨೦

[47] *["There is name in bhava and bhava in name. Therefore, reflect upon the name and reach bhava state to ultimately realise the beauty and excellence of the nectarine awareness within."]*

(Amritbindu-117)]

---

47 Oriya Divya Dhara Vol 19 Page 39

When we remember our mother, we are so elated. Mother is a word with so much of thoughts that when we simply remember her, we have a blissful feeling. Her sacrifices and services, her compassion and love etc. throughout our life are all remembered at once.

We call Lord Shiva as Ishwar. Shiva means auspicious and beneficial. He gives us peace and bliss. Scriptures ascribe many names and epithets to Lord Shiva. He is also described as the Supreme. We have seen His picture in which the river Ganges flows from His head. There is a snake around His neck. He is robed with a tiger skin. He holds a Trishul (trident) and a Damru (two-headed drum). The moment we think of lord Shiva, the above picture flashes through our mind spontaneously as *bhava*. While taking the name of Shiva, spontaneously the related thoughts come to our mind. But only mechanical chanting of a name without *bhava* may be futile. One must conduct himself like Lord Rama instead of only chanting Lord Rama's name.

He, who remains in a happy mood, becomes free from diseases. He, who has faith on God, will remain healthy and happy. We are not able to chant God's name with joy. He, who chants His name with love and devotion, gets wonderful results; he attains Him ultimately. But only mechanical chanting without *bhava* will not yield desired result.

God is a divine being. Divinity is there everywhere in everybody irrespective of the names. *Bhava* is more important than chanting of names. Since we do not possess adequate knowledge about God, we are not having divine feeling. Simply by taking a dip in the river Ganges without any feeling of divinity will not benefit much. *Bhava* is nectar like. He, who possesses *bhava*, really drinks the nectar. He, who knows the greatness and indispensability of God, will spontaneously have tears rolling down from his eyes while he thinks of God or chants His name. You should always possess divine thoughts. In other words, divine thoughts should overwhelm you. Such persons will attain God. All dirt will be cleaned when divine thoughts overwhelm you. Once you clean your heart God will appear.

Possessing ill feelings, people wish to attain divinity. How is it possible? Liberation means freedom from sufferings and attainment of peace and bliss. The elixir of *bhava* is nectar. That gives peace and bliss. All sufferings vanish. Since the sages are in divine state, divine qualities like piety, renunciation, service and righteousness are seen in them. At the time of death only the good thoughts will accompany and not the physical wealth that you have amassed.

Divya Darshan says, "Why should you suffer throughout in several births? Why should you not take to the righteous path and possess divine qualities which are God-gifted and present in all of you? It is imperative therefore to arouse the latent divine qualities in you by taking to spiritual path and acquiring true knowledge. It is stated that man has taken 84 lakhs of birth. After this life, how many more births he will take to be liberated is not mentioned in any scripture. The only remedy is in entertaining divine thoughts and chanting or remembering God's name. Try to acquire true knowledge by surrendering to Guru. In this birth, you can attain liberation.

[48]**Mukti:** Getting rid of all sufferings is Mukti. Getting rid of fear and doubts is Mukti. But real Mukti is realisation of the Self. If a person remains in dualism, he would be beset with doubts and fear. When someone admits of different names and qualities, that means, he is in dualism. If one goes on accepting dualism, suffering is bound to come. Mind shall get confounded and would encounter different kinds of unfounded obstacles. Man must acquire true knowledge which reveals, "Everything is but manifestation of Brahman." This is monism which means only Brahman is the eternal existence. All other things such as forms and qualities are evanescent. Therefore, Mukti is attained when one gets released from dualism. Man is born in dualism. When man confronts with multiplicities, all sorts of problems, doubts and despair come to afflict him.

Brahman is one. He is the creator of everything. In fact, He manifests as the movable and the immovable, the sentient and the insentient. God has multifaceted powers by which He has become man, animal, bird etc. Even the recognition of different powers is dualism. Only the unitary and

---

48 Oriya Divya Dhara Vol 8 Page 23

Supreme Brahman who manifests as everything is the final and flawless answer to all questions. This is Advaita Philosophy.

಄⋆಄

[49]A yogi normally remains away from home to live in forests in search of a congenial environment to do spiritual practice. They also wear different types of robes. Some move from one pilgrimage to the other to do spiritual practices. But this type of approach to spiritual practices may not be fruitful. By merely changing robes, spiritual practice is not complete. Some people wear white robes, some wear black and some others wear saffron. Some take to varied make-ups to appear as sadhus so that they could earn their livelihood. One thing is clear that those, who have uncontrolled senses and bundles of desires, cannot attain God. Those, who seek God with all humility and sincerity, can be successful. To attain God strong will power is essential. Results shall accrue according to our *bhava*. Since most of the people prefer to live in luxury and different material enjoyments, they remain away from God. A question can be raised as to why people do not make any effort to know or attain God. True, most of the people possess some knowledge about the material world. But they do not take any interest to know about God and His role functions. Since man is more inclined towards the material world and the material benefits, he carries many desires for the fulfilment of which he at times visits temples and takes recourse to some religious practices. A distressed person also prays to God out of helplessness and sees God in some form of his imagination. But the form of his imagination is not the real god. Seeing any imaginary form is not true god-realisation. Occasionally remembering God during the period of perils would not be of much use. God would listen to him, who always remembers Him. Many people go on asking for something or other from God. He, who knows God completely, cannot ask anything of Him. After acquiring knowledge, he can understand that God has sent all of us to this world after making all necessary arrangements. But due to lack of knowledge we are not able to make use of the gifts of God. If anything is to be asked for, that is knowledge only. By knowledge not only man can know more

---

49 Oriya Divya Dhara Vol 9 Page 5

and more about God and His Creation, he can also make use of all His gifts to live in peace and happiness and get rid of all sufferings. Ultimately, he can attain freedom.

God, to conduct His lila, has assumed the form of a thief, police and also the judge. He is one but manifests as all forms and qualities. We all are sitting on His lap. There is no question of not getting Him. But for a person who occasionally remembers Him during period of perils, God is far away from him. In order to attain Him, it is essential to evince interest to know Him more and more. A lot of things are to be known about Him. With an inquisitive mind one can go nearer to Him. Lastly the seeker would cry for attaining Him. He, who is eager to know Him, can get Him. Those, who are pleasure seekers and those who go to temples etc. only for performing some rituals for fulfilment of some desires, would not get Him. Those, who are under the control of three qualities such as *sattva, rajas* and *tamas*, would suffer. For attainment of freedom, one must transcend the three qualities. Such persons are not inclined towards the world of matters. They are not interested in food, clothing or in any kind of luxuries. They remain content with whatever they have. They do not worry for anything nor do they possess any ambition.

We come across pleasure and pain during God's lila. 'Kala' (time or God of death) is taking us forward to death. Everyone is controlled by Kala. No one can escape the clutch of Kala. Family priorities, office priorities and the dictates of our sense organs have kept us chained. We have never been independent. We are chained by ourselves. If we are afraid of somebody, that means we are chained. No one can bind him, who has attained liberation.

Man's biggest fear is death, but the liberated souls are not afraid of death. Those, who have transcended three qualities such as *sattva, rajas* and *tamas*, have conquered Time or Kala. They realise that everything is controlled and guided by Self. When you are being guided by mind that means you are bound by mind. He, who realises that he is different from the mind, means he is free from the mind. Attainment of full independence is not an ordinary matter. Man has remained chained since his previous births.

With every birth he gets more and more chained. When I (Sadguru Sri Sri Arjun) am speaking during satsang, you are listening, but you do not remember God afterwards. A lot of dirt is accumulated in you from your previous births. Those must be cleaned first. This is not easy. It may not be removed in a single birth. To attain purity, a single birth may not be adequate. You may have to take more births. When you would get full independence, at that time you would realise, "I am everything." If someone realises that he is That, then where is the fear? Why fear? I am all gods. I am Yama. Hence there is no question of fear for any god. The sages have attained that level. They have made so much spiritual practices in their earlier births and also in this birth that they have cut off all bondages and attained the highest level which means complete liberation. A free soul can only free others.

What Guru teaches you? Guru teaches you how to cut off your bondages. You have not started the process of lessening or cutting off the bondages. Had you started the process, by this time you would have reduced the bondages to a great extent. You are being prepared for that. When you have still weakness towards fish and meat, how can you say that you have cut off your bondages? When you still possess greed, how have you cut off your bondages? Those, who have no anger, desire, greed, infatuation, pride and jealousy and thus controlled their mind, are the real winners. They are the conqueror of time; they are Paramahansa. On knowing the Self, you are independent. Not knowing the True Self means you are still chained and subjugated. Knowing the Self means you are your own boss. You are the real master. You are the master of everything. When you consider some other as bigger than you or more than you, that means, you do not know yourself fully. Knowing the True Self is liberation. If you are under the clutches of wordly matters, then how can you be free? Now you imagine what the liberated souls have achieved. The realised souls after realising this Supreme Truth try to explain it before others for the benefit of mankind.

Those, who follow Guru's instructions, are living in proximity with God. They will be blessed by Guru. They can conquer Time. 'Kala' cannot reach them. In other words, there is no death for them. More powers are activated in them. If you would not get powers from God, then by which power you would be able to conquer your senses and Time? Therefore, in order to get rid of bondages and attain liberation you must believe in Guru and follow His sayings. Those, who are making efforts to realise truth, must purify themselves because God resides in a pure heart only. Therefore, keep your mind focussed on Guru and not on samsar. By Getting so much involved in samsaric affairs, we carry lot of burdens; enter into litigations, tensions and wrangling on various matters. Therefore, we suffer. Attachment is bondage. To acquire something in wrong ways is bondage. But the sages are free from all these. Hence, they are liberated souls. But the common people, not knowing the above truth try to earn happiness by cheating others or inflicting pain on others.

In this context, Divya Darshan observes that we all want to live in peace and happiness. But, we do not know what wellness is. Therefore, we suffer. Since you all desire wellness, you must know first what good is and how wellness can be achieved. While mixing with different types of people you must know that you are likely to be influenced by the other man and some of his qualities may get transmitted to you. If you mingle with gamblers, you may get addicted to gambling. If you mingle with wise men you will acquire wisdom. When you extend some services to Guru you are mingling with Him. Service to Guru includes taking care of Guru's physical wellness, carrying out His instructions and making efforts for the fulfilment of His mission. Massaging Guru's feet or giving some good eatables to Guru are not real service to Guru. Sincere obedience to His instructions is real service to Guru.

Observance of God's laws is also Bhagavat-seva. The opposite term of service is dereliction or disservice. Guru is a free soul. Service to Him can be physical, mental and verbal. By serving Him, you mingle with Him as a result of which His powers shall be transmitted to you. A disciple must think in Guru's way. Guru Nanak also laid emphasis on Guru-seva. It is told earlier that only a free soul can make others free. All the sages had served their Guru and therefore they had reached the highest state. Those, who feel ashamed to pay respect to Guru, cannot do any service to Guru. Ramakrishna Paramahansa told, He, who cries for God, would reach God.

We may take the example of mother and child. When the baby cries, mother rushes to the baby. When the mother cries, the children also cry. What a wonderful relationship!

Everyone must try to understand the greatness and importance of serving others. Through service, the servant rises to the position of God. Where there is master, there is servant. Divya Darshan therefore places service as the basis of all other divine virtues.

ဢ★ဢ

[50]In the scriptures it is written that God can be attained by Yoga. Yoga means relationship with God. Yoga is established with God in several ways i.e. by worshipping, chanting his names, remembering Him, discussing about Him, offering Him prasad (a sweet dish or any vegetarian eatable which is distributed to people after worshipping God as a blessing of God) and contemplating on Him. To create relationship with God, we make some efforts. This is called sadhana. For this we resort to various kinds of practices like different physical postures, breathing techniques, meditation etc.

There are various spiritual practices. Some practices give slow results and some practices give quick results. Keeping in view the situation and circumstances surrounding us, we should adopt the most appropriate practice. Spiritual practice is not a rigid single-track system. Our aim is to create relationship with God. Keeping in view our situation and circumstances we have to find some way to create relationship with God. Every moment, if we try to know the mystery behind each and everything, by that also we create relationship with God. Trying to know more and more about God means, we are in the process of attaining God. We must know who God is. Without knowing this how can one blindly try to attain God?

Divya Darshan says, "Try to know about truth which is present everywhere. Truth is God. God is the root of all truths of the Creation".

---

50   Oriya Divya Dhara Vol 19 Page 11

We must know who is called God. Where is He? Without knowing Him if we search Him here and there, it amounts to searching for diamond while sitting on the top of the diamond hill. We must know everything thoroughly. Knowing about each truth means we are gradually enhancing our knowledge about God. Even though we do not know fully about Him, whatever we know amounts to understanding God to that extent.

If we set out to meet someone without knowing his whereabouts or without having any information about him, where shall we go and how shall we find him? The scientists do not get anything new. But they know the titbits or truth of the matter. They examine atoms and molecules to gain detailed knowledge on that. The more we know about things, the more we get those things and understand their value. Accordingly, we utilize or get benefit from out of that knowledge. Knowing the whole truth means knowing God. Divya Darshan says, "Try to know Him who is named as God."

Hence for knowing anything, it is not necessary to leave your homes or families. It is also not necessary to do fasting. If you have sincere attitude to learn, that means, you are doing spiritual practice all the time i.e. for 24 hours. With this motive, if you do any work, that becomes your sadhana. If we know, we get. We know God in parts, not the whole. When we will know Him fully, we shall attain Him fully.

If you believe in God and make sincere efforts to know about Him, you will get more and more. Blindly doing anything may not yield the desired result. Hence knowingly doing any spiritual practice will bring positive results. Inquisitiveness is an essential quality by which an aspirant can move faster towards God-realisation.

⚬⚬✦⚬⚬

[51] [*"Man becomes lovable by casting off ego; free from grief, by giving up anger; affluent by relinquishing the desires and happy, by giving up greed."*

(Amritbindu-121)]

---

51 Oriya Divya Dhara Vol 13 Page 54

Ego is our biggest enemy. It does not allow us to live in peace. An egoistic person cannot endear himself to others. Our ego causes intolerance and prompts us to retaliate, be cruel and deceptive to others. The thoughts we entertain against others shall also get reflected on the minds of others and therefore, others will also have similar feelings towards us and consequently we shall be affected.

We all wish to have peace and happiness. But if we do not endear ourselves to others, how shall we get peace and happiness? We live in a society. If others do not love us, how shall we be happy? If our ego prohibits us to mingle with others, how can we enjoy social life? During our adversities, who will come forward to support or extend helping hands? If we cooperate with others and if we sympathize with others during their adverse situations, then only we can expect similar behaviour from others. Since we do not maintain good relationship with others but distance ourselves from them, others also reciprocate accordingly. An egoistic person is shunned by others. He burns himself internally. In fine, unless one loves others, one cannot be happy. Our ego stands as a barrier and keeps us confined. We should therefore introspect and analyse the same to thin it out.

Anger is another enemy that agitates our mind. Anger reduces the longevity of a person. Anger causes lot of damages to us. If somebody gets angry with us, we too get angry with him. But the wise men do not react to the anger of others. Anger is a killer of peace. Absence of peace amounts to sufferings. According to the Reflection Theory of Divya Darshan, our anger comes back to us as sufferings. In other words, to get angry is to welcome sufferings. Free from anger, the wise men remain unperturbed. But the ignorant men get agitated by anger. They are of tamasic category. Sattvic persons are normally cool and well composed. Sometimes they appear to be angry but for the good of others. By acting angry, they try to influence others to do or not do a certain thing. The tamasic people suffer more and frequently. An angry man not only suffers, but he transmits sufferings to others also. For example, out of anger, if we beat someone, we suffer and at the same time the other man also suffers. Not only that, we also incur sins for doing so.

Ignorant man commits such mistakes one after another. On the top of our Darshan emblem, it is written, "Ignorance is great sin". A wise man on the other hand analyses the cause of anger and tries to iron the same out. He does not react to the angry behaviour of others meted out to him. He remains happy always. He knows well that the angry behaviour is unwanted and is born of ignorance. It is evident that knowledge brings peace. There is no other way.

Multiple desires dog us always. After one desire is fulfilled, another desire crops up and goes on haunting our mind. People think how they can live without desires. It is undesirable that we desire multifarious things for our luxury and comfort being unmindful of the priorities of life and its goal. But the basic desire to live, acquire knowledge to get bliss and liberation or attain God are necessary and should not be forsaken. These desires are natural and essential parts of life without which the life's goal cannot be achieved. Merely for the sake of enjoyment of life (without understanding the meaning and goal of life), people go astray carrying a bundle of desires and make lifelong efforts for fulfilment of the same. Life, bereft of the real purpose, is a colossal waste. Their minds get preoccupied with cravings for something or other and their vision gets focused on the objects of their craze. For them, where is time for thinking about God or God-realisation! Where is time to ponder over causes of suffering and remedies thereof! Where is time to think of righteousness, justice, truth and duties!

It must be remembered that the sense-objects cannot keep us happy. They are all evanescent. If we can replace our material desires with desire for divinity or desire for self-realisation, all sufferings will vanish in this birth. If we can dedicate our whole life for acquisition of true knowledge and attainment of God, we can get real peace and happiness, bliss and freedom in this life itself.

Life's goal is clearly spelt out in the Vedas and Upanishads. Therefore, our quest should be to realise Brahman, by knowing whom everything becomes known and nothing more remains to be known; by attaining which nothing more remains to be attained. Hence, by giving up all desires that divert our attention from our goal, and making concerted efforts for God-realisation, we can attain the Supreme Brahman who is Bliss-Absolute.

Lord Buddhadev says, "Craving is the cause of suffering." We become happy when we get some money. There are sages who do not have clothings or money but still they are happier than us. It means that, not this money but there is some other wealth that brings happiness, peace and bliss. That is real wealth. For enjoyment of life we try hard to earn money but ultimately, we get sufferings. What is that invaluable and invisible wealth that can give us eternal bliss? That is the real wealth. That wealth is unlimited and inexhaustible. He, who gives up other desires, becomes a fit recipient of this unlimited wealth.

Greed is another big enemy that takes away our sleep. A host of thoughts swarm through the mind of a greedy person. His mind gets preoccupied with the targeted objects. He will be planning and contemplating all twenty-four hours. Where is the time for him to think of God or God-realisation? Where is peace and happiness for him who is perturbed by worries and anxieties? Out of greed, we run after material objects which last for a short period. Those things may be broken or may be stolen. We should have greed for something which is permanent, cannot be stolen or cannot wear out. Due to our greed, we suffer every moment. A worried man is never happy. An anxious person is never at ease or rest. By our greed we expect good things and happiness but end up with sufferings. Where there is real and permanent wealth, there is true happiness. There is bliss and freedom. We must give up greed for the mundane objects which are short-lived. For getting peace and bliss, we are to acquire right knowledge by which we should know about divine virtues and also about God. We should know the truths one after another and ultimately attain the Supreme Truth, who is Bliss-Absolute. Divya Darshan lays emphasis on renunciation, opposed to greed, by which true happiness can be earned. By renunciation, we can realise Him, by knowing whom nothing remains to be known, by attaining which nothing remains to be attained.

[52]A mere wishful thinking to attain God is not enough. One cannot attain God in that manner. One must honestly and humbly make spiritual practices with strong will in order to attain Him. An egoistic person cannot reach God. Hence egolessness is the key to reach God. After complete realisation, the sages make use of sattvic ahamkara to articulate their experience. They make use of sattvic ahamkara in order to benefit others. Sattvic ahamkara is not for asserting their position or greatness.

Mind suffers from many maladies. Those bring sufferings of various kinds. If the children do not obey us we get shocked and suffer. We go on pilgrimages at times to show others that we are dharmic. By visiting various pilgrimages if we are not able to cast off our ego then what is the use of such pilgrimages? If our inner dirt is not cleaned, then what is the use of pilgrimages? He, who is sincere in acquiring true knowledge and divine virtues even sitting at home and can cleanse his mind, he is really dharmic and is much better than someone, who is regularly taking holy bath. Without thought of God there is no peace and happiness in the world. Goodness is God. He, who remembers or chants God's name, becomes eligible to attain peace and happiness. On the other hand, he, who is infested with bad qualities, would forget God and shall suffer. Because of host of wrong doings due to bad tendencies he would always be afraid of somebody or other. On the other hand, the sages always remember God. Tears come out of their eyes when they chant God's name or contemplate on His greatness. They know that God is Peace-Absolute, Bliss-Absolute and all powerful. By Him everything in this universe has been created. Everything owes its origin to God. Everything exists because God exists. That is why the sages take God's name out of great joy. He, who follows God's laws sincerely, is a real devotee. A sincere devotee honours the laws of nature and conducts himself accordingly. He does not discriminate between high and low, touchable and untouchable,

He is weak whose mind is weak. Weak mind is volatile or unstable. Those, who have self-restraint (brahmacharya), are more intelligent and powerful. Those, who are goaded by their unbridled senses, are weak and remain at

---

52 Oriya Divya Dhara Vol 9 Page 12

the mind level. Many people do not know even what to eat and how much to eat. Very often they take their food in wrong combination. For example, fish or meat should not be taken together with milk or ghee. Fish and meat should not be taken at the same time. Many people suffer due to their faulty food habits.

He, who takes resort to goodness, can attain God. Wherever there are wrong doings, sufferings are bound to visit the wrongdoers. Those, who follow righteousness and justice, are real followers of God. Some have mastered occult sciences by which they attract large following. Some make use of tantra to show off their powers to impress people. But by doing so they cannot attain self-realisation. Common people approach such masters to acquire this type of knowledge, but they get frustrated later on. Even a short life with self-realisation is much better than any other achievements and a long life. If we do not pursue life's goal, what is the use of a long life? Those, who are followers of truth, are protected by the divine power. The wise men are humble, sincere and sweet. He is wise who can realise Truth. Reflecting and contemplating on God amount to taking shelter of God. God is all-pervasive. So is Truth that pervades the whole Creation.

By rendering services to Guru, mind gets purified. Most of you have no idea about God. How would you serve God? How would you reap the desired fruits? God has no specific form. In different religions, ideas about God are different. Hence people get confused. What is correct? Those, who resort to idol worship, would be groping in doubts. First, we should know our religion well and refrain from criticizing others.

You are disciples. Guru possesses more knowledge than you. If Guru is the Sun, a disciple is just a lamp. Guru is the source of infinite knowledge. It is not possible for the disciple to guess the level of His knowledge and wisdom. He, who serves Guru with all sincerity, becomes pure and divine. His heart shall be filled with devotion. Guru does good things always. He does everything good and beneficial for the entire Creation. If the disciple can observe this, his heart will get changed. The sages had realised the importance and greatness of Guru. Hence, they had prayed, "Gurur Brahmaa Gurur Vishnu Gurureva Maheswara; Gurur sakshat

Parambrahman tasmai Shri Gurave namah." The disciple who serves his Guru considering Guru as Brahman incarnate, all his ignorance and bad tendencies get destroyed soon. It is to be understood that God Himself has descended in the form of Guru to teach right knowledge. Guru's position is much higher than that of the parents. Hence the sages attach so much importance to serving Guru with sincerity and devotion. He, who knows this truth, gets his chitta cleaned quickly. On a clean chitta, God realisation is imminent. By His grace alone a disciple attains Truth. Satya (Truth) is explained by Divya Darshan in four categories; Temporal Truth, Partial Truth, Truth and Supreme Truth. This visible universe is a temporal truth. Ultimately who remains eternally is the Supreme Truth. Upanishad says that without His grace, He cannot be realised. A common man imagines God in innumerable fancies and forms. Vedas and Vedanta speak of God as one and second-less. He is the only Reality in this Creation. According to Kenopanishad, "The form you see is not God. But the power that enables you to see is God." Had you not possessed seeing power, how would you have seen? What our mouth utters as God, is not God. By whom the mouth is enabled to utter words is God. God is not a subject of experience by our senses. He, who has enabled the senses and bestowed upon them different powers, is God. The ignorant man without any knowledge about God prepares imaginary idols and believes that the idol is God. He is unable to know Him, who has created the man. He also does not believe in the existence of any other God.

When we are in peril, we remember God and pray for rescue. This is not true surrender. Realising the greatness of God and thereafter surrendering to God, is true surrender. A sense of love would sprout in his heart. Without His grace none can go to Him. Guru Nanak says that for them who are initiated, Hari naam gets vibrated in their hearts. By Taking initiation and chanting Ishta Mantra, all powers shall be manifested in the devotee. It is Guru who discloses the identity of God. The children do not want to go to school of their own. The parents try to send them to school. After some days or months, they get introduced to studies and evince interest to go to school. Thereafter the child takes care of his home-works etc. By God's grace the disciple gets attracted towards God and thereafter he crosses all hurdles to attain God. Without parents' blessings and Guru's blessings, one cannot get God's blessings. Therefore, parents' goodwill being so important, one must try to earn the same. Following Guru's instructions, one must chant God's name and remember Him always. He, who is able to chant God's name always, is really fortunate. The sinners cannot return to their heavenly abode or realise True Self. True Self cannot be realised without Guru Mantra. We are on the mid-way. We have come from somewhere. We must go back there from where we have come. Guru imparts that knowledge.

Guru Mantra contains lot of powers and meanings. The Ishta Mantra that Guru imparts us, emboldens and empowers us. There is Mahabhava in the Ishta Mantra. Guru explains that. If we do not have power to move along, Guru teaches the technique for a faster movement. Gurushakti inspires and protects the disciple from all sides. By this Ishta Mantra, we can realise True Self. Guru teaches all ins and outs for self-realisation. Therefore, the disciple must have complete faith, devotion and love towards Guru.

એઝ✲એઝ

[53]Many people do not know what exactly pilgrimage is. Generally, people think that a pilgrimage is where Gods or goddesses reside. But the place, where subject of Truth or God is discussed, is called a real pilgrimage. Chitta becomes purified if one visits a pilgrimage. If one goes to Guru and spends some time with Him, his chitta gets purified. By hearing about or chanting God's name, we are in contact with the Truth who is God. Hence God's name is so important. The truth, that is there inside as divine knowledge and divine thoughts is the real pilgrimage. Only some place however famous it may be, is not a real pilgrimage. From scriptural texts we get knowledge. But he, who has mastered all knowledge of scriptures, is the store house of knowledge. If we go to Him and be in contact with Him, we shall get direct knowledge. We get knowledge through service to Guru. In the process, the disciple becomes Guru. Therefore, Guru is the real pilgrimage. Truth is God. It is to be understood

---

53 Oriya Divya Dhara Vol 9 Page 18

that he, who regularly contemplates on Truth, really welcomes God. He, who attains Truth, attains God, because Truth is God. By wandering from one pilgrimage to another one may not get that much knowledge which one gets by reading scriptural texts. If one remains with Guru, one becomes purified and simple. He will automatically become a vegetarian and shall start taking proper food. Guru imparts knowledge on Truth. The disciple at that time takes a dip in the holy pilgrimage of Truth. He acquires knowledge on Brahman and becomes Guru. Guru's knowledge can be compared with an ocean. Guru Nanak was begging for Hari's name. Hari Naam is the Truth or Reality. The sages hanker after true knowledge. This knowledge gives us happiness, peace and bliss. But people are asking for money, buildings and children and even after getting all these, they remain unhappy. Happiness and peace may not come from out of external possessions. The ignorant men do not crave for freedom. They crave for good houses and children. Children would not bring us freedom. Guru Nanak says that, the samsar is a malady and for this Hari Naam is the only remedy.

If someone asks for money from God, is there any certainty that he would enjoy the money? He may die any day. Children may not be able to take care of their parents at old age. Material properties bring us sufferings here and hereafter. It must be remembered that unless one acquires true knowledge, impurities in him cannot be cleansed. Guru's words are pure light. Truth is light. Hence the disciple gets lighted by taking a holy dip in the pilgrimage of truth and knowledge. He always beams with peace and happiness. How can we say that we are knowledgeable or wise when we wear a gloomy look?

What is real wealth? Whatever helps us maintain the physical body and live peacefully is called wealth. Wealth in material form supports our survival. Wealth does not mean only food grains, money, gold and diamond. Good qualities or virtues are also wealth. It is subtle wealth or divine possessions. Normally the subtle wealth is called Vishnu whereas the wealth in material form is called Laxmi. Wherever there is Vishnu, Laxmi is bound to be there. All activities and processes in this Creation are based on truth. Truth and divine qualities are subtle properties. Instead of serving our master if we start cheating our master, it will not only cause harm to the master but eventually it will harm us. Spiritual knowledge is therefore essential to bring in happiness, peace and bliss. Wealth in material form can be stolen. For stealing the material wealth, lot of crimes like forgery, cheating, burglary of heinous nature are committed. Material wealth cannot give peace and happiness. But so far as divine virtues are concerned, truth breeds truth, love begets love and service begets service. In the process, there shall be multiplication of this subtle wealth. This subtle wealth must be acquired in order to attain God. The opposite of divine qualities are demoniac qualities. If we encourage dowry system, we will also suffer at the time of our daughter's marriage. If a master resorts to cheating or falsehood, his servant would also cheat him. Therefore, subtle wealth is especially important for a peaceful living. It would not only bring us happiness, peace and bliss, but also lead to our total freedom. Those, who do not obey their parents, are possessed by demoniac qualities and are not aware of Dharma. They are dipped in greed or delusion. Many people wish for increase in wealth and progeny. These are all cause of sufferings. The sages knew the causes of sufferings and that is why they were living in peace and bliss. A greedy, whimsical or self-centred person cannot possess the subtle wealth. The sages possess divine qualities which are subtle wealth. They help others by their subtle wealth. If I scold others I shall be scolded. If I cheat others, I shall be cheated. Most of the worldly transactions are based on cheating or maximising easy benefits.

Guru Nanak says, when you are spreading Hari's name, others are benefitted from it. Peace prevails there where God's name is chanted or contemplated on. The subtle wealth would not be destroyed by fire, water or air. Subtle wealth remains unaffected. We should acquire that wealth which shall permanently remain with us. That would give us peace and bliss not only in this birth but hereafter also. Divya Darshan never discourages anybody from going to the temples but whenever you are visiting temples you should consciously try to earn punya. When you make some sacrifice you get inner peace. If today you speak one truth, tomorrow you will speak two truths. Good qualities shall multiply. Subtle wealth shall multiply. But we are apathetic towards this subtle wealth. We are obsessed with material wealth that has a short life. We should know what real wealth is. By possessing divine qualities bliss and freedom is attained. Without possessing these qualities, how is it possible to attain bliss and freedom? Hence, Divya Darshan lays emphasis on acquiring knowledge and divine virtues. Many spiritual practitioners make lot of spiritual efforts and do lot of Yoga but it is observed that only a few possess divine virtues. If divine virtues do not blossom inside, all their efforts are in vain. We ourselves do not acquire divine virtues and do not tell others in support of divine virtues. The range of Divine virtues is so vast that its importance cannot be expressed in words. Those are available with Sadguru. In the books or scriptures little about it has been mentioned. But everything is known to Sadguru. He possesses all divine qualities. Man attains peace and bliss by means of knowledge. Ultimately, he can attain that Supreme Wealth i.e. God.

Without knowing this we resort to falsehood. Impure things are not accepted there. When man himself does not like bad or adulterated food, how God would accept or like those? Those, who resort to truth and righteousness, would attain heaven by their virtues. He, who possesses truth and righteousness, can attain Satya Lok. God is good. By goodness He can be attained. By means of bad qualities, He cannot be attained. We must be good so as to attain God. Truth is everywhere, with everyone. Knowing truth one after another means going nearer to truth. There are laws. When the applicable law is observed truth shall emerge. Hence everyone should aim at this subtle wealth which will bring in peace, bliss and freedom.

✿✦✿

[54]By serving others, real happiness is experienced. By chanting Lord's name also real happiness would come. The ignorant man is not able to get bliss because he does not know the importance of serving others and therefore

---

54 Oriya Divya Dhara Vol 9 Page 35

he is not interested to serve others. By serving others, one meets with Truth. The demoniac qualities slowly go away. He is purified. Greed and delusion go away. Through service one knows truths and thus one after another he reaches the inner truth. All crookedness and deceptiveness vanish. A sense of love shall overwhelm him. Therefore, sages laid so much emphasis on service. Virtues boost self-development.

Where there remains ignorance, there remains selfishness and greed. He, who is self-centred, cannot serve others. Even if we possess money, we are reluctant to help others at the time of need. Even if we possess enough food, we do not evince interest in feeding others. While you are doing spiritual efforts, you should realise the importance of service. You must serve others. You should consider this as instruction from Guru. In the scriptures also the sages have laid so much emphasis on service. By your wealth, by your knowledge and by your physical strength you can serve others. Man possesses everything but despite that he is unwilling to serve others. All arrangements have already been made for you to attain God. If man changes his approach to life he can serve others by which he can make himself pure.

Guru Nanak said, "Oh God! because you have given me the opportunity to serve, I could become pure."

By possessing the attitude to serve others, man can know that God has become the tree, only to serve us. By application of knowledge we know that we can serve the tree by applying proper fertilizer and water. By having inquisitiveness, we can acquire knowledge. By desire, anger, jealousy etc., knowledge gets veiled. Guru Nanak says that God in form of Guru is my saviour. Gurutattva is such a great wisdom that the ignorant men hardly understand the same. He, who realises Gurutattva, would become Guru. Guru imparts knowledge to the disciple about God. This means, Guru knows who God is. God in order to disclose His identity before others has become Guru. If He would have remained only as God, then who would have identified Him after He became many? What shall you call Him who discloses the identity of God? Because He discloses God's identity, He is called Guru. But He is God Himself. Hence Guru and God are one and the same. If I (Sadguru Sri Sri Arjun) say that I am God, can you understand? Guru knows how to explain things keeping in view the standard of the recipients. Initially a pupil does not know what a teacher is. If the teacher would first say, "I am your teacher", the pupils would not understand. Rather they would look at each other not knowing what the teacher says. When the teacher starts imparting knowledge by citing different examples; thereafter the pupils will understand that he who teaches is a teacher. Like this when Guru teaches about God, thereafter only He is called Guru. To explain to the disciples, he says that God has become Guru to impart right knowledge. Now you think when the disciple would know that Guru is God, how much *bhava*, how much peace and bliss he would get! Other animals like dog, pig etc. cannot know what God is.

Therefore, when a disciple proceeds on spiritual path, he should serve the Guru and follow Guru's footsteps or observe Guru's conduct. It is essential for the disciple to obey Gurus instructions. Knowledge level of the disciple is bound to increase if he keeps contact with Guru. Sharing of knowledge is the greatest service. He, who would be dedicated to serving others, would attain God.

When you consider 'Guru as Brahma, Vishnu and Maheswar', you would get His blessings. I (Sadguru Sri Sri Arjun) have told this at the time of initiation. If you ask questions to Guru, your knowledge level would increase. But if you ask questions to a pillar, shall you get answers by which you can add to your knowledge? One must surrender to Sadguru in order to realise the unitary Existence, i.e. God. Pure Consciousness appears as Guru. Guru Nanak says, "I was a mindless liar. But Guru has set me right. I realised Atman. By Guru, I attained the Supreme Truth and got rid of the worldly bondages." No stone or wood would give us liberation. Guru alone can liberate us. Blindly considering stone and wood as God, would not help. Do you know how God is there in stones and metals? The whole Creation is Brahmamaya (filled with Brahman). This knowledge can be had from Guru only. Therefore, it is Guru who can rid us of worldly bondages. Gurutattva is so great that an ignorant man cannot understand its true import. How to recognize a sage? How to know whether Guru has attained siddhi or not? If you go through the life history of the great souls and sages, you can know a lot. Hence keep on acquiring knowledge more and more, higher and higher.

છ⋆છ

[55]Purity is the most important pre-requisite for attaining freedom. An impure person cannot attain God. We follow different religious practices to attain purity. Self-realisation is the goal. To fulfil our desires, we undertake different kinds of worship and resort to fasting, celebrate various festivals and pray various deities. The importance of our inner purity for God-realisation is not properly understood by many. Therefore, we are not able to attain the required level of purity. We resort to outward bonanza to propitiate God but rarely think of internal purity. For ages man has been worshipping different deities but he is not able to cleanse himself because of which God remains far away. We confine ourselves mostly to outward decorations and eye-catching pandals. While we are supposed to keep our body clean it is equally important to keep our mind clean. Whatever is there in our mind gets reflected in our conduct. Mind becomes pure by telling truth, being kind to others and serving others. We do not pay much importance to cleansing our mind. That is why we are not getting blessings from God. It was the intention of the sages of yesteryears that through different types of religious practices, the mind of the devotees would get purified. It is stated in the puranas how Savitri, by dint of her devotion and wit, could get back the life of her husband Satyavan. Savitri was pure and innocent at heart. She was a dedicated wife. She was also quite knowledgeable. She could outwit even Yamaraj and got back her husband alive. But even if many are worshipping, that kind of purity, devotion and knowledge is rare. In such case, how can death be conquered? He, who has got blessings from Devas, can proceed faster towards self-realisation and attain immortality.

According to Divya Darshan, whatever is good is pure. If anything is not good, it is impure. Good qualities include all divine virtues. He, who possesses good qualities, will become pure. We do not like any injustice.

---

55 Oriya Divya Dhara Vol 9 Page 47

For wrong doings, a person is punished by the court of Law. If we obey our parents and elders and follow the scriptural instructions, we can become pure. But by cleaning our bodies we think that we have purified ourselves. By some outward worship, we think we have become pure. All good thoughts are divine thoughts. He, who keeps contact with good things, gets divine blessings. But we get ourselves more involved with bad things which drag us towards desire, anger, greed, vanity and jealousy etc. By this we become impure and get sufferings. To get rid of sufferings we should seek the help of divine powers. But we take shelter of demoniac qualities. Knowing this, the sages always instructed the mankind to be good and do good. Then only man can be pure and move on the path of self-development ultimately to realise his own self. At times, we behave in cunning manner. To propitiate God, we offer coconut, banana etc. and ask for boons. The personal godheads are quite intelligent, more intelligent than us. They can understand our evil design. They would never bless us unless we are pure and innocent. Those, who are pure, are helped by the divine forces. Our sense organs and organs of action are divine powers. When one gets support from the divine forces, one may do or achieve miraculous things to the surprise of others.

The Mantras that are chanted in the yajna (any ritual done in front of sacred fire with mantras) are meant for various Devas. By chanting such mantras, we establish contact with Devas. By doing so, we get purified. There is no need for burning ghee. There is no need for the ancillary arrangements. If a devotee fixes his thought on God, that is enough. By this practice he can get the benefits of yajna till his death without spending a pie even. To entertain noble thoughts in mind and heart is real yajna. Yajna also means satkarma or noble deeds. One must continue his contact with what is good. The most important thing is that our thoughts should move towards divinity. External worship or any pompous arrangements do not yield such benefits. He, who knows like this, would be inclined towards goodness by resorting to noble actions and noble thoughts. He would concentrate more on good actions, good expressions and good thoughts. Man has been doing karma throughout his life. Righteous karma is yajna. Knowing this, one should try to be good to attain goodness i.e. God.

He can become pure and get blessings from Devas and move on the path of self-development to realise God within. No outward display is necessary; no big celebration is necessary for self-realisation.

Purity of heart and mind is of utmost importance to get rid of sufferings and attain self-realisation. To attain purity, people stop eating non-veg food, even onions and garlics. But they do not mend their ways and turn towards goodness, good actions and good thoughts. How can one get blessings from Devas until and unless he possesses divine qualities? One cannot get rid of sufferings unless one realises True Self. In other words, liberation is impossible without self-knowledge.

೧‌✦೧

[56]A life without a sense of devotion is devoid of peace. Where there is devotion, there is peace. When we obey somebody, when we are guided by his advices and instructions, we are regulated by him. It is our Dharma to abide by the instructions and advices of our elders. Therefore, we get peace. Where there is no devotion or obedience, there is no peace. Therefore, life without devotion is no life.

Bhakti or devotion means paying respect and obeisance, doing things according to His will or trying to fulfil His scheme of things. There is renunciation, restraint, service, truth, discipline and humility in devotion. Therefore, through devotion we are observing Dharma. Through devotion, we make ourselves more disciplined.

According to Advaita Vedanta, Brahman is one and only one. We should have devotion towards the unitary and eternal Brahman who is Supreme. True devotion comes after experiencing the Advaita Tattva. The following nine categories of bhakti are discussed in the scriptures.

"Shravanam, Kirtanam, Vishnoh Smaranam, Paadasevanam, Archanam, Vandanam, Daasyam, Sakhyam, Atmanivedanam"

The last category of bhakti is Atmanivedanam which is self-surrender. Self-surrender is possible when we worship the unitary Supreme Power.

---

56 Oriya Divya Dhara Vol 11 Page 48

Self-surrender is not possible when we worship many gods and goddesses. Many people are there who weep before some god or goddess. Weeping is not the surest sign of true devotion. Therefore, true devotion comes only after experiencing the non-dual Supreme Brahman. True devotion only can get us freedom. All other eight categories of bhakti are based on dualistic convictions. Only the last category of bhakti i.e. self-surrender is non-dual. Only the realisers know true devotion. While explaining the Truth to others, the realisers descend some steps and express about God's greatness etc.; but they always remain established in non-dualism.

The aspirants should consciously observe what the sages or the spiritual masters are doing. How they conduct themselves, how they talk and how they behave are all worth noticing. By doing so, the disciples can learn a lot. In many occasions, I (Sadguru Sri Sri Arjun) say, 'OK, it's all right.' Such spontaneous approval of mine is from a different perspective. I am able to tell so because I have already reached that stage.

જી✦જી

[57]This Creation is a product of renunciation. By and through renunciation, God's play goes on. Brahman renounced His subtle state and appeared as the gross Creation. From the gaseous state, water was formed. Brahman relinquished His unqualified state and assumed different qualities in different forms. Renunciation is going on incessantly in this Creation. It goes on not only in the animal world but also in the plant kingdom. A seed germinates and grows to become a full-fledged tree. Leaving the previous state, things evolve continuously. Everything has been created from Brahman and ultimately gets merged with Brahman. Man, due to his ignorance, is unable to know from where he has come and where shall he go. He simply wants to live on good food and enjoy. Divya Darshan advocates knowledge. This Creation is full of knowledge. The jiva, by means of knowledge passes through renunciation, restraint, spiritual practice, service, truth, love and forgiveness to complete its journey. Renunciation may be construed as the beginning of the journey. We move

---

57 Oriya Divya Dhara Vol 19 Page 42

forward step by step. This quality of renunciation is there since one's birth. But since the ignorant man does not understand the importance of renunciation, he becomes scared when he hears about renunciation. But instinctively he does renounce so many things every day. When he craves for earning wealth, he does not bother to take his food even. Everyone possesses the quality of renunciation. But one will be benefited more if he knows which things are to be relinquished to reach his goal of self-realisation. One must renounce one's present identity to realise the Supreme. Body-identity must be renounced to realise Self.

There are five sheaths in us such as- physical sheath, vital sheath, mental sheath, intellectual sheath, and blissful sheath. The spiritual practitioner must transcend one sheath after another to reach the blissful sheath. Finally, the blissful sheath must also be transcended to realise the unqualified Brahman. Body loses its significance then.

He, who cannot renounce the mundane matters, cannot reach the unqualified Brahman. The sages have renounced so many things. That is why they have become great. Even though they live in the samsar, they stay unattached. "I am not this physical body." He, who has realised this, has renounced to some extent. To leave the present state and move to a higher state is renunciation. One need not renounce any material object to reach Brahman. One should renounce one's greed, attachment, and ego to move higher.

Hence Divya Darshan says, "Oh Mankind! To get rid of sins and sufferings, try to know Brahman by acquiring the related knowledge. By acquiring right knowledge, you will become powerful and will cross all hurdles that may come on your way to the goal."

One must take shelter of the divine power to muster up more power. To acquire divine power, one must acquire divine knowledge.

Man wants to live always in peace and bliss, but he suffers. Divya Darshan says, "There is bliss in renunciation. By acquiring true knowledge, you will be capable of removing all dirt from within and enjoy bliss. The more you acquire divine knowledge, the more you get divine bliss." Where there is no renunciation, there is no liberation. Renunciation is the basis of liberation. Where there is no renunciation, there is bondage. Bondage is the cause of suffering.

Therefore, Divya Darshan calls upon everyone to be awake and enhance the awareness within. Divya Darshan further asks everyone to give up all negative qualities and try to realise the divine Self. The main negative qualities are ego and consequent self-vanity. Man suffers due to these qualities. He gets entrapped and wails. Man's six enemies are- desire, anger, greed, attachment, vanity, and jealousy. Because of all these negative qualities, man becomes more and more reactive and revengeful. He, who can give up all these negative qualities, lives happily and proceeds on the path of self-development.

Divya Darshan never asks its followers to quit anything to be on a spiritual path. It is enough if one develops a sense of non-attachment towards worldly matters.

By acquiring divine knowledge, man can get happiness, peace, and bliss. Ultimately, he will be merged with the Supreme Self. Mundane knowledge and attachment to matters bring us sufferings. Everyone should make determined efforts to acquire self-knowledge.

જ⁕જ

[58]Human body represents architectural excellence of the Supreme Brahman. The goal of human life is attainment of self-knowledge for liberation or God-realisation. That is why man has been bestowed with the instinct of inquisitiveness from his very birth. By this, man will come to know truths one after another to realise the Supreme Truth. For this man must move from lower truths to higher truths. Until he gets blessings from the parents, he cannot get blessings from Devas. Until he gets blessings from Devas, he cannot get blessings from the Supreme Brahman. Once he knows a specific truth, he will gradually know the next higher truth. We must make a beginning. We should start from lower truth and move to next higher truth. We own what we realise. We are benefited to the extent of the knowledge we

---

58 Oriya Divya Dhara Vol 11 Page 51

attain. This is called blessing. In other words, the level of peace and happiness increases with the increase in the level of knowledge. Knowledge means knowing the truth. Truth is accompanied by peace and bliss. Hence everyone should try to enhance his level of knowledge about truth. Ultimately, one will realise the Supreme Truth. Anybody, who has strong will or eagerness to know the Supreme Brahman, will realise Him one day or other.

Those, who possess divine qualities, will be blessed by Devas. To serve, obey, respect and love the parents are all divine qualities which people naturally have. But there are deviations in many cases. Without the blessings of the parents, none can move higher. Hence the sages give so much importance to service. Serve not only your parents but others also. Get the blessings of all. That will take you higher and higher, from lower truths to higher truths. Ultimately you will realise the Supreme Brahman. Also be kind-hearted and care for the plants and animals. Particularly those, who are on the spiritual path, must be service-minded. Then only God's grace will come. For example, you may serve some patients who require physical help like dressing their wounds, cleaning their beds, washing their clothes and utensils etc. Due to some reason or other, if you are not able to do this type of physical service, you may pray for his good health. Planning and creating congenial conditions for others' comforts also come under service. If you cannot do anything directly to serve others, you may render some financial assistance also. You may also get things done by requesting others for necessary assistance. Always pray for the wellness of others. Serving others including members of family, neighbours, kith and kin should be the way of life. By doing that you will get love and goodwill from all sides. Even if there may not be any material benefits by doing service to others, the goodwill and love that you receive, although not tangible, is more valuable than anything else. By that, you will get blessings from the divine powers and will attain the Supreme Truth. Seva or service is the basis of all other divine qualities which are always operational in the kingdom of nature. You may refer to the Darshan photo (the emblem of Divya Darshan) in which service is there in green colour as the base.

By service, we get blessings. Through service we are meeting with truths. We become intimate with the persons we serve. We come to know about the physical, mental, financial and domestic matters of the persons we serve. In other words, by service, we come nearer to truths. Through service we meet a person. We know about his requirements and his problems. We learn about the medical procedures and administration of medicines he is going through. When we come closer to a patient, we know the ancillary truths. We also come to know what is there in his mind; his feelings etc. The sages say that by serving one and all, self-realisation is possible.

A question arises here. That is, when we are not able to see God, how to come in His contact and how to serve Him? We ask such questions due to want of adequate knowledge about God. Man asks such questions with the notion that God has some gross form like humans. Whatever worships we make, are also service. Whatever arrangements we make to worship God come under service.

By not evincing interest to know about God, we are distancing ourselves from truth and are guided by our imaginations under the pretext of devotion. Divya Darshan says, "You should try to know about Him whom you are worshipping." Unless we understand His requirements, how can we render necessary services to Him? Whatever services we may be rendering to God, we should know whether our actions are helpful for our self-development. Whether we are moving towards the goal or are we deviating from the goal?

We must know whether we are on the correct path, whether we are doing things right for our self-realisation. By whatever name God may be called, it is to be understood that God is there everywhere and in all beings. Hence do not ill-treat anybody. Swami Vivekananda said that service to mankind is service to God. Thus, by serving others one will come across truths after truths and will ultimately realise the Supreme Truth.

If you want to make progress in your spiritual efforts, it is essential to serve others. By that you will earn *Punya* or virtues that will sail you faster towards the goal. All your negative qualities will wane away slowly if you keep on serving others. All other divine qualities will be activated in you. You will be eligible for blessings from the Almighty. Remember this and serve all considering that you are serving God's Creation and thereby God.

Sometimes it so happens that while serving a patient, the patient scolds you or physically assaults you. Do not feel bad for that. He is not in a mental condition to understand what you are doing to him. Never mind. You will earn virtues for the services you are rendering. You will be blessed by God. It is not desirable to calculate the benefit accrued to us on account of our service. God also knows that the patient is ignorant about the importance of service being rendered by you to him, but he needs it. Hence consider that God has made you an instrument to help him.

Your first and foremost duty is to serve others. It is a very powerful tool that will take you forward. You will get blessings of God. What more is required! You are doing your duty by way of service. This is your Dharma. All our spiritual efforts should hinge upon service. There is another dimension of service which takes you towards your goal. That is disseminating right knowledge to others. For that whatever arrangements we make for satsang is also Service. Divya Darshan carries on the mission of imparting right knowledge to the people. He, who dedicates himself for fulfilment of this mission, is also doing great service that will take him nearer to the goal. By this service you are doing good to the society that includes your neighbours, family and friends. By this service of carrying the message of right knowledge and divine virtues, the society at large will be benefited and everyone will live in peace and attain freedom. People will live fearlessly and blissfully. Now you can understand what a noble mission you all are involved in. You all are born for this purpose. In fine, by serving others you are earning virtues. Your virtues will take you to the goal. He, who sincerely does this, will be liberated in this life itself. Those, who are doing things half-heartedly, may not reach the goal in this life. They may have to take more births. Therefore, everyone should try day and night to do more and more service and earn virtues for a faster self-realisation. He will get blessings of Sadguru. At the time of initiation, I (Sadguru Sri Sri Arjun) had told, "Prepare yourself to get God's blessings." Remember this always and conduct yourselves in the righteous way.

❀✦❀

[59]*["By mere outward worship, you do not get His blessings. Only by strong faith and sincere obedience to His Will, His blessings shall be showered upon you."*

(Amritbindu -53)]

By worship, most of the people understand it as observance of some rituals along with a set of procedures and formalities relating to the rituals which are traditionally handed down to us by our ancestors. In course of time, entertainment and extravaganza too have become additional dimensions of our worship. The sacred purpose of worship in most of the cases is relegated to the background. Hence, people do not get the benefits as much as they should get. Indiscipline and internal wrangling distance us from actual worship.

God has gifted human being with a rare and fair form. Behind his birth, there is a definite purpose. If one repeatedly contemplates on this, one can realise the Truth. Sincere effort for attainment of the goal is the first and foremost Dharma or duty of man. Man is born to go upward and not downward. At the end of his upward movement, he can realise the Supreme Brahman. This is the very purpose of human birth. His goal is not just to eat and survive.

Man is not able to know about himself. He is not very clear about why he eats; what and how he should eat and by surviving what he wants to achieve etc. Man is supposed to know all these answers without which his living is purposeless. If man understands the purpose of his living, he will get rid of sufferings. Ignorance is the cause of sufferings. He habitually commits mistakes and prays God to open escape routes for him. It does not work.

Purity and sincerity is necessary for worshipping God. Without it, worship is fruitless. Everybody should know what worship is and why to worship. Without knowing, if somebody worships, he will not get the results thereof. According to the scriptures, He, who is the source of all energy, is to be worshipped. By worshipping Him, the devotees get His blessings.

---

59 Oriya Divya Dhara Vol 13 Page 24

By worshipping, people come to know more and more about Him and His Laws by which the entire Creation is being sustained and regulated.

Now the question is whether it is necessary to worship merely to maintain the body and survive? The answer is an emphatic 'No'. Many people worship ignorantly and pray for getting rid of sufferings, but they do not get the expected result. After knowing the right way, if somebody worships, he will get good result.

Worship is respect to and compliance of God's instructions and Laws. By doing so, man obtains knowledge and gets purified. By the good impulses and virtues acquired in the past several births, one has got human birth. Man must still purify and evolve himself in this birth and try to reach his goal of self-realisation. Therefore, worship is essential. It earns the worshipper good impulses and virtues. True worship is not concerned with any material gain. It is concerned with inner purity.

True worship is righteous and skilful performance of duties with a view to attaining the life's goal. In other words, any action that does not lead one to attainment of life's goal of self-realisation is not true worship. Without a destination, the journey of life is a wasteful fiasco.

In the Taitteriya Upanishad, the sage named Bhrigu in his childhood asked his father Varun about his duties. In reply Varun said, "Try to know Him from whom everything has emanated, by whom everything is sustained and in whom everything gets ultimately merged." This is the goal of human life. In this, man's total requirements will be fulfilled. If you ask anybody regarding his choice between happiness and sufferings, he will opt for happiness or peaceful living. Whatever is to be done for getting peace and happiness is called duty or karttavya. All actions should synchronise with karttavya. Due to ignorance if people do contrary things, how shall they get happiness? According to the Law of Karma, a person will suffer or get punishment for his wrong doings. God even cannot save anyone from the results of his wrong actions. He will not break His own Laws. In view of the principle of reward and punishment in the Law of Karma, people should carefully choose their actions for getting peace and happiness. God has given parents, friends, sisters and brothers so that one can live happily with their cooperation and goodwill. Scriptures provide knowledge for the people to get peace and happiness. Therefore, before worshipping God, man should first introspect and try to root out his bad qualities. That is real worship and by doing so, he will get divine blessings.

The sages say that Man is scion of immortality. God has made all arrangements, ab initio, for him so that he can live in peace and happiness. He has also filled in him some divine virtues which get him peace and happiness and ultimately, he can return to God. But man is beset with demoniac tendencies and therefore he has been suffering. It must be remembered that divine qualities must be inculcated to acquire right knowledge. This is called true worship. But people do not evince adequate interest in knowledge as a result of which they are not able to perform right actions. The result is suffering. God also does not save us from this. For acquiring knowledge if somebody prays God for knowledge, he will get knowledge. God is Knowledge-Absolute and by giving knowledge to man, He opens the whole world to him. Some principles are to be followed to earn wealth i.e. to get the blessings of Goddess Laxmi. Similarly, some principles are to be followed to acquire knowledge i.e. blessings of Goddess Saraswati. The more we observe God's laws, the more we get peace and happiness. Brahman has manifested as so many gods and goddesses with specific powers. By worshipping a single deity, we should not expect that he or she will fulfil all our wishes. Therefore, we must worship the source of all powers i.e. Brahman. It is to be remembered that our wrongful actions impelled by ignorance bring us sufferings.

Hence knowledge must be acquired to get rid of sufferings. We must refrain from wrong doings. Then only we can live in peace. To get God's blessings we should possess right knowledge and divine virtues such as renunciation, restraint, spiritual practice, service, truth, love and forgiveness. We must always be humble and grateful to the Almighty who has been doing so much for us. By worshipping Brahman, we can get the blessings of all other personal godheads. Due to want of spiritual knowledge we are not able to repose faith on the Almighty. Faith is the propeller of further advancement in the spiritual journey.

The sages from time immemorial have been imparting true knowledge. He, who will follow that knowledge, will get peace and happiness. The secret key to peace and bliss is with Guru. If Guru is satisfied with the disciple, the disciple can get peace and bliss on getting right knowledge from Guru.

Due to ignorance we are not able to discriminate between virtues and vices. Our vices outweigh our virtues. Sufferings are on the rise. The sinners may be placed in the wombs of lower creatures in the next birth. The sages have introduced Pancha Yajna (five sacrifices) by performing which sins can be reduced and virtues will increase. Of the five, Rishi Yajna or Jnana Yajna is the best. By performing this Yajna, Brahman can be realised. Every day if you study some scriptures and discuss among yourselves, your spiritual knowledge will increase. Your bad qualities will slowly go away. The uniqueness of knowledge is that by it all your accumulated sins in the previous births and present birth are destroyed. It is the power of knowledge-fire. With the advent of the light of knowledge, the darkness of ignorance vanishes forthwith. Therefore, ignorantly worshipping some deity will help none. Right thoughts, Right expressions and right actions are the real worship that shall lead one to the life's goal. All these come from right knowledge imparted by the sages, scriptures and Sadguru.

౮౩✢౮౩

[60]Now I (Sadguru Sri Sri Arjun) am going to tell you something about bhakti. There are a large number of devotees. Some of them are quite knowledgeable persons. But one should know what true devotion is. The devotion of common people is limited only to some occasional rituals, visiting some temples and pilgrimages periodically, singing in praise of God and praying God for fulfilment of certain desires etc.

When we find some good qualities in someone or come to know about his greatness, we like and respect him. We like gold because we know it is a precious metal. We have some knowledge about God. Hence, we respect Him. True devotion will come after knowing about His greatness and His indispensability for the Creation as well as its constituents. True devotion

---

60 Oriya Divya Dhara Vol 14 Page 24

means love and respect. Without knowing about God, devotion cannot come. How can we respect somebody about whom we do not know anything?

It is seen that only during the time of adversities, quite a many remember God. After that they forget. This is because they do not know anything about God. People remember God when they expect something from God. But a person with knowledge about God and His greatness, cannot forget Him. He, who realises the greatness of God, will hesitate to do anything wrong for he knows that he will be punished for wrongdoings. When the knowledge of a devotee increases, he will be convinced that he is living only because of the support of God. He is the essence of everything. He is the vital energy. He is Truth, Consciousness and Bliss. Without Him, nothing can exist. On knowing this, a devotee will surrender to God.

Man speaks about self-surrender, but he forgets thereafter. People worship God in various ways but thereafter they forget. When you are used to think that everything is done by you by means of your qualities, knowledge and power, in such case, where is the question of surrender? Hence, quite a good percentage of persons who claim to be devotees know very little about God and His greatness. Some people wear different types of robes and assert that they are devotees. But a real devotee does not attach any importance to any distinctive clothing, sandal paste or vermillion marks. He does not attach much importance to the body and its decorations. A real devotee knows that everything belongs to God and therefore he likes to lead a very simple life. Wearing a coloured cloth does not make one a devotee. He, who leads a simple life with his mind always fixed on God, is a real devotee. Then only he can realise how great God is. God is everywhere. A true devotee will obey God's Laws or the Law of Eternity. It is essential for a devotee to acquire as much knowledge as possible about God and His powers. Then only he can realise that God is the very essence of his life.

જ⋆જ

[61] Being compelled by necessity and impelled by nature, we have committed lot of sins in course of several births. We have already enjoyed the fruits of our actions in our previous births and some are carried over to our present births. Ignorance is the cause of all sufferings. But it is regrettable that man is not trying to get rid of sins and consequent sufferings. He is not evincing interest to even know how to earn virtues.

By serving others, virtues can be earned. This is the surest way. Imparting right knowledge to others is a way to serve because by doing so the recipients' sufferings will get reduced or eliminated. Therefore, receiving right knowledge amounts to earning virtues.

This Creation is full of continuous changes. Many come and go. Nothing is permanent in this world. The Creation is a dynamic process. But in this changeable world, there is an unseen principle of service that is going on always in and through the process of change. Service goes on unabated. Everyone in this Creation serves one another. They are all made for service. With our limited knowledge, we cannot know that whatever we are doing are all for service. In a family, don't we serve each other? Service is going on between husband and wife, father and son and so on. We serve the plants by watering the same and applying fertilizers to them. The plants also serve us by giving fruits and flowers, and the life-saving Oxygen. The Creation is sustained by service to each other.

Since we do not have clear idea about Service, we do not know that we are serving others and therefore, we do not have the necessary attitude of service. If so, how can we expect good results of our actions? How can we earn virtues?

The best and highest form of service is service to Guru. Guru is the embodiment of knowledge. Knowledge is power. Everything is possible by knowledge and spiritual practice. Hence service to Guru is so important. At times, you feel shy and reluctant to serve Guru. It is a sin to avoid serving to Guru. Some of you also neglect in serving your parents. It should be remembered that through service, one can easily

---

61 Oriya Divya Dhara Vol 14 Page 36

reach God. Who can serve? He, who has love and devotion, can serve others. If you have not served others, God will not help you or serve you in your spiritual journey. The more one loves somebody, the more one serves him. Service will lead you to bliss. Bliss is the outcome of love. We wish peace and bliss but do not serve others. How will it be possible? Man has not understood the importance of service and love. It is love that impels someone to serve others. Enriched with spiritual knowledge, one can love others without any return or without any condition. This is the Dharma of every human being. This love leads one to eternal and infinite bliss. But due to ignorance, we distance ourselves from serving others even though many opportunities are available to us. The sages and spiritual masters lay emphasis on service and that is why, they always advise us to serve others. Because Brahman or Atman is also present in others. Due to ignorance, we are unable to comprehend the essential points laid down in the scriptures.

By doing service to others, our internal organs (Mind, intellect, chitta and ahamkar) get purified. Through service, one gets in touch with truth physically, mentally and spiritually. Bliss is inherent to Atman. Through service, one comes closer to Atman resulting in more and more divine bliss. The sages without any self-interest serve others. That is why, they are always blissful. While the wise men realise Atman and remain blissful, the ignorant are confined only to physical bodies, sense organs, mind and intellect. Therefore, the ignorant cannot enjoy true bliss. Hence Guru always inspires you to acquire self-knowledge and get liberated from all sufferings.

Atman eternally pervades everywhere. Atman manifests as mind, intellect and conscience. Only the spiritual mendicants can understand this. The common people may not understand it. He, who loves Atman, also loves all the manifestation of Atman easily. Realisation of Atman, which is self-realisation, is essential for getting permanent bliss. The realisers love all as they experience Atman everywhere and in all beings. According to Upanishad, the spouse is dear not for the sake of the spouse but for the Atman; son is dear not for the sake of son but for the Atman. Therefore, by serving others, you are worshiping Atman or Brahman. Hence, Divya

Darshan says, "serve others with love, humbleness and without selfishness or ego." Through service, you can purify yourself and reach closer to truth. God will inspire you, strengthen you and bless you. If you do not accept God, it means you do not know what truth is. He, who knows truth, lives with righteousness and love; he respects God and realises Him ultimately.

If you love Him, you will remember Him always. God loves you always. You will be His and He will be yours. Ultimately you will be united with Him. This is called liberation or Moksa. He, who follows the Law of Eternity, finally attains Him. Acquire more and more spiritual knowledge; you will be blessed; your divine eye will open; you will have more patience to listen.

The ignorant are almost deaf as they do not listen to or understand the deep and subtle spiritual subjects.

Therefore, acquire more and more knowledge, practice desireless service and realise Truth.

ℰℬ✶ℰℬ

[62]**Samskara (Past impulses):** Can the illiterates understand scriptures that contain the tattva of the highest level?

In reply, Sadguru said that no generalization can be made in this regard. All can understand but may not fully. Some persons may understand well even with a brief explanation on the subject. There are also persons who grasp very little even after elaborate talks. It must be admitted that the understanding power differs from person to person.

Another point is that if one does not have interest in any particular subject, he will not understand even a small thing. If one evinces interest to know, one can learn higher things also. A teacher's first duty is to create interest among the students. The subject must be explained in a very simple and clear manner. If some subject is explained properly, even people with less qualifications and past impulses can understand partly if not wholly. Persons with good past impulses can grasp things quickly. Examples are

---

62 Oriya Divya Dhara Vol 15 Page 35

there that some dull-witted persons also become wise after coming in contact with sages and wise men. During the lifetime of Lord Buddha, there was a ruthless brigand named Angulimala living in the jungle; he had been unleashing terror in the area and causing untold sufferings to the people. After a brief interaction with Lord Buddha, he got totally transformed and finally surrendered to Lord Buddha. There are umpteen examples of transformation of bad people to good people.

The sages can very well read the minds of other persons. They know the past, present and future of others. But generally they do not disclose the same. In urgent cases, they may give some indications only.

It should be remembered that the past impulses of a person get activated in this birth. Due to sins committed in the previous births, a rich person may be born as a poor man and lead a life of penury. Therefore, it should be our conscious effort to garner good impulses by resorting to good karma and righteous conduct to ensure peace and happiness. Persons are placed in different categories due to guna and karma (Shrimad Bhagavad-Gita). Man's conduct is a mirror of his past impulses. The wise persons treat everyone with equal vision. The three qualities such as sattva, rajas and tamas are the outcome of knowledge or past impulses.

Persons of tamasic nature normally conduct themselves as demons and lower animals. An ordinary person normally possesses rajasic qualities. While tamas represents ignorance, inertia and laziness, rajas represents passion, activity, ambition and avarice. Sattvic quality represents goodness, calmness and knowledge. All good qualities such as love and affection, service or helpful attitude, truthfulness, sincerity in duty and compassion etc. are seen in a person of sattvic quality. In other words, different levels of knowledge come out as nature or qualities of persons. Therefore past knowledge or past impulses (samskara) play a predominant role in the present life. Past samskara is the driving force behind all activities and ambitions in the present life. By spiritual practices, a seeker transcends all three qualities. He becomes Knowledge-Absolute. He realises that he manifests as all these three qualities such as tamas, rajas and sattva. Thus he reaches the state of Brahman. He gets established in the Supreme state which is known as Pure-Consciousness.

The sages rise above all differences like castes and creeds etc. They go beyond knowledge and ignorance. Nothing remains to be attained. Nothing remains to be known. They go beyond all dualities like victory or defeat, profit or loss, honour or dishonour etc.

☙✳❧

[63]The sages had realised Supreme Brahman. After realisation, even while living in this physical world they possessed non-dual devotion. They are aware of the truth that the Supreme Brahman pervades everywhere and in everything. While explaining about the Supreme Brahman, they take recourse to dualism.

The spiritual aspirants should minutely observe the sages to know how they behave or deal with different situations, how they speak and respect others.

Many people believe in God. They worship God throughout their lives. But they are not able to realise God. Many people have surrendered to Sadguru and taken initiation. They follow the instructions of Guru, but they do not reach the state of Guru. What prevents the disciples from attaining the highest state? The disciples go through different scriptures and hear so many things from Sadguru but many disciples do not pay attention to Guru's conduct, his actions and his expressions etc. as a result of which they do not get complete knowledge. Along with knowledge, divine qualities should also be acquired by the disciples to gain faster progress towards the goal. The disciples follow some instructions and not all instructions of the Guru. He, who follows all instructions of Guru, will be benefited more.

When I (Sadguru Sri Sri Arjun) purchase something, I do not bargain. I do not sort the vegetables while buying. I do not complain even if somebody gives me less by manipulating the weights and measures.

---

63 Oriya Divya Dhara Vol 18 Page 7

How a disciple should conduct himself?

The disciple has less knowledge. If he possesses strong inquisitiveness, he can know more very quickly. Guru's instructions should be followed in toto. The disciple should know that by following Guru's instructions, he will get Guru's blessings. His thinking should be "I am not doing a favour to Guru by following His instructions. Guru's instructions are tonics or nectarine elixirs for my self-development." Everybody must take care of his own body (by proper diet and physical exercise etc.) as per requirements to remain hale and hearty. A sick disciple cannot follow Guru's instructions and therefore cannot progress on spiritual path.

You should remain always humble whether in the presence of Guru or elsewhere. You should have self-restraint relating to food habit, speech and mind. You should have good relationship in the neighbourhood. Always try to maintain a safe distance from the wrongdoers and negative people. Pay respect to the sages and superiors. Those, who restrain their senses, become more powerful and can attain the goal faster.

Doing more physical labour is harmful. On the other hand, a lazy person cannot do his duties properly. Excess sleep means wasting time. Sleep is essential to give rest to the body and mind. Some jokes or humours also provide rest to the mind.

Food habits: It is good to take vegetarian diet. In the initial stages, emphasis is not given by Divya Darshan on diet. Divya Darshan lays emphasis on inquisitiveness and acquisition of knowledge. Without this, only intake of vegetarian diet will not help in improving knowledge. A spiritual aspirant must take controlled diet.

❧✶❧

[64]There are some sages who have taught us about the material world and the behavioural aspects. They guided the mankind on the social systems based on moral standards or ethical values. The purpose is to make a harmonious social living.

---

64 Oriya Divya Dhara Vol 18 Page 43

There are some sages, who speak on still higher planes of existence. Those people who have good impulses (samskara) will be able to understand the preaching of such sages. Those subtle thoughts are nectar-like. There is death for the gross, but the subtle thoughts or knowledge do not die. Common people cannot understand the subtle thoughts expressed by the sages.

Majority of the people are on Bhakti path. The influence of Bhakti on our society is quite predominant. It will be correct to say that there are fewer persons on jnana marg. In future, more and more persons will be attracted towards knowledge and shall take to knowledge path. So far as spiritual knowledge is concerned, our present society is still in its infancy. Many people are still unable to acquire true knowledge despite observance of so many rituals and so-called dharmic practices.

This is Kali Yug. Satya Yug is bound to come. Divya Darshan is born at the juncture of Kali and Satya. Hence it is the duty of all of you to acquire true knowledge and spread it. By doing so, you will acquire more and more punya. Knowingly or unknowingly, you are committing some sins. You can correct yourselves by acquiring true knowledge. You must be conscious that you are spreading true knowledge imparted by Sadguru for the well-being of the people. Others may or may not accept this, but you must continue your efforts with courage and confidence as a matter of duty. Sadguru is watching your activities and movements. Lord Jesus had said, "Let them listen who have ears; others need not." This means, those, who are conscientious, shall listen and take to their hearts. The devotees in general are worshipping different personal godheads. But Divya Darshan emphasizes on possessing divine qualities and expressing them in conduct.

Imagine the situation in the society when there were no coins or currency notes. How were the people managing their transactions? They were managing things by trust, truth and divine qualities. They were helping each other. They used to believe each other. They were living in peace. In this Kali Yug, many people due to their demoniac qualities have greed for wealth and therefore try to grab other's wealth. Hence there are disturbances and litigations in our present society. People do not believe each other. Many people resort to cheating to satisfy their insatiable hunger for wealth. In such situations, how can we get peace? It is reiterated that demoniac qualities take away our peace. By simply clamouring for Satya Yug, it will not come. Truth must be welcomed and held in heart with reverence.

❧✦❧

[65]Since we are in human form, we consider ourselves as jiva. Man is the most advanced creature of this Creation. Since man is in nature, he is not able to know his Self although he has been contemplating on wherefrom he came and how he came. It is never easy to reach the true answer. Only a few who sincerely tried to know and made intense spiritual practices were able to know the Self. The Law of the Creation is – "Like form, like qualities; like qualities, like form." Hence the qualities of a jiva find expressions in a jiva.

The sages had, after realising the Truth, expressed that the Creation has come from Brahman. Brahman has taken the form of jiva. Brahman is there in the jiva in an invisible state. But due to ignorance, man is not able to understand and appreciate this. Even the jiva does not know what exactly he is.

The gross body and the subtle body taken together is called jiva. Once man loses his gross form, his power gets enhanced in subtle body. Since the gross body is an outer covering of the jiva, his power also gets restricted to the gross body. There is causal body inside the subtle body. The causal body is more powerful than the subtle body. Once the causal body is transcended, the spiritual seeker by the grace of Sadguru reaches the Supra-Causal state which is Pure Consciousness. All powers are present in that total state.

The subtle body is powerful. The mind, the intellect and the *Tanmatras* are active in the subtle body. In the causal body conscience is active. You are Brahman even though you are not able to realise this truth due to ignorance. Everything is there inside you. People misconstrue the mind for Self.

---

65 Oriya Divya Dhara Vol 15 Page 19

But the True Self is beyond nature and transcends everything. The three qualities such as sattva, rajas and tamas are called Prakriti. The jiva gets manifested in the ambit of nature or Prakriti. The jiva has come from Brahman. Jiva is not actually a part of Prakriti. He is Purusha with coverings of Prakriti. Everything in the kingdom of nature is changeable or evanescent. The gross body impacts the jiva so much that he is unable to know the True Self. By spiritual efforts, the more man transcends the coverings one after another, the more he would be able to know Self. There are two ways such as good and bad. Once somebody does good, remembers good and contemplates good, he will acquire good impulses and shall attain goodness that is God. This is called self-development. On the other hand, he, who resorts to bad thoughts, expressions and actions, accumulates bad impulses that would keep him farther from God. It would lead to his regression which means the process of self-development gets impeded. Instead of moving towards peace, happiness and bliss, he plunges himself into sufferings.

We have taken innumerable births in the past and all along we have considered our gross bodies as our 'Self'. We are not aware that there is a subtle body inside the gross body, and there is a causal body inside the subtle body. This means, both causal body and subtle body are present inside the gross body. The Supra-Causal body, which is beyond all bodies and at the same time all-pervasive, controls everything. In other words, Brahman has taken all these forms. He is the causal body, the subtle body as well as the gross body. This is the process of manifestation. The manifested object, due to its insentience, is not able to know its source. Brahman is beyond Prakriti or nature. This means, He is beyond the three qualities. Therefore, He is unqualified or attributeless, whereas in the visible universe every form has a quality embedded in it. Due to inadequate knowledge, we even cannot comprehend the gross world and the things therein.

Scriptures speak of four quarters or steps of Brahman.

1. The attributeless Brahman (Supra-Causal)
2. 'Om' (causal)

3. From 'Om' to tanmatras (sense, touch, sight, taste and smell) (subtle)

4. From tanmatras to five gross elements (gross)

The lower three steps constitute Prakriti. In the visible universe, while we can see earth, water and fire, we cannot see air and ether. The personal godheads come under Prakriti and have specific powers. The subtle body is endowed with the powers of personal godheads. From 'Om' to the five gross elements, everything comes under Mahatattva or Buddhitattva. For the sustenance of the Creation, intelligence is necessary. The Devas belong to Buddhi tattva. When the jiva assumes gross form, his powers gradually get reduced. Hence the jiva is not able to know Brahman. Whatever is happening in the ambit of Mahatattva, man is not able to comprehend. Hence, he suffers.

To get rid of sufferings man is to not only know the gross body but also the subtle body and causal body. Ultimately, he would know Self to get rid of all sufferings. Man's subtle body gets connected with the gross body. The subtle body rarely thinks of the causal body. He, who would know that he is different from all these which are mere outward coverings, would be able to know Self and would get rid of all sufferings. The causal body is an equilibrating state of the three qualities such as sattva, rajas and tamas. This is the state of Sat-Chit-Anand. The subtle body carries the qualities like desire, anger, greed, infatuation, ego, jealousy etc. But once the causal body is realised, one can get bliss. The sages and seers remain in Nirvikar state as well as in Anand state. The originating point of the three qualities is called Maya or Adya Shakti. Maya has two powers. One is veiling power and the other is projecting power. Due to this, we consider something as the other. In other words, due to veiling power the form of a rope gets veiled, and it is projected as a snake. Therefore, the truth remains unknown. This happens due to absence of adequate light or knowledge. When light is focused on the spot, the super-imposition of the snake on the rope vanishes but the rope remains as before. Brahman is eternal; Jagat is a super-imposition.

Goddess Durga is called Mahamaya. In this entire Creation, the play of three qualities is always on. He, who would get the blessings of the three qualities (three powers in one) or Mahamaya, would get rid of all sufferings. Once the spiritual mendicant would know the primordial energy of the three qualities such as sattva, rajas and tamas, he can unravel all mysteries. Knowing the gross universe is like knowing only first step of Brahman. Knowing the subtle universe means knowing the second step of Brahman. Knowing 'Om' is, knowing the third step of Brahman. Knowing Brahman is, knowing the fourth step which means total knowledge. Sattvic thoughts are like 'Soma rasa'. Projection power starts from the quality of rajas. Dissolution comes from the quality of tamas. When the three qualities balance each other, there is equilibrating state.

Sense organs are created from out of sattvic and rajasic ahamkara. *Tanmatras* are created from out of rajasic and tamasic ahamkara. When man shall know the Self fully, he would get rid of all sufferings. This is called self-realisation. Paramatman manifests as Prakriti. Once man knows this, he can also understand the Brahman who is beyond Prakriti. Hence every spiritual mendicant should make sincere efforts to get the blessings of Prakriti to realise the Purusha who is none other than the Self.

❧✦❧

[66]A spiritual mendicant, in his quest for knowing more and more, meets relative truths one after another and ultimately he realises the Absolute Truth. Brahman, Atman and God are different names of the Supreme Truth. Realisation of Brahman is same as realisation of True Self. Commonly it is also called God-realisation. This is our goal. And for achieving the goal, we resort to various kinds of spiritual practices. Most of the people complain that they are unable to concentrate during meditation. Other worldly thoughts deflect their mind. About 90% of the people are of this category. This is the reason why very few people become successful.

Among millions of spiritual mendicants, one or two may be reaching the Supreme state. Why so many aspirants are unsuccessful? The reasons must be found out.

---

66 Oriya Divya Dhara Vol 20 Page 23

Where are our defects or shortcomings? After knowing this, we must take remedial steps to streamline our sadhana. We must therefore know why the failure rate is so high. Unless we rectify ourselves, how can we succeed? I (Sadguru Sri Sri Arjun) find that although many disciples are attending our classes, only four or five are grasping well. Others are progressing but their progress is not satisfactory. After a few years, it will be known how many of you will succeed.

Whatever we do to attain any goal is called sadhana. It is essential that we must be keen to attain the goal. The spiritual mendicants must have love, sincerity, and inquisitiveness towards God. If we do not possess these qualities, our progress will be awfully slow. Those, who are not attending classes, how will they learn? Those who are not making any effort will be unsuccessful. But I believe that a good percentage of the disciples of Divya Darshan will be successful.

Those who do not know about God, whom will they get? Hence, before we start our spiritual journey, we must know about God. In absence of proper knowledge about God, we imagine someone as God and accordingly carry on our sadhana which leads us nowhere. Many people are not interested to know about God, but they are interested to get something from God. "I must reach out to God"; this feeling should be strong from the beginning itself. Once one attains God, one cannot ask for anything from Him. Hence instead of trying to attain Him, merely expecting anything from God is meaningless. One should not carry out his spiritual sadhana for fulfilment of desires. His desires may be fulfilled but he may not attain God. Further, he may be carried away by desires and thus deviate from the goal of attaining God. While doing spiritual practice, one must introspect if there are any flaws in one's approach. For this, knowledge is essential. Due to want of knowledge, many become unsuccessful in their pursuits.

I trust the success rate will be high for the Divya Darshan disciples. Divya Darshan imparts knowledge in a methodical way from individual survival, harmonious living in the society and finally self-realisation. Divya Darshan teaches about lila and greatness of the Supreme Brahman with a dualistic approach and finally about the realisation of the unitary existence. Divya Darshan lays emphasis on believing in the existence of God, putting faith on God, having sincere devotion towards God and loving God who is the unitary, infinite, all-pervasive, all-powerful Supreme Brahman after knowing whom everything becomes known; nothing more remains to be known also by attaining Him everything is attained; nothing more remains to be attained. He is the Self; He is Bliss and Pure-Consciousness. Divya Darshan emphasizes on acquisition of knowledge and blossoming of divine virtues. This is the duty and Dharma of every human being. This leads to the goal of self-realisation. Therefore, Divya Darshan imparts knowledge in a very systematic and simplified manner. Divya Darshan upholds the scriptural essence and never contradicts other paths or systems of philosophy. Divya Darshan proves the existence of God, the unchangeable essence, by its 'Theory of Change'. Once we know about God's greatness and indispensability, we will be automatically attracted towards Him. It should be remembered that man performs his sadhana with a view to attaining a specific goal. But only after reaching the final destination he gets rid of all suffering. The benefits from out of spiritual efforts are vast and limitless. By taking shelter of the Almighty, this goal can be achieved. God has infinite powers that are ineffable. Once the spiritual aspirant knows about this, he will have greater keenness to attain God. The spiritual aspirant gets convinced that due to God's grace and all types of support, he is surviving. Therefore, he will have greater devotion and love towards God. Because of God, everything in this Creation is well-regulated and synchronized. "If I take His shelter, I will get greater strength and power." With this conviction, he can make spiritual progress faster.

Regarding concentration of mind on a specific object or subject, Divya Darshan says that mind gets more and more attracted towards something which it considers as more valuable. When someone comes to know that diamond is more valuable than gold, he will leave gold and run after diamond. Most valuable thing in this Creation is God. None can even imagine the value of God. The wise know that God is invaluable. Hence, they get always attracted towards God. A spiritual aspirant who does not have any idea about the indispensability and value of God will not be firm in his spiritual practice. A child does not know the difference between a five rupee note and a five hundred rupee note. Similarly, how can somebody be keen to attain God if he does not know the value of God? A common man gets attached to worldly matters and considers worldly pleasure as a yardstick of his success. It must be remembered that human birth is for a great purpose, i.e. attainment of Brahman. If you know about God more and more, your mind will get attracted towards God more and more leaving behind all worldly matters. You will concentrate more on God. You cannot force your mind to stick to God. The sense organs such as- ears, skin, eyes, tongue and nose will keep on dragging mind towards sound, touch, sight, taste and smell. It is essential therefore to train the mind on spiritual subjects particularly about the greatness and glories of God.

Due to inadequate knowledge about Brahman, we imagine different Gods, ascribe them different forms and worship them or meditate upon them. Due to lack of proper concentration, we feel drowsy and leave our meditation there. While meditating, different forms come to our mind. We get confused and disturbed at that time.

When we face some adverse situation, we remember our friends and expect them to come to our rescue. At that time, we apply our mind and intelligence to contact a friend who has got the necessary knack to solve our problem; we consider his capability before contacting him. Likewise, when we will know about God's infinite powers, our mind will seek His help to come out of any problem. Mind will place more faith and confidence on Him. Therefore, if we seek His help, He will guide us during our spiritual journey. "God will give me courage and power." He, who thinks like this, will progress faster, get His blessings and attain self-realisation.

True knowledge or self-knowledge is the highest knowledge in spirituality. It is not enough if the spiritual aspirant only acquires knowledge about God's existence and His greatness. Self-realisation or realisation of True Self is necessary. Unless God is realised, we remain half-way. We know something about gold, and we know how to prepare ornaments from out of it. But the scientists, who know this element thoroughly, can put it to more important uses. The truth is that we can enjoy something to the extent we know about the same.

The spiritual practice in jnana-marga rests upon listening, meditating and repeatedly contemplating. Divya Darshan says, "True sadhana is to make efforts to know Him, whom we are keen to attain." In other words, doing karma with proper aptitude to attain God-realisation is Sadhana. Otherwise, all efforts will be directionless and slow. What destination can be defined for a whimsical or aimless wanderer? Man suffers a lot. But if he does not make efforts to come out of sufferings, he will continue to wail and mourn.

A spiritual aspirant should be strong enough to face any adverse situation during the spiritual journey. There are many who withdraw themselves half-way on the sight of some obstacles. I (Sadguru Sri Sri Arjun) am ready to give all my knowledge to the disciples; but they are not ready to receive. I grieve for them. I have come with the sole purpose of imparting true knowledge. I am calling upon them to face towards me, but they are turning their faces away. The disciples do not understand that I have come to save them from all sufferings. Repeatedly I speak to them, but they are asleep like Kumbhakarna; even more than Kumbhakarna! They are caught up in the snares of illusion. It is said that to wake up Kumbhakarna, a number of drums were beaten close to his ears; many horns and conches were blown to create a big noise. I am always trying to wake them up. But they are unable to hear me. I am therefore sad for them all, and not for me. I believe that at least now they will wake up.

We should do good to the whole world by spreading true knowledge. By doing so, we will be benefited and the whole world will also be benefited. For performing this big and noble task, we must be strong enough. If you acquire true knowledge, you will be strong because knowledge is power.

If you put your selfish interest first and thereafter think of others' interest, things will go awry. Those who work for fulfilment of personal desires cannot contribute to the well-being of the society. Rather they become obstacles to common interest. One must be sattvic to progress on the path of sadhana. Therefore, be good and do good to others. Sacrifice your self-interest for the sake of others. By doing so you are preparing yourselves for attainment of your goal, i.e. God-realisation. Those, who are going to the frontiers to fight battles, are given intensive training first. Similarly, when you are going to accomplish big tasks, you must prepare yourselves physically and mentally.

Try to organize conference of Divya Darshan every year at different branches. All branches must support the centre. If the centre becomes strong, branches will also be strong. There must be regular contact between the centre and branches.

(Gurudev in his valedictory address to the disciples in the second Annual Conference at Sunabeda on 12.06.1988 gave vent to his feelings in the following words.)

> *"I am determined to wake you up from your deep slumber even at the cost of my sleep. In your dream also you should remember that Guru is waking you up. You should remember that I have dedicated myself for your well-being. I have come with that purpose. I expect that during my lifetime, some of you should get enlightened. Whether my wish will be fulfilled or not is only known to the Almighty."*

๙๛

> [67] *["We try to keep the body clean but rarely try to clean our mind. When mind becomes impure, everything appears differently. Therefore, along with body, the mind is also to be kept clean and pure."*
>
> *(Amritbindu-51)]*

Cleaning the exterior i.e. the physical body is necessary but not sufficient unless the internal organs such as mind are kept clean. These two aspects are inter-connected. Unless kept clean, body will not remain healthy and disease-free. A healthy body has a positive impact on the mind. If the mind is calm and well-composed, good thoughts come. When the physical body

---

67 Oriya Divya Dhara Vol 20 Page 50

is unwell, lot of negative thoughts come. Keeping the body clean and fit should be a daily habit. Similarly, even if the body is healthy, but the mind is not healthy, many unwanted thoughts swarm in. Therefore, both body and mind should be kept clean otherwise one will get diverted from the goal of life. During journey, if we quarrel with people, our movement may get retarded. We may not be able to reach our destination. Therefore, keeping the mind balanced and cool is so important to undertake a journey that leads us to the goal of life. Realisation of True Self is the goal of life. There are so many devotees who take early bath, put sandal paste on their foreheads and visit religious places on a regular basis. All these will not yield results unless internal purity is there.

Therefore, Guru's instructions and also instructions laid down in our scriptures are to be followed sincerely to keep our mind clean. By regularly attending satsang and by remembering Guru's instructions and living up to them, our mind remains clean and composed. Those who adhere to such practice get blessings from Guru and attain the goal.

After mind becomes fully clean, the physical aspect becomes secondary. If someone's mind is clean and pure, normally his body also remains free from diseases. Bliss gets reflected on a pure mind. On the other hand a wicked mind prompts one to indulge in negative activities to suffer ultimately. Those who are not able to attend Satsang or visit *ashram*, they should chant Ishta Mantra in their homes. By this also, mind becomes clean.

The above things are easy to do. But we do not want to learn about the Law of Eternity and therefore do not observe the same. Without observing the Law of Eternity, how can we attain the blissful state? The Paramatman is there in all of us as the Atman. He, who realises like this, realises True Self.

Without having any knowledge about God, how can we attain Him? Knowledge is essential even to know the worldly matters. "God is there as Self inside me." This thought should be very strongly entrenched in the minds of the spiritual seeker.

Without this, no other way will help us realise self. Divya Dasrhan says, "Keep your mind clean and pure so that the Parmatman in you will clearly shine out. If you realise God inside, you can also see Him outside everywhere and in everything."

For all spiritual seekers, this internal purity is especially important.

❧ ✶ ❧

Messages to Spiritual Aspirants

[68]**His message to the disciples:** "The whole world is looking for divine knowledge. You are all born for this purpose. Remember always that without self-knowledge, peace is not possible. Self is Peace-Absolute. He, who knows the Self, gets peace. Therefore, always try to know Him, the Peace-Absolute. Remember, Vedas, Upanishads and the precepts of great teachers have not been properly understood and appreciated by the people so far. Divya Darshan aims at reaching out to the people to revive that divine knowledge. Remember and understand that this knowledge which I have brought from Satya-Loka (from the plane of Truth) will raise you to the stage of God realisation. Try for your development and of the society as well. That will be your best austerity and spiritual practice. Continue with your good works, austerity and spiritual practice. Good rewards are assured. I (Sadguru Sri Sri Arjun) have come to wake you up so that you can get rid of sufferings by acquiring self-knowledge. I am resolute to wake you up even at the cost of my sleep. *(The spirit of His above statement bears resemblance with that of Socrates who said, "I have come as a dragon fly to wake up the lazy horses by my stings.")*

You should think, "Ishta Mantra is our Guru. He is always with us. You can get everything from Him. I am advising you to keep on trying to spread the true knowledge of "Divya Darshan". Try to bring "Divya Darshan" to the reach of educated mass. Even after I leave my gross body, I shall be there always with you. You will get whatever you wish. Those, who are involved in the development of *ashram*, should keep on trying more. Rewards are in store for them. Good efforts will never go unrewarded in the kingdom of God. Remember, Truth can be realised by Truth. You are born for that. You are born to engage yourselves for the development and spread of "Divya Darshan". After I leave this physical body, you must endeavour to fulfil my mission."

On 21.06.1986, at Sunabeda, he addressed the disciples to remain united for the noble cause.

"Stay united in the Sangha. Sangha is required for maintaining unity and order among the members/disciples. If Sangha becomes strong, a lot of work can be done for the welfare of the society. Every member must be aware of this. He, who works for the Sangha, earns lot of virtues and at the same time the society also gets benefited. Man cannot carry any wealth with him at the time of his death. Only virtues remain with him. Virtues are the only assets, although invisible. The virtuous man gets blessed by God. The sacrifices we make here earn for us virtues that help us hereafter. It is the duty of every person to earn virtues instead of accumulating wealth. He, who is not keen to acquire virtues and in turn indulges in sinful activities, is animal-like. It is also a virtuous deed to maintain discipline in the Sangha. We help each other in the society we live. He, who sacrifices for the sake of the society, is virtuous. Proper bonding with the Sangha is essential.

Members should cooperate and participate in the Sangha activities. Members sacrifice time and their domestic works for the sake of the Sangha. By that, they earn goodwill and virtues. Those, who dedicate themselves for such noble and spiritual purpose, get divine blessings. It is said that due to virtues, we go to heaven and due to vices we go to hell. Virtues give us peace and happiness. Vices bring us different kinds of sufferings. According to Socrates, "Ignorance is a great sin." He, who is not conscious of vices and virtues, is in fact committing sins since he is ignorant. Making efforts for self-development is a divine quality. He, who is not trying for self-development, becomes a sinner even if he does not consciously commit any sin. Sangha inspires all members to work for their self-development as well as that of the society. Sangha leads us on the path of righteousness so that we become free from sins and sufferings. There is no dearth of people who take pride even in wantonly committing sinful activities. But people with conscience derive pleasure from good works done for others in the society. They know that virtues build up their inner strength resulting in happiness. Vices and virtues are all set to overwhelm us. It depends upon us which one we are to choose. The sages of yesteryears always alerted us against sins and had all along shown us virtuous paths which we human beings are to follow. Realising this truth, Lord Buddha gave a lot of emphasis on Sangha and had formulated various guidelines for fine-tuning the Sangha and its activities. Lord Buddha had preached, "Sangham sharanam gachchhaami." Therefore I advise you to distance yourselves from sins and be afraid of sins. Do not indulge in any activities which are detrimental to the interest of Sangha. Remain united and strongly move ahead on the path of righteousness to achieve self-development of yourselves and of the world at large."

During a discourse at Sunabeda on 25.07.1987, he spoke thus. "Reluctantly I am expressing this because you are all curious to know. Even if I leave this mortal body, I shall reside in the hearts of my devotees for their self-development. That divine power incarnates taking the form of Guru. He is present everywhere. Be careful. Never disbelieve the divine power. I have descended for that purpose. It matters little for me whether you accept me as your Guru or not. I have come to serve you all. I will be rendering my service to you whether you accept or not. Parents, however great they may be, keep on serving their children. My motto is to serve you all. Do it I must."

⌘

[69]We usually attach more importance to the body and its get up, and identify ourselves with that. We do not attach much importance to knowing Truth. Our outward get up does not speak about our personality. Our conduct is more important because by this, others know what type of persons we are. He, who has realised truth, goes beyond the birth and

---

69 Oriya Divya Dhara Vol 7 Page 40

death cycle. He goes beyond the range of karma (action) and its results. The person, who realises truth, becomes simple, magnanimous and kind-hearted. Without realising Truth, those who only dress themselves to look like an ascetic, invite troubles for themselves. The scriptures all along emphasises on knowing Truth. Truth is the essence of life, and it must be realised. Therefore, everybody should acquire true knowledge or self-knowledge. Divya Darshan says, "In whatever situations you may be, try to acquire self-knowledge." To attain liberation or Moksa, there is no better way than acquisition of self-knowledge. Anything other than self-knowledge is subject matter of Maya. Realisation of truth is not possible by analysing the subject matter of Maya. We are stuck up with performing some rituals. We do not try to know the power, whom we are worshipping. Divya Darshan says, "Whatever faith or religion you may belong to, liberation is impossible without self-knowledge." By acquiring self-knowledge, one can attain everything. He will reach the goal by the grace of Guru. Nothing more shall remain to be known or to be attained after realising Atman. He, who is keen to know Atman, can realise Atman in this birth itself.

Guru is making all arrangements for you so that you can realise your Self faster. Divya Darshan tries to reveal everything but you are so unfortunate that even if God comes to you, you are not ready to recognize Him. God is always there in you and around you. You are not able to recognize Him because you do not know who and what God is. How unfortunate you are! Guru cannot give you anything more. God is not separate from you. Guru cannot hand over God to you. Guru can give you only knowledge by which you can recognize Him. Guru is always giving you that knowledge, but you are not interested to receive the same. You alone are responsible for your sufferings. If you so will, you can realise Him in this birth. Otherwise, you may have to take many births. I am always thinking how my disciples will receive knowledge. Sleep does not come to me when I think over this. When I wake up also, I think of how you will all receive the knowledge I am imparting. But you are not listening to me. When I am sincerely doing my duty, you are hesitant to reciprocate. "I wish, one of my disciples attain enlightenment during my lifetime!"

It is bad luck for you that even if Divya Darshan is revealed for you, you are not able to take maximum benefit from out of it. Divya Darshan is there to fulfil the will of God and to spread knowledge about the Law of Eternity. Divya Darshan is for you all. I have come with the total spiritual knowledge which I impart to you all. I have planned well so that you could receive the same within a short time and attain liberation. But if you disown this, you will be distancing yourself from your goal.

Your progress is slow. With present knowledge, you are not able to understand and appreciate the value of Divya Darshan. If Divya Darshan does not work here, I will impart it elsewhere. Guru comes with a mission, carries out His mission and goes back by His own Will. Guru is beyond birth and death. In this, many mysterious things are there. I am not telling those things since you may not believe them.

You should remain always alert and never neglect in acquiring self-knowledge. Then only, you will reach the goal faster. I wish you well.

જ⭑જ

[70]**Message on the eve of New Year:** "New Year Greetings to all of you.

In this New Year, stick to your spiritual practices for the self-development of others as well as yours with renewed vigour and vivacity, impulse and exuberance. Accept that this is your duty as well as Dharma that shall lead you to the goal. To conduct yourself with this approach is your austerity and spiritual effort. When you proceed this way, you may come across many adverse situations. Never get disheartened or depressed. Adversities enhance and strengthen your ability. It must be remembered that the more one has undergone sufferings, the more eligible one becomes to receive God's blessings. Remember that sufferings and pains are the ornaments of the lovers of God. The more the sufferings, the more one shines with beauty.

Go ahead. Never retreat. Guru is always by your side and is noticing your deeds and determination. Divya Darshan is God's Manifestation, Law and

---

70 Oriya Divya Dhara Vol 17 Page 3

Will. Observance of this Law amounts to acting according to God's Will. The more an aspirant follows this Law, the more dutiful, pious and virtuous he becomes. By dint of these virtues, he shall realise his True Self. There is no doubt about it. Do not bother whether in this life span you would achieve or not. Day or night, each is a mile-stone. The more one progresses, the more he would be near to the goal. Keep this thought in mind that you are definitely progressing. Wealth, properties, prestige and fame are all transient. Whatever is done for self-realisation is permanent, auspicious and nectarine as it includes the subject matter of personal living, peaceful social living as well as self-realisation, all in one. Please convey my heartiest good wishes and blessings to all spiritual aspirants and try to keep the light of Divya Darshan ablaze. Ashram is the temple of Self, temple of knowledge and temple of divinity.

❧✦❧

During the first Divya Sammelan (1987) at Sunabeda, he said to his disciples, "I have enkindled the light of Divya Darshan; you keep it ablaze to welcome Satya Yug. Divya Darshan shall bring in Satya Yug."

In January 1989, after he returned from Kumbha Mela (Prayag), he said to some of the disciples, "I have come to impart knowledge but you are not able to recognize me." Afterwards you would say, "He came; he departed; we could not know him." On 28 February 1989, he exited his mortal body.

❧✦❧

[71]Every saying of Guru is power-packed. Gurushakti would be activated in Him, who remembers Guru's sayings, and conducts himself accordingly. This is truth. I had got by heart the gospels of many sages and great persons. I have been inspired by those powerful words and reached this stage. The realisers express their experiences after attaining the Supreme. I had followed their words and have become Guru. The words of the great Greek philosopher Socrates "Ignorance is a great sin", was a great source of

---

71 Oriya Divya Dhara Vol 6 Page 19

inspiration to me. I was convinced that knowledge must be acquired to dispel ignorance and the consequent sins. Hence Guru's sayings should be registered fully in the minds of the disciples. Guru's powers are encapsulated in the teachings. He, who would follow the teachings, would also become powerful.

Many sages have told so many good things. Those are all inspiring, but all such teachings do not lead to self-knowledge. Only the teachings of the true realisers lead to self-knowledge.

There are many powerful sayings in 'Amritbindu' (a small book containing the teachings of Sadguru Sri Sri Arjun). All the ways for attaining self-knowledge are shown in Amritbindu. You should all try to delve deep to understand the essence of Amritbindu. When we are going to acquire self-knowledge, we must become powerful from every side. Unless all inert powers are activated in us, we cannot attain the Supreme Self. But it is seen that the disciples also do not remember the teachings of Amritbindu properly. Therefore, full powers are not activated in them. Again, only getting by heart is not enough. One must realise its essence and try to conduct oneself accordingly.

Many scriptures are written for the peace and happiness of mankind. But facts are not discussed in detail in them. Divya Darshan explains truth in four steps; such as temporal truth, partial truth, Truth and Supreme Truth. There are six systems of philosophy. Every philosophy comes out with some modification or development over the level of knowledge discussed earlier. Wherever any gap is there the next philosophy clarifies the same. Vedanta Darshan came as the sixth darshan fulfilling all the deficiencies in the previous five systems of philosophy and thus provides a complete solution.

But the essence of scriptures is not understood properly now-a-days. It is because the language and style in them appear to be difficult in the present-day due to the growing predominance of the mundane knowledge over the spiritual knowledge. Now-a-days, man must be taught ab initio and in detail to make any philosophy comprehensible. Divya Darshan therefore explains the essence of spirituality in a straight, simple and shortest manner so that even the common people and busy householders can understand and appreciate.

The values of scriptures are not recognized fully now-a-days. The commentaries thereof still remain incomprehensible. An intelligent and wise person can understand from brief hints on any subject. But to explain things to the ignorant person, it must be made simpler with examples and dilations. Divya Darshan fulfils all deficiencies by imparting different levels of knowledge in the simplest manner. This is the uniqueness of Divya Darshan. It is a sin to consider yourself small or insignificant. You will play the role of Vyasadev and impart true knowledge in the society. Prepare yourself fully. You can do it. You have come for this purpose i.e. to help me in this holy mission.

Everyone, whether with low level of knowledge or high level, has the intrinsic power. Everyone is a rightful recipient. Many obstacles may come on the way. You are going to acquire true knowledge. You are born to do good to the society. The disciples are spreading knowledge about God and spirituality. They are the real heroes. I congratulate them. The simple style of Divya Darshan is unique. It must be understood and appreciated. Those who are doing God's work are fortunate. They are guided by God. They would be successful.

You must assess the social environment etc. while carefully presenting Divya Darshan. For this, knowledge, courage and power are required. Divya Darshan is going to achieve wonders. True knowledge would be spread in the society. Move forward with patience, courage and vigour. The knowledge must be spread in both cities and villages. By this you will be blessed and the whole world will be benefited. You are going to execute God's Will. You are taking lot of pains for Divya Darshan. Continue with this attitude always. I am always with you. Remember this.

ರಾ⋆ೞ

[72] He, who is obedient to the parents and prays to God at least twice, i.e. in the morning and evening, gets Guru's blessings. Brahman willed to be

---

72 Oriya Divya Dhara Vol 19 Page 14

many. But before manifesting as many, He kept Himself as Guru because after manifestation, whatever forms will be created, corresponding qualities will also appear therein. The manifested forms will be unaware of the true and original state of Brahman. Guru therefore reminds all of us about our True Self. Guru teaches us that we are not these transient forms but the eternal Brahman. Guru imparts true knowledge. Mother is a Guru who imparts preliminary knowledge. In other words, God came as mother first. Hence a child should be given good samskara from the beginning. People commit mistakes by inculcating bad habits in the child. They, in many cases, offer non-veg food to the child even if he is not interested in such food. Sometimes the parents teach wrong things to the innocent child like greed, vanity and falsehood.

The second Guru is the father. Father also teaches so many things. The child easily imitates the parents' behaviour or qualities. The third Guru is the schoolteacher. The teacher teaches different subjects in the school so that the child after he grows up will be able to properly earn his livelihood. The fourth Guru is Karna Guru who imparts God's name. The fifth Guru is the Sadguru who teaches us about self-realisation. Even from books, we learn so many things to improve our knowledge. He manifests as different creatures in this Creation. From everything, you have so many things to learn. Guru manifests as such. Guru is there inside us. When we question ourselves, it is Guru who, remaining as conscience and our Atman, imparts answers to us from within. Guru is everywhere. When you feel that Guru is inside you, true knowledge will come from within. Guru can assume physical form and impart knowledge. Guru can also remain in invisible state and impart knowledge to you all. He, who realises Guru, gets total knowledge.

I (Sadguru Sri Sri Arjun) have come to this stage by the knowledge I got from my Guru Socrates. Even if I had not seen him, I was thinking that he is with me. By that I got knowledge from him. Even if he had died about 2500 years ago, I could get knowledge from him. I had not seen even his photograph. I saw his photo for the first time pasted on a wall on one of my friend's house. Guru's name was printed at the bottom of the photo. When I saw the photo of my Guru, tears rolled down my eyes.

God manifests as different Devas and bestows upon them various powers for our well-being. He, who knows this, will live happily. Even if we possess diamond but if we are ignorant about its use, it is like not having the diamond. Similarly, even if all Devas are there with us, since we do not know about them, we suffer. Like this, Guru is also there with us and in us.

The number of disciples is increasing day by day. Try to build an *ashram*. I will be sad if I see people do not get a place to sit when I come next time. Hence, donate money for the *ashram* for a suitable accommodation.

Still some of my disciples have not quit drinking habit. They must quit that otherwise Guru will be blamed. Stop drinking and make your family life a heavenly experience. Otherwise it will be hell. I have come for your happiness, bliss and freedom. There are many disciples in this village. I am happy with you all.

Divya Darshan is the simplest path. Most of the disciples have become good. They will go up in life. Those who cling to bad habits will go down. Divya Darshan is for self-development of one and all. The entire village should develop. Share your knowledge and experiences with others so that they also come to right track and develop.

Take care of Guru when he comes to you. Follow his instructions. All disciples are equal in the eyes of Guru. Serve your Guru or always remain alert to serve him when required. Last year when I came here, many people did not know me. This year the number of people knowing about Divya Darshan has increased, and you have all taken greater care of me. If any disciple goes on a wrong path, try to correct him. Guru will be blamed for the wrongdoings of any disciple. A father reprimands his children in order to bring them to the right track. It is because the father loves his children and wishes for their well-being.

Everyone must try for the development of Divya Darshan. Do not be too elated or too depressed while encountering different situations, favourable or unfavourable. I know that you have spent some money for organizing some functions. Do not worry for that. You will get good results for that. Go on spreading the message of Divya Darshan.

Try to circulate the literature of Divya Darshan more and more among others. Amritbindu is a small booklet but it contains the messages of Satya-Loka. It is a treasure house of knowledge. It contains all essential points that will help the reader enhance his inquisitiveness and ensure self-development. I wish the disciples take all my knowledge and utilize that knowledge for the self-development of the people at large. I will be happy to see changes taking place among the people.

❧＊❧

[73]What I have realised is all by His grace only. While speaking about God no particular form should be attributed to Him. It will suffice if you know Him as 'Om'. Spread the message of Truth. To get His grace you have to possess divine virtues. You should also talk to the people about the importance of divine virtues. In Amritbindu, it is mentioned that Truth is peace; truth is bliss and the basis of liberation. The more you know how truth is present everywhere and in everything, the more shall you be benefited. Never discriminate between high and low; never entertain the feeling of casteism.

Always be humble. By this you would become more powerful. Muster up more power and become more powerful. Always remember that only by truth and love, it has been possible to uphold this Creation.

You should always think that Ishta Mantra is your Guru who is always there in you. By Ishta Mantra you can get everything. I tell you repeatedly to spread the message of Divya Darshan far and wide as soon as possible. Educated mass may better understand the philosophical import and truth of my preaching. Even when I would not be available in gross form, I would be always with you in my subtle form of knowledge. Whatever you would wish for, you would get for sure. Those, who are engaged in building *ashrams*, should continue the same with greater vigour. Their sacrifice and labour shall not go in vain. All their virtuous deeds are preserved in the

---

73 Oriya Divya Dhara Vol 8 Page 30

kingdom of God and good results are in store for them. Remember that by knowing, upholding and adoring truth, you can one day realise the Supreme Truth. You are born for this purpose. Even after I relinquish my gross body, you should continue with your good deeds for the sake of Divya Darshan. The whole world is looking for this knowledge. You must understand that you are born for the purpose of disseminating true knowledge as propounded in the form of Divya Darshan. Remember that without self-knowledge there is no peace. Self is Peace-Absolute. He, who realises Him, shall get peace. Hence, make spiritual efforts to know Paramatman. Many obstacles may come on your way. These obstacles are also His lila. Once you know this, you would not break down.

Truth is there in you. Therefore, search for truth inside. You may end up with frustration if you search for Him outside. Bliss is well inside you.

I have come to do good to to mankind by imparting true knowledge. You will do the rest. All powers are within you. Do never forget that I am always there in you. I am there and shall be there. Body or no body, it is immaterial. I am not sad for myself. I am sad for you all. I am neither happy nor unhappy. I am beyond; I am free from all dualities.

Truth triumphs always. Everyone is entitled to attain peace and bliss one day or other. Never get disheartened. It is difficult to realise Truth. But if you have strong inquisitiveness, you would definitely attain. Divya Darshan is inside you.

Earning money is not a sin. But it is a sin not to utilise money for noble purposes. Earn money and do service to the people. Many people do not have clear concepts about how to earn money and how to spend.

Every disciple should contribute a handful of rice for the purpose of *ashram.* Do not pressurise them who are financially weak. Contribution to *ashram* may be in any form. Always try to give free teaching of Divya Darshan. Free tuition is the best way to impart true knowledge. Spiritual knowledge is true knowledge. Without true knowledge spiritual knowledge is incomplete. Make efforts to impart true knowledge in schools and colleges.

Always try to be self-dependent. All spiritual seekers irrespective of their caste or creed belong to spiritual community. Everyone of you should try to articulate your knowledge and experience so that the message of Divya Darshan can spread faster and in a more effective manner.

Unity is your base; stay united.

ღ⭑ღ

[74]The sages, to maintain discipline among the growing disciples and make them walk on a goal oriented and right path of spiritual journey, had created the concept of 'Sangha'. By a purposeful living, efficiency level would increase and a lot of work can be done. Sangha should get registered. By Sangha, the members can be benefited; the society can also be benefited. If we are organized, not only we can move on our path with greater strength, the society shall be strengthened and can move on towards greater peace and happiness. Sangha has a permanent existence. Even after the world gets transformed, the words of truth shall always remain. Sangha should be strong so that it can cross obstacles and move ahead for attainment of common goal. Therefore, the sages have attached so much importance to Sangha. By working for the Sangha, you would earn peace and happiness along with virtues. The society would also be benefited in the process. Man does not carry anything with him while he departs except virtues. Virtues are our real assets here and hereafter, invisible though. By dint of your virtues, you would earn blessings from the godheads.

By your sacrifices you earn virtues which are hidden assets for your future life. All of you should try to accumulate virtues. By remaining united and doing works or making sacrifices for the Sangha, you would earn virtues. To live in the society, everyone requires to be helped by others. He, who knows the importance of sacrifice, would be ready to sacrifice for others. Sacrifice is a divine quality. When the Sangha convenes periodic meetings for deliberations on special programmes and various organizational issues, the members should participate and put forth their ideas. It is also a

---

74 Oriya Divya Dhara Vol 8 Page 33

virtuous deed to sacrifice time for Sangha even at the cost of domestic works. Those, who sacrifice time, labour and money for the Sangha, are fortunate because the godheads become pleased with them and bless them. We know that due to virtues earned by us, we go to heaven. By committing sins, we shall be consigned to hell. In other words, virtues yield us peace and happiness while vices bring us misery. It is said that ignorance is a great sin. He, who never ponders over what virtue is and what vice is, commits sin only. To think over self-development is a divine quality. A person, who is not trying for self-development, is a sinner even though he does not have any other vice. Hence to get rid of sins, it is necessary to get organized in Sangha. Many people keep themselves away from Sangha when the question of some contribution arises. The wise people keep on consciously and instinctively acquiring virtues. There are many who feel proud with their wrongdoings or vices. The conscientious people become happy to earn virtues. Every moment we earn either virtue or sin. In the scriptures, there is mention about Deva-yan and Pitru-yan. The virtuous go to higher lokas by Deva-yan and get peace and happiness while others go by Pitru-yan and get sufferings. Hence the sages and seers always caution us to remain away from sins and to consciously keep on earning virtues. Sins bring sufferings. Therefore, everyone should honour the guidelines of Sangha to move on the right track and earn virtues. By doing so, you would earn virtues and simultaneously earn divine blessings. You would be rewarded with peace, happiness and bliss. Sangha should be protected at the cost of personal sufferings. By your sacrifices, if others are benefited, it is a virtue. History shows that many kings and emperors sacrificed their lives for the sake of their kingdoms. Many sacrificed their lives in the independence movement for the safety and sovereignty of our nation. Their names are remembered even today. Only the wise and conscientious realise the importance of sacrifice for others. Sacrifice is always bigger than only financial contribution. Your deeds of sacrifices would spread very soon far and wide while your financial help may not even be known to your neighbours.

In a Sangha the members draw inspiration from each other. You would proceed on the path of self-development. At times, you quarrel with others and stop talking to them. But a wise or realised soul is ever ready to fall at the feet of other great persons. Those, who are in illusion, are committing sins and are bound to suffer. When I tell you all to stay organized, I do not talk only about any institution or nation. It also includes a family. If everyone would remain conscious of earning punya or acquiring virtues, the home would be transformed to heaven. Even two persons may form a Sangha. The aim is to earn punya. Lord Buddhadev had realised this truth and therefore he reiterated the importance of Sangha by preaching, "Sangham Sharanam Gachchhami".

Your attitude should be, to be on the right track to move straight for self-development. The ignorant men cannot understand this. Do not be lax in the matters of earning virtues and walking on the path of Dharma. It is the attitude of renunciation that earns for us virtues fast. One should fear sins. Therefore, consciously refrain yourselves from sins. I trust that you would stay organized in the Sangha by which you can proceed on the path of self-development faster along with the development of the society. My blessings are always with you.

༒

[75]*(On 1ˢᵗ of January 1989, Sadguru Sri Sri Arjun had laid the foundation stone of Divya Darshan ashram at Antarjholi (Near Gunupur, Odisha) and had addressed the gathering. A brief extract is given below)*

We have heard that people of Satya Yug used to live in peace and happiness. There was no theft or burglary. People were adhering to justice and fairness. They were observing the principles of Dharma. But now in Kali Yug, the way of living of the people is almost opposite. It is said that after Kali Yug, Satya Yug would come. Now it is the peak of Kali Yug. There are instances of unfair and unjust way of living style of the people. There are frequent occurrences of cheating, theft, deceit, cruelty, arrogance and exploitation. Man seems to seek pleasure from inflicting pain on others. Divya Darshan's mission is that everyone should live in peace and happiness.

---

75 Oriya Divya Dhara Vol 6 Page 24

Everyday temples, mosques and churches are being built. The number of devotees is on the rise. Paradoxically, instead of peace and happiness, suffering is on the rise. Instead of facing light people are facing towards darkness. Everyone should ponder over this. After Satya Yug, true knowledge has been undergoing a declining trend. Hence now-a-days, there is acute crisis of absence of true knowledge. Earlier kings and emperors were patronising the *ashrams* but now-a-days, there are very few *ashrams* left for imparting true knowledge. We have distanced ourselves from true knowledge and almost lost our great heritage. The sages and seers in olden days were imparting true knowledge. The present-day education is altogether different. There is no teaching on character building and ethical values. There is no teaching on the goal of human life or any discussion about true knowledge or even about how to get peace and happiness. Accumulating material wealth with narrow selfishness is given top priority. Many people resort to Dharma only for fulfilment of their desires.

If man acquires true knowledge, he can live in peace and happiness. Satya Yug will come again. We have heard that telling lie is a sin. But we are not aware of the actual implications of sin because of which we go on committing sins without hesitation. We always seek happiness but we do not know the source of peace and bliss. How shall we get freedom from sin?

If we make regular arrangement for dissemination of true knowledge, our children would also acquire the same. If we do not make a congenial climate now, how can our children evince interest in true knowledge? We must be good. If our neighbour is not in peace and happiness, we would also be disturbed. If any thief is there in the neighbourhood, we would be afraid to sleep peacefully at night. Hence, people in the neighbourhood should also be good. If we clamour for Satya Yug but conduct ourselves like demons, Satya Yug will not come. When more and more people will take to the path of truth, Satya Yug shall come.

Ashrams are temples of wisdom. If more and more *ashrams* come up and disseminate true knowledge, the society will have more saints and sages who would impart knowledge about peace and happiness.

Can the deities in the temples give us true knowledge? We worship different deities only to fulfil our diversified desires. By that, our desires shall increase which would bring us more sufferings. But *ashrams* would give us true knowledge. It is seen that people come forward to donate for temples and not for *ashrams*. They are under the impression that by donating to temples, the deities would be propitiated and shall promptly fulfil their desires. They believe that their offerings shall return to them manifold.

But knowledge received from *ashrams* shall make us more knowledgeable, courageous and powerful. By knowledge we can ultimately free ourselves from the worldly bondages. By knowledge we can discriminate between truth and falsehood; good and bad. Hence dissemination of knowledge is the best option. More and more saints, sages and wise men would come out who in turn shall impart true knowledge to the society and the world shall be benefited. *Ashram* is for dissemination of knowledge which is invaluable. Those, who patronise the *ashrams*, are virtuous indeed. They multiply their virtues by supporting the *ashrams*. *Ashram* is a light house that would keep on showing light to others. We must establish *ashrams*. We must set things right in our homes. By building *ashrams*, we can repay the debts owed to the sages or rishis. We must spread the knowledge of truth, justice and divine virtues. Then only Satya Yug would be back. Remember Divya Darshan is God's Will, Law and Light.

❧✦❧

[76]Ignorance reigns supreme in all spheres. Incidents involving greed, ego, pride, jealousy, cruelty, vengeance etc. raise their ugly hoods every now and then almost everywhere. Most of the people have distanced themselves from Truth. In this scenario, right knowledge or spiritual knowledge is the only panacea that can heal the ailments caused by ignorance and bring in peace to the society. While imparting spiritual knowledge, one must carefully observe the standard of the recipients. The knowledge that is imparted should be quite simple to touch their hearts and inspire them to walk on righteous path. To explain the true knowledge lot of patience,

---

76 Oriya Divya Dhara Vol 12 Page 58

courage and depth of knowledge is required. He, who is knowledgeable and virtuous, can present Divya Darshan precisely. I (Sadguru Sri Sri Arjun) bless you all. May you all shine with Gurushakti. You are Vyasa of the present time. Let all powers of Vyasa be there in you. All disciples should respect the senior disciples, who are engaged in spreading Divya Darshan. Senior members are more knowledgeable and experienced who are at the helm of affairs of the Sangha. If the members support the senior disciples, they will feel emboldened and encouraged to do Divya Darshan works faster and in a more effective manner.

You have all learnt something about Divya Darshan. It is a great and befitting spiritual philosophy that paves the way to peace, bliss and liberation. Divya Darshan is God's Will. Divya Darshan spreads true knowledge and divine virtues aiming at bringing Satya Yug on this Earth. No doubt, it is a great challenge for the Sangha. During this three days' programme, different aspects will be discussed about the existence of God and His greatness. Discussions will also be there on the Law of Eternity or Sanatana Dharma, Truth, Consciousness, ignorance, Knowledge, divine virtues and spiritual practice. You will very clearly understand the importance of the journey of human life and its goal. You will know about your duty and righteousness that will lead you to your goal of self-realisation. I urge upon everybody present here to listen to the discourses with rapt attention. In a spiritual congregation of this nature, you should not leave your seats and move here and there unless it is very urgent. Discipline is of utmost importance to become a good disciple. Any sort of indiscipline in a jnana yajna is nothing less than a sin. Try to disseminate to others the knowledge you gather from here. Let others in the society be benefited.

You have all sacrificed your time and money to be here continuously for three days. This attitude should remain with you always. It is a great opportunity for you to listen to series of discourses at a stretch for three days. You can spread this knowledge in the society for its betterment. May the Almighty give you enough strength and courage to march ahead with the banner of Divya Darshan to create awareness in the society about true knowledge and divine virtues, and welcome Satya Yug. My blessings are always with you. I am always there with you. Never forget this. Go forward.

A small booklet containing the essence of Divya Darshan is just published. Each of you must procure a copy because Guru's words are power-packed. By retaining those words and repeatedly contemplating on them, the latent power in those words would be transmitted to a disciple.It is essential that you should remember Guru's sayings. If you forget Guru's teachings, how can you call yourself as disciples?

Before Divya Darshan was born, I had got by heart the sayings of some great men. Those sayings were continuously inspiring me as a result of which I could come to this stage. True knowledge is there in the sayings of great men. Truth remains hidden in those sentences. That truth must be welcomed, contemplated upon for total assimilation and illumination. This is the Law of Eternity. He, who follows the instructions of the sages or great men, observes true Dharma. Their teachings are for the benefit of the entire mankind. Those teachings must be received properly. They are enlightened souls. Hence, their teachings are based on their self-realisation. Truth or true knowledge is the essence of their teachings. Those are precious gems. He, who assimilates the true knowledge, enriches himself.

I got knowledge from my Guru's saying, "Ignorance is a great sin." I came to this stage because of my Guru's words which were deeply entrenched in me. You see, how much power is there in Guru's words! But due to ignorance we are apathetic towards the sayings of the sages as a result of which we are getting deprived of true knowledge. He, who understands and appreciates those sayings, becomes pure, great and powerful. Therefore, I am telling you to grasp everything that Divya Darshan preaches. Amritbindu contains inspiring sayings of Divya Darshan in a very compact manner. It is full of self-knowledge that coincides with the essence of all scriptures. If you try to understand those sayings, more power will come to you. Many more treasures are there in Divya Darshan which are yet to be published.

You are on your way to self-realisation. Always remember it. Unless you possess more and more power in you, you cannot reach the goal of self-realisation. In order to reach the destination, necessary preparations must be made for the journey. Since you are going to attain big things, you must keep yourself on your guard. During the journey, you may have pleasure and pain. You may not be able to imagine how much and what all are needed during this great journey. Guru is making all arrangements to enable you to reach your goal. There is power in Guru's words or instructions. If you properly assimilate the same, you will have more courage and inspiration that will help you reach the goal. Try to read Amritbindu regularly and understand the same. Guru will take care of the rest.

৩✦৩

[77]I am imparting true knowledge in a very simple but comprehensive manner that I have brought for you from Satya-Loka. The purpose is to enable you to easily attain self-knowledge or self-realisation. This is the simplest spiritual process. If you disown this, there is no other simpler way than this by which you can get rid of sufferings so quickly.

Divya Darshan is before you all with this purpose. In the past it was there. In future also it will reappear.

During my lifetime people cannot know me (Sadguru Sri Sri Arjun). People will come to know me after I leave this physical body. I am speaking about subtle subjects which are not easy to grasp. Hence people will not recognize me when I am alive. People could not recognize Jesus and Socrates during their lifetime. Those, who speak about gross world of matters, are accepted and adored very quickly. Gross subjects can be understood very quickly. They also demonstrate some miracles. But their teachings do not last long. It takes hundreds of years to understand and appreciate the subtle thoughts. The world needs peace, happiness and freedom now. Divya Darshan is showing the way to freedom. Divya Darshan does not speak only about God. Divya Darshan teaches man to free himself from the body consciousness. All have to be self-dependent. Only sitting and counting beads in the name of God will not help. When food will not be available, one may forget God. Therefore, you have to

---

77 Oriya Divya Dhara Vol 18 Page 63

work and at the same time acquire knowledge. You have to arouse the divine qualities from within.

⋯✳⋯

[78]In the primordial age, the people were living in caves. They did not know the use of light. Only during the daytime, they were getting light and heat from the Sun. Otherwise, there was darkness all over. They were hiding themselves in caves, which means they were living in darkness. We are living now in the darkness of ignorance. We are seeing the Creation, but we are not able to see the Creator. We are seeing our shadows but not the Self.

Someone from the crowd comes out of darkness and having seen the light shows us light. But without knowing the Truth, we see the illusory forms and believe them as Truth. We should search for the Truth. He, who realises Truth, is wise. He is Sadguru who has come out of the darkness of ignorance and makes us realise the light of Truth.

I was also ignorant one day. By my past impulses and Guru's grace I realised the Truth. Some people misunderstood me. It is quite natural for them to misunderstand because they did not know the Truth. Socrates, Jesus, Dayanand and many others were misunderstood and were killed. People living in ignorance cannot understand the greatness of knowledge and Truth. The ego of the ignorant men stands in the way to knowledge and Truth. That is why the sages say that those who have not surrendered to Guru cannot get higher knowledge or Truth. Sadguru shows us the path of righteousness and inspires us to move forward. He lives ordinary life as we do. He moves with us and wears normal dress as we do. He loves everyone. He has come to save us and lead us to our eternal abode. We should follow his instructions.

I have come to serve you all. I have come to live up to God's Will. I enjoy doing that. Freedom is not a small achievement. It is the goal of every human being. There remains no doubt or fear there. I trust you will all

---

78   Oriya Divya Dhara Vol 19 Page 18

make spiritual efforts and work sincerely for self-development. My good wishes are always with you.

ᏬᎨ✦ᏭᎧ

[79] Today (18th July, 1985), I am going to tell you something on my 53rd Birthday. I have come to impart right knowledge through Divya Darshan. Lot of teachings are there in the scriptures on Dharma, Artha, Kama and Moksa. Moksa or Nirvana is the goal. Some seekers go to the forests or some secluded places to carry out their sadhana. Some seekers remain in the society with family and do their duties and observe Dharma to get liberation. Dharma is a precursor of Moksa. Unless it is known clearly what Dharma is, it is not possible to observe the same correctly. Unless Dharma is observed properly, it is impossible to attain Moksa. Moksa cannot be an outcome of any ritual.

Divya Darshan says that in order to attain Moksa, it is not necessary to renounce the home and family. In the first verse of Ishavasya Upanishad, the sage has spoken about fulfilment by renunciation. According to this Upanishad, whatever we come across in this Creation belongs to God. God pervades everywhere and in everything. Nothing is yours. The five elements such as earth, water, fire, air and space belong to God. The sage says, "Enjoy everything but do never forget that everything belongs to the Almighty. Think that God has given you all these things for your survival and happiness. Therefore, do not eye on someone's property. Greed for anything is a sin."

The above-mentioned verse of the Upanishad succinctly teaches us how to live in the world in a detached way, considering everything as God's property. Nothing belongs to us.

The sages were living with non-attachment. Everyone should try to find out the paths which the sages or spiritual masters had treaded on to cross the worldly bondages to attain the highest state. The seekers should seek guidance from them and follow their instructions sincerely.

---

79   Oriya Divya Dhara Vol 18 Page 12

Lord Buddhadev has spoken about four truths to get rid of sufferings.

- ❖ There is suffering.

- ❖ There is a cause of suffering.

- ❖ Suffering has come; it must go.

- ❖ If the cause of suffering is known, its eradication is possible. It will go away. In other words, in a specific situation, suffering has come. In a different situation, it will go away.

Sadguru is Truth-Absolute. He, who takes shelter of Sadguru, will slowly be free from defects. Complete surrender is essential for the purpose. Then only Gurushakti will be transmitted to the disciple. Those who have complete faith on Guru will get His blessings. But it is unfortunate that there are many persons who are unwilling to acquire true knowledge. Then how will it be possible to cross the worldly bondages and attain liberation? Those who have not surrendered to God or Guru will continue to suffer.

"Dhammam sharanam gachchhami"; Thus, Lord Buddhadev was laying stress on Dharma in his teachings. Divya Darshan says, "Surrender to Dharma. Take shelter of Dharma. Dharma protects us; Dharma nourishes us; Dharma brings us peace and bliss." It is therefore necessary to know what Dharma is and how to take resort to Dharma.

If we do not steal, we will not be punished. If someone commits any mistake or sin, we ask him to feel sorry or beg excuse. God is kind. He will finally dispense justice to us. By committing sins, we suffer and move downward. By doing noble deeds, we earn punya, get peace and bliss, and move upward. Dharma is the only path that leads to the goal of Moksa or liberation. Everyone must take recourse to Dharma. But who will give us knowledge about Dharma and its observance?

God is Truth-Absolute. He is the Truth of truths. He is the Supreme Truth. But in the Creation, changes are always going on. Jagat itself is a product of change. Hence, according to Divya Darshan, Jagat is a partial truth. There is a Creator who has brought Jagat into existence. Everything has a previous state. For example, there was sugar cane before sugar was produced.

The man had also some previous state. Man has come from Brahman and shall go back to Brahman. Man should take shelter of Truth and Dharma to go back to Brahman. First, he must try to become Deva. Finally, he will realise Brahman.

I bless you all. Take shelter of Satya and Dharma. I have come with that purpose. My purpose will be fulfilled if you follow my teachings. You should try to progress on the path of self-development. Try to understand God's will and do good to the world.

☙ ★ ❧

[80]In earlier occasions, I have told you the purpose of my birth. We all want peace and happiness. But in turn we get sufferings. This indicates that we do not possess knowledge about how to get happiness and peace. We undertake different kinds of activities with a view to getting happiness. But the result is unwanted suffering. What may be the reasons? Where are our defects? It is true that unless we have knowledge about a thing sought after, we cannot get that. The sages descend on the Earth only to teach about how to get peace, bliss and freedom. Peace, divine bliss and freedom are the birthright of everybody. For attaining this, one must take shelter of Sadguru and take instructions from Him. Unless one attains the state of happiness or peace, how can one attain blissful state?

It is a matter of pride for us that God has descended as Sadguru in order to impart spiritual knowledge to mankind that will enable everybody to get rid of all sufferings and get peace, bliss and freedom. It is quite embarrassing for me to speak about myself. I am happy that by arranging Satsang on this occasion, you will get inspiration and courage to go for attainment of Truth. If you go through Amritbindu, you will find clues by which any householder can peacefully and harmoniously live in the society and do spiritual practices for attainment of the goal i.e. Moksa. In my childhood, I used to say, "Vanquish all fears of the world." I had not collected this above statement from anybody nor read it from any book; the above statement automatically reverberated in me. Those, who consider anything

---

80   Oriya Divya Dhara Vol 18 Page 17

as impossible, have not even reached the first step of knowledge. The sages never die. They are always there. Their teachings have been inspiring and guiding us for our individual, social and spiritual progress.

There are certain feelings which are not to be articulated publicly but still I must say that I shall be residing as the 'Self' of the disciples even after I relinquish this physical body. I shall be ensuring your self-development and guiding you to the goal. That divine power has descended in human form as Guru. He is eternally there everywhere. The spiritual seekers should never take Gurushakti lightly. He, who maintains regular relationship with Gurushakti with faith, devotion and love, shall attain liberation. One must surrender to Guru.

I have come with this purpose. Whether you recognize me as Guru or not, it matters not. Parents, however big they may be, keep on serving their children. I have come to serve you all. Whether you take my service or not, I will be serving you all.

જ⋆ଓ

Theory of Rebirth

[81]**The subtle body:** Inside the gross body of the jiva there is a subtle body. The subtle body is called *jivatma*. The subtle body is invisible. The subtle body contemplates; experiences pleasure and pain, peace and happiness etc. It also tries for fulfilment of desires. It should be remembered that there is not only a subtle body inside the gross body, there is also a causal body and inside causal body there is Supra-Causal body. The subtle body is constituted of 18 principles such as- Intellect (Buddhi, the discriminative or determinative faculty), Mind, Ego (Ahamkar), five *Tanmatras* (*shabda, sparsha, rupa, rasa, gandha*), five sense organs (ear, skin, eye, tongue and nose) and five organs of action (*Vak, Pani, Pada, Payuu and Upastha*).

The subtle body acts through the gross body and strives to fulfil its desires or achieve its goal. The gross body is regulated by the subtle body, subtle body by the causal body and the causal body by the Supra-Causal body. Supra-Causal being is named as Brahman. Brahman exists in unmanifest state without any form. Therefore no qualities or forms are attributed to Him. He is attributeless and formless. Example of how subtle body acts in the background of gross body is cited below.

I am writing this. Who is actually writing? The answer is – The subtle body. Writing is backed by some preceding thoughts. These preceding thoughts are expressed in form of writing.

Whose thoughts are these? The answer is – The subtle body. To translate the thoughts into writing, a physical body (hand) is used as an instrument. I am saying something. Who is saying this? The answer is – The subtle body. The physical body is converting the same to sound. Another example – Suppose I am reading a book. Who is reading and understanding? The answer is – The subtle body. Reading is done through the physical eyes whereas understanding happens by mind which is a part of the subtle body.

Likewise, the subtle body experiences all sorrows and sufferings, all happiness and fears, all peace and bliss which come as the consequences of our past actions. But all works are done through the physical body. It may be mentioned here that a physical body which is composed of five gross elements gets decomposed easily whereas the subtle body does not get decomposed so easily. Actually, the subtle body is the Jiva. Since Atman resides inside the subtle body, it is called *jivatma*. After the physical body is destroyed, the subtle body that remains is called *pretatma* or the spirit. The subtle body possesses all knowledge and experiences gathered throughout the past life. The subtle body enjoys the fruits of all his actions while in the physical body and also after it gets separated from the physical body. In other words, after the *jivatma* leaves the physical body and becomes *pretatma*, it is bound to experience pleasure and pain, fears and anxieties etc. The subtle body in *pretatma* stage also can see its parents, brothers, sisters, wife, children, friends and relatives. It is because in the subtle body all faculties such as intellect, mind, senses and *tanmatras* are present and active. Many people disbelieve the subtle body (*pretatma*) and its existence, mainly because it is invisible. People also disbelieve the existence of Atman. People accept that it is the physical body that does all activities. They are under an erroneous notion that after a person dies, nothing remains as subtle body or *pretatma*. (This 'nothing remains' is definitely an unscientific idea)

The gross body has form. Since it is made of 5 gross elements such as earth, water, fire, air and space, it is subjected to hunger, thirst, excretion etc. But the subtle body is different. There are no such five gross elements in the subtle body. In a sense, the subtle body is therefore more powerful than the gross body. A subtle body need not have to take food or drink. It need not excrete. Since *jivatma* is worried about food, drink and many other necessaries, it remains restless and his mind as well as intellect gets puzzled more often. But the mind of *pretatma* is free from all these worries and anxieties. A *pretatma* has greater concentration power. The will power of a *pretatma* is stronger than that of a *jivatma*. But a *pretatma* carries many unfulfilled desires. Even as a *pretatma*, he or she remains attached to the family left behind. A *pretatma* in most cases wills to get back to its place through rebirth. It is a fact that *pretatma* exists. What is called *jivatma* here in the physical body is called *pretatma* after death of physical body.

We shall discuss here how a *pretatma* is keen to keep touch with samsar. There are mainly three types of *pretatma*s.

- ❖ The first type is sattvic in nature. They possess divine virtues; they follow the path of righteousness.

- ❖ The second type is rajasic in nature; they are like ordinary human beings living in samsar with some kind of devotion to God to get good results from Him.

- ❖ The third type is tamasic by nature; they are cruel, arrogant, lustful, infatuated and greedy etc. In other words, they possess demoniac qualities.

Sattvic and tamasic *pretatma* can take different forms by its will power. But Rajasic *pretatma* generally takes the help of the physical bodies of others to fulfil its desires. However, a *pretatma* of sattvic and tamasic categories can enter into others' bodies very fast but occasionally. Now a question may be raised as to why the sattvic or tamasic *pretatma* seems to be more powerful. The sattvic *pretatma* is on the virtuous path. The *pretatma* belonging to this category is empowered by divine qualities. Therefore, it can take different forms as and when needed. We might have read in various mythologies that the demons were assuming various forms. They are besieged with negative qualities such as- lust, greed, cruelty etc. They acquire different types of powers based on mantra and tantra. Their will power, although in opposite direction, is also strong. Therefore, in order to satisfy their desires, to take revenge on others or to find sadistic pleasure, they assume different deceptive forms. Only by will power, all these things become possible.

We experience different kinds of dreams. The body at that time lies on the bed. The question here is- Who was seeing the dream? The answer is- the subtle body.

This indicates that the *jivatma* or the subtle body is different from the physical body. By yoga practices also this can be experienced well. In the state of *samadhi*, the yogi gets delinked from the body. In our day to day life also, we may observe that when we get engrossed in some thoughts, we lose body consciousness. At that time we are not aware whether we are sitting or walking. All these prove that the *jivatma* is different from the body. Due to the presence of the subtle body the physical body gets activated. Even from the life of Jagadguru Sri Shankaracharya, it is learnt that his subtle body had entered into a king's physical body. After remaining there for a few days, he left the king's physical body and re-entered his own physical body. In the Yoga science as well as Tantra science, mention is made about assuming other forms.

Ayurveda which forms a part of Atharva Veda also admits of Preta-tattva. Preta treatment is also a part of Ayurvedic treatment. Tantra also includes preta-tattva. Tantra deals in supersensuous knowledge which means things happen beyond the realm of our sense organs. Hence people disbelieve and also are afraid of tantra. Mantra is a part of Tantra science. However, the Tantra science of good olden days has been diluted or distorted in course of time and has almost lost its pristine glory. That is why many people are averse to tantra now-a-days. Tantra shastra, in fact, is a superior science.

Since many do not know about the nature of the preta (spirit), if any patient becomes delirious and talks in an incoherent manner, people approach a tantrik who at times creates a fuss. He even thrashes and whips the patient with fearsome poses and postures. Instead of curing, more often he makes the patient's condition worse. Preta or spirit exists in a different realm subtler than this physical world we live in. Unless proper study is made on physical science, Tantra and Ayurveda, it shall be difficult to know whether the patient is facing problem due to a spirit or due to any other physical ailment. The more someone goes deeper and deeper, the more will he be able to understand that behind the world of matters and the world of spirits, there is another Supreme Power called Brahman or Atman whose existence is transcendental.

ೞ⋆ೞ

[82]To get this human form we have passed through innumerable stages of the process of creation. It is altogether a different form without any resemblance with the earlier forms we had possessed. In the stage of nebula, there was no formation of the Earth we live in now. But after we were born on the Earth, we could see the Earth. Lot of changes have occurred in the Earth since its inception. We are now seeing innumerable plants, birds and animals of different shapes and sizes. Birth or creation precedes evolution; evolution precedes birth or creation. There is a continuous chain of transformations. Rebirth, being a product of this process, occurs just as birth occurs.

Rebirth: Rebirth implies birth after death. The sages of India so emphatically and convincingly expounded the theory of rebirth. The theory of rebirth is an important part of the Indian Philosophy. The ancient sages of India had taught to the mankind right knowledge on Truth and Dharma, observance of which can ensure a righteous living and release from the shackle of ignorance to attain the supreme goal of life which is liberation where there is no worry and uncertainty, no doubt and desperation, no sorrow or suffering. Rebirth implies continuation of life beyond death till the goal is attained. Even after the physical body ceases to exist, the subtle body continues to be driven by the Law of Eternity. The undying consciousness continues its journey to become one with the Pure Consciousness. Without self-knowledge, the theory of rebirth cannot be comprehended. Without rebirth, knowledge and Dharma will not find its true and complete expression. Only the sages understand what rebirth is and how it occurs. Common people cannot easily understand this.

Changes are always there in the Creation. Forms are getting changed. That is why we come across new forms or appearances. Everything was pre-existing. No existence has come out of non-existence. Let us take

---

82 Oriya Divya Dhara Vol 18 Page 31

the example of water. Water particles are so tiny that they mingle and move with air. Water particles are not visible to an ordinary eye. They form vapour or cloud when they get condensed. Further condensation makes water droplets. Water becomes visible, so also ice. There are thus so many states of water. Their previous birth was Hydrogen or Oxygen. It can be well imagined through how many stages things are processed to form ice. The ice, in order to go back to its previous state, must become vapour. This means lot of actions and interactions for transition from the visible to the invisible and from the invisible to the visible are always going on in this Creation as a result of which we come across multifarious changed forms and changed qualities involving repetitive births and deaths.

Let us take the example of a tree. It was there as a seed. It became a seedling. Thereafter its trunk along with branches gradually grew with leaves, flowers and fruits. Again, the seed remained in the fruit. You can well imagine how many stages it has passed through to become a seed.

Take the case of a candle. When it burns, we get light, some smoke, which mingles with air and becomes invisible thereafter. After some time, the candle gets burnt and there remains no candle. In fact, nothing has been destroyed. Everything has been converted from the gross to the subtle. The candle gets converted to fire, smoke or carbon di-oxide. The previous birth of smoke is fire. The previous birth of fire is the candle. At every stage the form is different; so also, the quality. This shows that everything has a previous birth as well as a subsequent birth.

Nothing gets destroyed. Matter is converted to energy and energy to matter. When we can not see the form and quality, we call it death. When we come across certain form and quality for the first time, we call it birth. In the process of conversion of matter to energy and energy to matter, we experience multifarious objects with different qualities.

Every living being passes through three stages namely, childhood, youth and old age. The appearances and qualities differ from one stage to other. The same person exists in the body which is passing through different stages. Death is the destruction of the physical body. The jiva inside does not die but takes another form. The jiva relinquishes its physical body and gets another which is new. That is called birth. Thereafter, incessant changes happen till the goal of liberation is attained.

೮<del>ᵉ</del>✦೮

[83]What happens after death? Where has one come from? Where will he go after death? People do not know the answers clearly. But it is a fact that the person who died will be born again. He, who is there now, shall also remain in future, but in different form.

The sky was clear. Some changes occurred in the atmosphere. Cloud was formed and then we saw cloud in the sky. Cloud was there before we could see it. It was there in subtle state, in the form of vapour or water. In certain conditions, cloud is formed and becomes visible. It is just a transformation from the subtle to the gross, from the invisible to the visible state. There is no question of any birth or death here in case of cloud. Similarly, when a jiva quits the physical body, it remains in its subtle form. Likewise, the subtle form also takes a gross form under certain conditions. Anything that is present now shall also exist in future through transformation. Birth and death are only passing phases like the invisible becoming visible and the visible becoming invisible. Only changes occur from one state to the other. When a jiva undergoes the so-called death, it leaves the physical body and remains as a subtle body which is called a spirit. When the subtle body again assumes a physical body, we call it birth. Those who have earned virtues in their lifetime, move higher to the region of light and those who have committed vices, go to the region of darkness. Those, who are inclined Godward and possess divine qualities, are virtuous. In the puranas, descriptions are there about heaven and hell. The sinners go to the hell whereas the virtuous go to the heaven.

According to Divya Darshan, the fruits of actions are enjoyed by the *jivatma* in the physical body and thereafter by the *pretatma* in the subtle body. To experience the remaining fruits of his earlier actions,

---

83 Oriya Divya Dhara Vol 16 Page 33

he is born again on the Earth according to the law of nature. When a person dies, some of his desires remain unfulfilled. He comes back to the world again with his carried over desires. Thus, he is born again and again.

It is Ishwar who awards the fruits of actions according to the Law of Action. He also creates favourable and unfavourable environments, pleasant and unpleasant situations for different persons for enjoyment and suffering corresponding to the fruits of their actions. There is no certainty that a human will be born again as a human. According to the amount of sin one has accumulated, one may be born as an animal or any other lower creature. Similarly, by the strength of virtues one may be given human birth. Now the question is – "How the subtle body enters a specific womb?" A subtle body may be remaining in Pitru-Loka or Deva- Loka. It may come to the Earth through rainwater, enter any plant, any fruit or leaf etc. When the fruit or leaf is eaten by an animal or human being, food is converted as blood and then to seminal fluid. During the process of union, it enters the pre-determined womb. As it appears, it is an overly complex and unpredictable process that happens by the law of nature. There are several ways through which a subtle body can enter a womb and is thereafter born as someone's son or daughter.

You have come alone and shall return alone. You are here to enjoy the fruits of your actions. Similarly, your wife and children have also come here and joined you to reap their fruits of actions. The fruits are not interchangeable. Therefore, never choose any wrong path for the sake of your family. Refrain consciously from sins. Acquire as much virtues as possible in this birth itself. You can free yourself from all bondages and sufferings in this birth if you acquire right knowledge and conduct yourself accordingly. It is always advisable to approach a Sadguru for true knowledge and correcting yourself. Knowledge is an immensely powerful instrument by which all sins will vanish. All bondages and sufferings will go away. You will attain absolute peace, bliss and freedom.

⋄✳⋄

Pretatma (spirits)

[84]Inside the gross body, there is a subtle body which is known as invisible spirit. After death, the gross body is destroyed but not the subtle body. Now we will discuss about what the subtle body does and how it remains. When the subtle body remains in a physical body we call it *jivatma*, man or animal etc. Without any physical body, this subtle body is called *pretatma*. In other words, the *jivatma* becomes *pretatma*. *Pretatma* in a physical body is called *jivatma*. The subtle body can enter another physical body. At that time, we say that a spirit has entered into the body.

This Creation is normally explained in four steps. The visible universe is gross and the other three steps are subtle. There are many invisible things in the subtle world. The subtle bodies remain in the subtle world. There are many a *pretatma* who remain unconscious after death for a long time even for months and years. Therefore, they even do not know that they are already dead. Such a *pretatma*, when it regains consciousness, starts remembering the past happenings just as, after we wake up from slumber, remember things and undertake our different priorities.

The subtle bodies would try to talk to us, but they are unable to speak out and we too cannot listen to them either. They may be thinking why we are not replying to them. Even though they may be standing near us we are unable to see them. They may be thinking whether we have become blind and deaf. The spirits also see that we are crying after their death even by calling their names. Then they feel, probably they have died. For many days and years, their attachment towards their physical bodies and their houses, families and children remain. That is why they would not leave their places years after their death. They would be carrying the desires for the good of the children, for example, education of children, marriage of daughter etc. Because of such attachment, they may take birth in the same house, relatives' families, or elsewhere according to the Law of Karma to reap the results of their past actions. There are some spirits who give some indications of their visits to our houses by way of some sound of utensils,

---

84   Oriya Divya Dhara Vol 10 Page 43

swinging of a hanging object or some other sounds. We do not welcome the visits of the spirits to our houses. If we get some indication of the presence of any spirit in our house, we call a Tantric who carries out different rituals to oust the spirit from our house. We also call by the name of the spirit and ask it to go out instead of disturbing. The spirit who has visited the house out of love and affection just to see its children, feels hurt by the hostile attitude of its own relatives. Thus, gradually the spirit loses interest in the family and quits. The spirit wanders hither and thither for fulfilment of its individual desires and aspirations. The spirit would continue to reap the results of its past actions. In due course, the spirit is bound to take birth in a different form in appropriate surroundings according to its past actions. Many spirits remain in *Preta-Loka* for long period i.e. for years. Once the subtle body is born in a physical form, it is no longer a preta or spirit. Family members also perform different rituals for the dead to get release from the preta state, but it is just a transfer from one type of bondage to another i.e. from the subtle state to the gross state. There is no liberation in either of the states. Whether subtle or gross, one remains in worldly bondage.

Some believe that one takes rebirth immediately after death. If it is so, then why do people perform rituals after death of their near and dear ones? Further, there would not have been any need for a *Preta-Loka*. According to one's karma, he gets into the Pitru-Loka or Deva-Loka. At the appropriate time, he is reborn. There are instances that some boys and girls narrate the details of their previous births. But not all remember their previous births.

Incidents happened in the morning are forgotten by the people in the evening or on the next day. There are people who suffer from diseases for a long time and stay bed ridden. Mainly due to old age and chronic diseases, memory power becomes feeble. Some of them are ignored and neglected by their family members resulting in dispassion. Such persons easily forget their past lives and past connections.

Some persons die young, may be due to accidents. Till death, they were quite active and had good memory power. They remain in Preta-Loka with all their memories about past lives. Some of them take rebirth after a short stay in Preta-Loka. Therefore, quite a small number of persons can remember their previous births.

Some spirits in order to express themselves, give vent to their feelings before their relatives by entering into the physical body of a living person. Normally people are afraid of the spirits. They call the tantric and perform rituals to drive the spirit out. For doing so even they torture the physical body. It is not desirable to torture anyone. By affectionate handling, the spirit would narrate details and give its identity also.

In the following paragraphs, some of the incidents that Sadguru Sri Sri Arjun had experienced are narrated.

Case no. 1

During those days I was working as a teacher in Kujendri High School (Near Gunupur, Koraput District). By that time I had completed two years of my married life. That day, it was 7 P.M., a dark evening. My wife and I were sitting in the backside of our courtyard. Suddenly there was a jingling sound. In that lonely place, on hearing such a sound, I became a little alert and could not just ignore the unexpected jingling sound. I asked my wife to go inside. She started bursting into laughter. Her gait, posture and talking style suddenly changed. I could know that some *pretatma* (spirit) has entered her body. I was having some herbal roots. On the touch of the roots, normally the spirit quits the body. But all of a sudden, she threw away the roots. I stood there well composed without anger or ill-feeling. I asked her, "Who are you? Why have you come here?"

She replied, "We were moving in this area and I just came here". After hearing the reply, I had a doubt. "Why is she speaking in plural terms?" I thought. I asked her, "Who else have come with you? Where are they?" She replied, "My mother-in-law and some friends went away that side. I took this side."

Question- Have you got a mother-in-law also? "Yes", she replied.

Question- When did your mother-in-law die; before you or after you?

She replied, "Before me".

"Probably like this, they live in family in the world of spirits," thus occurred to me.

I asked further, "How did you die?"

"During delivery time, I could not bear the pain. Hence I died. My husband did not arrange any medicine."

I thought to myself, after death also, she is carrying bitterness against her husband. How shall it go! Unless knowledge comes and ignorance is dispelled such type of ill-feeling would remain. In this world man nurtures ill-feelings due to ignorance and ego and suffers from that. In the other world also he suffers due to carry-over of such attitude and feelings. One thing is clear from this that the spirit has still link with the family or the society in which it lived earlier. The spirit carries all memories of its past life. Although we say that a person has died, it is clear that he or she has not died but changed the form. He/she was living earlier in the physical form and now also he/she is living with same knowledge, same temperament and same attitude although in ethereal body that is invisible. Therefore pain and pleasure continue here and hereafter depending upon the mind-set or level of knowledge. It is an ethical practice in many places not to go for re-marriage or to have a second wife. Because the first wife who is no more will be grieved in the other world after seeing her husband in love with someone else. This is also applicable for the woman who accepts a second husband. If the spirit continues to be saddled with such type of agony, anger and ill-feelings, the process of her self-development would not be possible. In such case, life after death becomes a hell. I asked, "Do you have any children?"

She told, "Yes".

Here in this case it should be remembered that the spirit had said, "Due to labour pain I died." If she had died, who is answering now? It is clear from this that the *jivatma* cannot die. The living is always living. Living being cannot die. Only form changes from the gross to the subtle and from subtle to the gross. Further I asked her, "What do you eat? Where do you stay?"

This *pretatma* was uneducated. She did not clearly tell about her food habits. She told, "We stay in lonely places, dilapidated houses or on the trees."

I asked, "Are you frightening people?"

She replied with tone modulation and dramatic gesticulations, "The people say that the ghosts have big eyes! They have so big heads!"

I told her lovingly, "No, No, so beautiful you look!"

I asked, "Can you appear in your form before me?"

She told, "Yes."

I became conscious. I immediately said, "OK, OK, afterwards you would show your own form."

She went on speaking very openly to me without reservation.

I told, "Will you daily come like this?"

She said, "Yes, I would come."

Afterwards she left my wife's body. My wife came back to her own senses subsequently. I was quite happy. I narrated this instance before some of my friends. The spirit had given word to come next day but she did not turn up. Some experienced persons told me that I should not have made the incident public. Afterwards, I went to her village and cross-checked her statements and all were found to be true.

About 35 years ago I had this long and open hearted dialogue with a spirit. I still remember her free, candid yet painful expressions about her family. I still love the way she shared her grief with me that day. When I think of her, tears roll out of my eyes seeing the level of her ignorance and the resultant sufferings she was undergoing. When would she be free from all these samsaric thoughts and start seeking her higher goal!

༄✦༄

Case no. 2

I recollect one more incident of super-imposition of a spirit. While I was on duty at Sunabeda, I got a message that a spirit has entered into a woman's body. I reached there and found that 4 to 5 persons had gathered there. The woman was crying and telling something. I asked her politely, "Wherefrom have you come?" She replied, "From Cuttack District." She also told her name. I asked, "What for have you come?" She replied, "To tell about my daughter." I could not understand anything from this. I asked the husband of the patient, "Whose name is she uttering? Do you know her?" He replied, "Yes Sir, she was my first wife."

I further asked the spirit, "What has happened to your daughter?"

She started sobbing more and more. She started, "My daughter is 9 year old. She is staying in my father's house. She is not fed well. She is not properly dressed also. My husband is living comfortably here. I could not tolerate the sufferings of my daughter. That is why I have come here to tell." She continued, "My legs are aching; feet are burning."

I asked her, "What happened, mother? Why pain?"

She was not able to speak properly due to tiredness. In a feeble voice she told, "I covered this long distance on foot." (The distance is about 500 Km from Cuttack to Sunabeda)

She was looking tired. Her husband standing nearby was looking guilty and ashamed. From his gestures one can understand very well that he had committed some wrong. He was also looking frightened lest the spirit (his first wife) should narrate more details. I asked for more details from her husband who affirmed that she was telling about his daughter who is staying away from him.

The spirit felt thirsty and asked for water. She further said that as she died of some disease, she was feeling thirsty. Water was given to her. I asked her husband about the cause of her death. Her husband replied that she had died of cholera. It is of common knowledge that cholera patients normally feel thirsty. The spirit now is feeling thirsty because she had died of cholera. I questioned the husband why he was not bringing his daughter to stay with him or not sending money there. Her husband promised to remit money to her daughter regularly. People present there were shouting, "Drive her out immediately."

I had sympathy with the spirit. She had come to tell about her daughter's sufferings. She had walked a long distance for that. She was in grief. How could I drive her out? The spirit asked for some tobacco mixture. It was given to her. Repeatedly she drank water. One hour had elapsed. I consoled her assuring that her husband would take care of her daughter from then onwards. I advised her to leave that body. I had to repeat my advice two or three times intermittently. Again she asked for some tobacco mixture which was given to her. She drank some water also. After moving a few yards, she fell down meaning thereby that she had left. Afterwards, there has been no such problem in that family. This happened at H.A.L. Township, Sunabeda. Likewise, there are some more experiences with the spirits who enter into the physical bodies of other persons. If a subtle body, as discussed above, can enter into another physical body to express itself, there is no wonder that it can also enter into an ovary and take rebirth. A person takes birth according to his desires and also the results of his past actions. There is no end to desires. By the time he dies, some of his desires still remain unfulfilled. A jiva goes on desiring something or other till his last moment. These residual desires are the driving force behind his onward rebirth. The results of his good deeds or bad deeds, virtues or vices are to be necessarily experienced by him; he assumes a different physical body and thus his identity gets changed. In reality, there is no such thing as death; it is only transmigration from one body to another. Disappearance is called death and reappearance is birth.

❧ ✳ ❧

Case no. 3

In yet another incident, during 1979, a married lady was waiting at Gurudev's quarters at A/64, Sunabeda to take initiation as she had some personal problems. While the process of initiation was going on, a *pretatma* which was residing in her body became active. Gurudev privately enquired from the relatives present there, who told that the *pretatma* was giving frequent troubles. Even she used to demand non-veg food regularly. It was clear that the *pretatma* was an evil spirit of tamasic nature. The lady who was actually taking initiation was by that time overwhelmed by the *pretatma*. The *pretatma* started telling her problems. "I entered into her body when this girl was five year old. Her uncle had sent me here. Since then I am residing in her body. She will not have any son of her own. If she will give me one of her daughters, I shall leave. For last eight years her husband has been trying to dislodge me through tantra etc."

Gurudev after listening to her gave some good advices. The *pretatma* agreed to quit on one condition. She told, "First you liberate me." Gurudev told her to chant "Jai Sadguru" and leave her body. But the spirit was unwilling to leave. She insisted on taking initiation and Ishta Mantra. She further told, "If I take initiation and get Ishta mantra, no tantric can utilise me for doing harm to others." After she was initiated by Gurudev she left. Gurudev subsequently gave initiation to the lady who had by that time regained her consciousness. The *pretatma* never came back.

⚜

Some questions and answers on rebirth:

Question- If a person takes rebirth after death, why everyone is not able to recollect his previous birth?

Answer- At the time of death, everyone's condition is not same. Some people suffer for long time and their memories become weak. Again in the subtle state he spends days and years. Thereafter in the mother's womb also in different situations and surroundings and on a stage to stage basis, it grows over a period of time. All past memories are lost in the process. The more the period of stay in *Preta-Loka*, the more is the loss of memory. Further if a child dies and takes rebirth, he also cannot say anything.

Question: Then which category of people can recollect their previous births?

Answer- Those who come back early to a particular place or parents, due to their strong will power, they can recollect. Those who die of accidents at young age, their memories remain fresh and due to will power again they may come back to the same house and recollect experience in their previous birth.

Question: Whether man takes rebirth always as a man or any other category?

Answer- Depending upon the degree of virtues and vices, past impressions and will power, man takes rebirth. Changes are going on every moment. Normally man is progressing or getting refined through births. Evolution takes effect due to this principle. The nature helps one to take him to the place wherefrom he has come. But due to bad tendencies or unfavourable situation, if somebody commits lapses, there are chances that he may be demoted. Again after some births he gets refined and comes back to the human birth. In this process, one day, he reaches the highest state. An example may be cited here. Due to negligence a student does not cope with the required standard and is detained in the same class. If he discontinues his efforts, he may forget what he had studied before. His standard goes down further to that of a still lower class student. He has to put in more efforts to make up his lost standard to get promoted to higher class. Due to indulgence in wrongdoings and vices also man moves downward until he corrects himself and reverses the trend.

As long as changes are there, there is Creation. As long as Creation is there, there would be changes. As long as changes are there, there are rebirths or repetitive births. The so called births and deaths are only the effects of changes that take place perpetually. If there are no changes, the question of Creation does not arise.

God or Brahman manifests Himself from formlessness to forms and again from forms to formlessness by His Will Power. Even in atoms also due to this dynamic or vibrant process of change, new rays, particles and sub-particles are incessantly created, get modified, arranged and rearranged for further creation from subtle to gross elements and objects containing various properties and colours. That is how this universe has come into existence, everything of which is a changing or passing phase. This means the process of birth, death and rebirth is perpetually happening in this changeable Creation. Further, nothing gets destroyed due to the principle of conservation of energy. Matter and energy are one and the same or kinetic phases of one and indivisible Potential Energy. Birth, death and rebirth are the phases of a grand cycle of change. There is no new creation. There is only new appearance and re-appearance. There is no dissolution. All dissolutions are for re-creation. There is no death. Every death is for rebirth or reappearance. True destination of everything is changeless Self.

Doubts and Clarifications

[85]The most important thing for a man is to appreciate and assimilate Guru vakya. The Sadguru descends on Earth only for the well-being of mankind. He considers everyone as His children. But we are hesitant to obey Guru's word. Due to this we suffer. We are not able to discriminate between good and bad due to our ignorance.

Who is a Guru?

The highest and the supreme Tattva is Gurutattva. There is nothing weightier or more precious than Gurutattva. Guru always wishes good to the disciples.

Which duty is to be performed by the disciple on an urgent basis?

Whatever karma we do, we get into bondage. We should undertake on a priority basis such karma by which we can get rid of the worldly bondages. Divya Darshan says that karma is the cause of bondage. Karma is also the cause of freedom. Hence desireless karma should be performed. All karma should be performed for God's sake. By desireless karma man can be released from the bondages.

Man does not want sufferings. He wants to remain hale and hearty. He wants happiness, peace and bliss. By wishing well to others and doing good to others, the knots of our bondages slowly get eliminated. If you are suffering, this means you are committing some mistakes somewhere. Every moment, you must introspect and try to find out where you have erred and

---

85 Oriya Divya Dhara Vol 20 Page 62. Also includes selected questions and answers which was published in our book 'Divya Darshan - The Philosophy Divine' (2017).

thereafter try to rectify yourself. Freedom (Moksha) is inevitable if you become good and do good.

What is the essence of freedom?

Man gets knowledge from his karma. In our daily life, we perform some daily and some occasional karma from out of which we gain knowledge. Slowly man gets attracted towards spiritual knowledge and gets inclined to know Brahman. Hence all our karma should be directed towards true knowledge or knowing Brahman. By doing good actions, our chitta gets cleaned. When our chitta gets cleaned, knowledge springs up. By acquiring true knowledge, one gets liberation or Moksa. Mukti is a common word which is used differently. But Moksa is union with Brahman. It is called Mahanirvana.

True knowledge is a matter of experience. Unless true knowledge is acquired, one cannot think of Moksa. Hence Knowledge of Truth is essential for Moksa.

What type of karma will do good to us?

If we walk on the path of Dharma, good things will happen to us. After death also dharma remains with us. Dharma protects us. Dharma brings us peace, bliss and freedom. By doing so, we gather more and more virtues (Punya). You must try to know which karma is to be undertaken to be on the path of Dharma. Desireless action is Dharma. Liberation is inside us only. He, who is keen to attain the same, will attain.

Who in this world is pure?

He, whose internal organs such as mind, intellect, and chitta are clean, can be called pure. He, who believes in God, will have compassion for others. There are persons in whom in certain specific circumstances, some good qualities are seen. This means that there are good qualities in him which are dormant but flickers of the same are seen in some situations. One must try to blossom all divine qualities in oneself. Those, who possess divine qualities, can be called pure.

What makes one infatuated?

Due to infatuation one's conscience gets eclipsed. This infatuation is for various forms and qualities. This is inferior to love. Love takes place between Atman and Atman. There is no selfishness in love. Infatuation is a big intoxicant like wine. Those who get attached to forms and qualities will suffer. There is no liberation in this state. True love means unconditional self-surrender.

What is the essence of samsar?

Human birth is rare; and not that easy to get. He, who acquires self-knowledge and do good to others; those, who know the Creator and Creation and always work for the well-being of others, enjoy peace and bliss.

Some questions and answers:

1. **Question-** Whether there is rebirth?

    Answer- The answer is lengthy. A separate chapter is there in the book, 'Divya Darshan, The Philosophy Divine' by Sadguru Sri Sri Arjun. However, some hints are given below. If examined in depth, it may be seen that the Darwinian Theory of Evolution is an affirmation of the Theory of Rebirth. The incessant flow of the grand process of evolution bringing out newer and newer products of the Creation with all potentials for further refinements, developments and promotions into higher and higher grades or categories through innumerable modifications such as generation, operation and dissolution in this grand laboratory was upheld by Darwin in his Theory of Evolution. When body becomes bereft of the functional consciousness, we call it dead. It is the presence of Consciousness that keeps the body fresh and alive. Here the question arises, can the Consciousness which keeps the otherwise dead cells alive itself die or become anytime non-existent? Whether the energy operative inside can become anytime non-existent? True, the gross body dies and gets disintegrated. But the subtle body remains intact. According to the Law of Karma, the subtle body assumes another form in due course and again comes back to the world. Being born once is as much a wonder as being born many times. There is a set of principles that eternally remains as the cause of the creation or destruction, birth or death, virtues or vices, happiness or sufferings, bondage or freedom. By the same Law, rebirth is possible. That Law is perpetually operative without human intervention. That Law was there before human beings (or any other matters, plants and animals) came into existence. That Law of Nature binds all of us until we seek and attain our true self, the synonyms of which, among others, are peace, bliss and freedom. The answer above is indicative only.

2. **Question-** People talk of God. But whether anybody has seen Him? If the answer is yes, then why God is not being seen now?

   Answer- The formless and attributeless entity also known as Nirguna Brahman expresses Himself in innumerable forms. Although He does not have any specific form, due to His greatness, He can assume many forms. The visible universe is His gross form. Man cannot understand this due to ignorance. Knowledge is essential to realise His manifestation. The sages have adopted different methods to explain the concept to the learners by bringing in the concepts of personal Godheads, Ishwar and Vishnu etc. A devotee according to his thought perceives the form. In other words, that meditated form appears before him. That is how many devotees are stated to have seen Shiva, Vishnu, Rama and Krishna etc. Great devotion is required for this. In the *bhava* stage only it becomes possible. According to the *bhava* of the devotee, different forms appear before him. He is commonly known as Bhagavan. One must move to the higher stage of *bhava* to see God. There must be unstinted devotion. Without this it is not possible to see God. This sounds unbelievable but it is true. There is Reflection Theory in science. This Theory is also applicable in case of *bhava*. Whatever be our *bhava*, similar results shall of course ensue.

3. **Question-** It is said that if one treads on the spiritual path, one may not get food for survival. To what extent it is true?

   Answer- It is said that during Satya-Yug, people were telling truth and living in peace and happiness. During Tretya-Yug also people were living happily. The question is- Why the people now are not happy. That means, during those days people were telling truth and that is why they were living happily. Now-a-days, people have distanced themselves from truth and that is why they are suffering. Truth does not mean only speaking the truth. Truth means- truth in conduct, truth in speech, observance of righteousness and justice. Without all these, man cannot live properly. If opposite qualities such as mischievousness, injustice and untruth prevail in the society, how can anyone live peacefully! The present day society is facing this crisis. In this unfavourable surrounding, if anyone treads on spiritual path, he may face some ridicule or resistance. His words may not be given much weight. But this does not mean that he should leave the path of truth, justice and righteousness. Even if he suffers, his sufferings will be much less than those who are on the opposite track. If in a family, the children tell lies, wife tells lies, and the husband also tells lies then how will the family run? Husband may not go to his work place but may tell that he is returning from duty. Wife after preparing food may tell that there is nothing to eat. Children may go to cinema hall and tell that they are returning from school. How chaotic the family atmosphere would be? If wrong doings are resorted to, everything like medical services, postal services, transport system, factory, electricity, commercial activities, schools and colleges shall get disturbed. There would be chaos, strikes, vandalism or hooliganism. The social system shall break down and there would be untold sufferings. The world is going on due to truth, love, faith, loyalty, good conduct, dedication, righteousness and justice. Man is therefore able to live with peace and happiness. In other words, spirituality is our life, property and everything. If there are aberrations, there will be disturbances leading to the destruction of the social fabric. Ultimately sufferings shall be the logical outcome.

4. **Question-** Whether God is there? If He is there, whether He is benevolent or baneful?

(This is not an ordinary question. It is related with knowledge on Brahman. Without some knowledge about the Creation, the answer to this cannot be comprehended well. Still, the answer which relates to post- Creation is briefly presented below.)

Answer- Vegetable kingdom preceded human birth. Otherwise from where man would have got his food? Before the vegetable kingdom, there was of course mineral kingdom and so on. If we examine still further, we see that before a baby is born, milk is stored in the mother so that the baby would take it as food after birth. Whatever has been created are to be maintained for which all pre-arrangements have been made. He, the basis of everything, remains at the beginning, middle and the end of everything. By Him, the process of creation, operation and dissolution is on. He is the controller of destiny of all. He is named Ishwar. He is also known as Sat-Chit-Anand or Truth, Consciousness and Bliss. Everything in this Creation is made in a preconceived and precise manner. The wise realise this and therefore call Him blissful and benevolent. Due to fragmented knowledge, an ordinary man understands neither the Creator nor His Creation. He conducts himself in a very casual and capricious manner and accordingly gets uncertain results thereof. According to the Law of Karma, good actions yield good results and bad actions return as bad results. Many do not understand this mysterious Law of Karma. People raise the question like why some are born lame, blind, incapacitated and poverty-stricken. Actually man suffers from himself i.e. due to his own Karma. There is no loophole in the Laws of Nature. The sages knew this well. When our level of knowledge shall get enhanced, we would also realise that God is always blissful and benevolent.

5. **Question-** If God is doing everything and therefore we have got nothing to do or bother about, then why do we suffer?

Answer- The realisers can only say that God is doing everything. On realising this truth, they lose their sense of individuality or doership. They have crossed over the feelings of happiness or unhappiness, success or failures, ego or doership, sins and sufferings. But we are only uttering the word God without understanding the real importance of God and with that scant and superficial knowledge we say, "We have got nothing to do or bother about since God is doing everything." On the other hand, we are saddled with feelings of sufferings, pleasure, ego, anger, greed and delusion. With such mind-set how far is it correct to say that God is doing everything? We have simply heard the sayings of the sages but we have not lost our ego or sense of individuality so far. He, who has surrendered his sense of individuality, who has nothing to own in absence of a sense of 'I' and 'mine', can alone say that God is doing everything (that means there is no separate existence of I' and 'mine'.)

6. **Question-** What is the benefit of approaching a Guru? Whether knowledge cannot be acquired without a Guru?

   Answer- People carry with them different kinds of samskara (past impulses). Therefore, all cannot understand a subject equally. In other word, the same subject is understood differently by different people. This indicates that whatever we know is very little and therefore more knowledge is to be acquired for a proper understanding. We also gather knowledge by seeing, listening and reading. Besides, Guru is also in everybody's heart. When some question arises in our mind, at times we get the answer from within. It has been told earlier that knowledge is Guru and Guru is knowledge and the medium through whom we get knowledge is called Guru. By reading any book, when we gather knowledge, the book is our Guru. When we get knowledge by listening from the teacher, he is our Guru. Our mother is our Guru. Our father is our Guru. We learn many things from them. Vivekananda had said, "Whoever is more knowledgeable than you, is your Guru." Those, who have strong samskara, can understand things by only seeing, even before seeing. Without Guru, it is difficult to learn anything. Further, there are persons whose power of understanding is not much. They cannot understand things easily from different sources discussed above. It is definitely desirable for them to approach a Guru for knowledge.

   According to the Greek Philosopher Socrates, he, who has forgotten, is a disciple and he, who remembers is Guru. By taking shelter of Guru, the disciple gets strengthened by knowledge.

Knowledge is power. By taking shelter of Guru, the disciple gets encouraged, inspired, emboldened and empowered.

7. **Question-** If God is said to be everywhere even in earth, wood and stone, what is the harm in worshipping a stone?

Answer- That God is all-pervasive, only sages or realisers have experienced this. Whereas we have simply heard that God eternally pervades everywhere. He, who realises the all-pervasiveness of God, worshipping is not necessary for him. There is no need of invocation or immersion.

But all others should worship God. We should also know what worship is and how it should be performed. We should also know about Him, whom we are going to worship. On the other hand, if we go on worshipping without knowing about Him, we do not get the desired results. The more we know about Him, the more we get His blessings. How to know about Him? The answer is- God has given us the instinct of inquisitiveness. We should get our doubts clarified by enquiring from knowledgeable persons. We should also read scriptures like Shrimad Bhagavad-Gita, Vedas and Upanishads etc. If we repeatedly contemplate on the knowledge we receive, our level of knowledge shall increase and our mind shall turn Godward. Our faith and devotion shall also be strengthened. It should be remembered that after knowing the greatness of God only, we shall have proper faith, devotion and love towards Him. Consequently, we would surrender to Him. Listening, recollecting, contemplating and meditating etc. arouse divine thoughts and feelings and thereby we stay attached to God with strong faith and devotion. This is real worship.

8. **Question-** Whether there is any place like heaven or hell? If the answer is yes, where is it?

Answer- Heaven or hell does not relate to any particular place. In a nutshell, suffering is hell whereas happiness is heaven. Normally people believe that the personal deities or the Devas are there in the heaven. Heaven is a subject matter which is very subtle and corresponds to intellect and conscience. The thoughts of conscientious people are also of higher planes. They can understand the subtle things. The subtle are long-lasting. If somebody understands and appreciates the subtle things and conducts himself accordingly, it means that he is enjoying the nectar and getting heavenly bliss. On the other hand, the gross objects are perishable and therefore bring in sorrows and sufferings. Persons attached to gross or mundane things wail and mourn when they are dispossessed of their material wealth. They are not aware of the value of subtle things. They almost live in hell. Blissful life is true life which knows no death. Death is opposed to bliss. The subtle are more powerful or energetic. He, who knows the subtle kingdom, is more powerful and happy. Generally the spiritual aspirants evince interest in the subtle and they take to the path of divine virtues. Such spirits can move anywhere. It has been stated that the pious go to heaven by the divine vehicle known as Deva-yan. That means they go to Deva-Loka where the personal godheads reside. The righteous persons enjoy heavenly peace and happiness even after their death since they live in heaven. But persons, who hold on to opposite qualities and indulge in sinful actions, remain attached to the gross world due to their lesser level of understanding. The gross matters being changeable always bring in sorrows and sufferings due to obvious reasons. In a nutshell, good or bad results mostly come depending upon the standard of knowledge, actions and lifestyle. Bad results arising from own actions bring in sorrows and sufferings to the doer. Good actions similarly bring in happiness here and hereafter. The former is hell whereas the latter is heaven.

9. **Question-** What is concentration of mind and how will it come?

Answer- When mind becomes single pointed on the object or subject of meditation, it is called concentration. God has given us this power of concentration from the beginning. Therefore everyone possesses this power. Had there been no concentration, we would not have been able to walk, read, talk and even eat. Those, who are not able to do these and are abnormal in their behaviour, are called mad or insane. That means everybody with a sound mind has got the power of concentration. Our concentration gets disturbed due to the following reasons.

❖ Everything around us is changeable, that too, every moment. Our mind gets impacted due to such changes.

❖ We possess different types of negative qualities such as- lust, anger, greed, infatuation, pride, jealousy and so on. These qualities sometimes become active and therefore our mind gets diverted towards different subjects and objects. In a nutshell, our mind gets distracted due to our unguarded thoughts and desires.

Now let us learn how to guard ourselves against the multiple thoughts swarming through our mind. There are motives behind our actions. If mind considers something worth doing or valuable, it gets attached to that. In other words, the more the mind considers something as valuable, the more the mind gets attracted towards that. Once we know that gold is more valuable than silver, our mind gets attracted towards gold. Mind will shift from gold to diamond once we come to know that diamond is more valuable than gold. Similarly, once we know the value of education we shall be interested in education. Once we know the value and greatness of God, we shall be attracted towards God. Similarly, once we know the value and indispensability of the object of meditation, our mind will be fixed there otherwise it will shift to other mundane matters which it considers as more valuable and useful.

Therefore, we must know why we are meditating on God. Who is God? Why is it so essential to realise God? God is the most powerful, most knowledgeable, all pervasive eternal essence. He is most valuable. Isn't our consciousness more valuable than any type of material possessions, be it gold or diamond? He, who understands the import of all these, can truly meditate with unwavering concentration.

10. **Question-** To gain true knowledge, is it essential to adopt yoga practices?

Answer- Yes, yoga is necessary. But people do not possess clear idea about yoga. Generally people think of Astanga Yoga of Patanjali (such as- yama, niyama, asana, pranayama, pratyahara, dharana, dhyana and *samadhi*) as yoga. Some say that to fix mind on God is yoga. But quite a many cannot appreciate this. They express their inability to sit for hours for yoga *samadhi*. Some others say, they cannot count the beads while chanting God's name. Some are also averse to continued repetition of mantra. They take the plea that they have got other important works to attend.

Particularly the householders are averse to such types of yogic practices. They say, in whatever positions they are, they are all right. According to them, there is no urgent need to adopt yogic practices. According to Divya Darshan, establishing relation or link with something is yoga. Yoga or the link may be with a thought or with any object. Everybody wants to live well. Everybody seeks peace and happiness. Everybody seeks good things in life. Hence it is essential to establish link with what is good. But only God is eternally good. Divine knowledge is essential for establishing contact with God, who is good. Divine knowledge helps for self-development. In the scriptures, the Eternal Truth is named as Brahman, Atman or God. Therefore according to Divya Darshan, trying to realise the Truth is yoga. By this, mind shall establish link or contact with the Truth and shall be ultimately merged with Truth. One should evince interest to know and meditate so that link would be established with Truth. The more we know about Truth, the more we acquire knowledge. In other words, knowing the Truth is knowledge. By yoga, the light of knowledge is enkindled. Man is always in yoga. But he is unable to understand this. Once he appreciates the ways and infallibly practises yoga, he shall be blessed with divine knowledge that leads to peace, bliss and liberation.

11. **Question-** The sages speak of 'Paramananda' that means Supreme Bliss. Whether everyone can experience it?

Answer- Yes. It is possible. We derive pleasure from out of mundane matters. Everyone has experienced this. But this is temporary pleasure as the mundane materials are subject to change every moment. Due to change, creation, sustenance and dissolution do happen. He, who effects the changes, is not subject to change. He is named as Brahman, Atman, God, Ishwar etc. We enjoy or experience the end products but we do not know the Creator who is the basis as well as the cause of all these. The pure and virtuous souls, like the wise sages and the enlightened yogis, realise the Supra-Causal Existence and experience Supreme Bliss. This Bliss has no end. It is eternal. There is no iota of sufferings here. This Bliss is known as Sadanand, Atmanand, Brahmanand, Paramanand etc. People who are possessed of demoniac qualities are steeped in ignorance and are bound to suffer. On the other hand, those, who possess divine qualities and have inquisitiveness to acquire knowledge for realisation of Truth, are qualified to get God's grace and they attain Supreme Bliss.

12. **Question-** If one does not quit samsar (worldly life bound by the Law of Karma with the chain of death and rebirth occurring in a cycle), for him God-realisation is not possible. How far is it true?

Answer- Yes, it is true. One has to renounce while living in samsar. We are habituated to living in the samsar; we are bred and brought up here. How can we survive without samsar? This appears to be a worrying point. That is why we are all so much attached to samsar. He, who clings to the samsar, gets samsar but not God. But the spiritual aspirant need not worry about this. Leaving the samsar appears to be an unpalatable proposition. But it is not. We have to understand this statement properly. One need not go away from samsar. Where can he go?

Only thought process or mindset need to be changed. According to Ishavasya Upanishad, this entire Creation is created and pervaded by the Truth-Absolute called Paramatman. This means that whatever we see, hear and experience are all His. He regulates everything. Which one is ours? Everything belongs to Him and Him only. Hence our duty is to use and enjoy all that He has given us. At the same time we should never forget that these are the gifts of God. We should never think that we are the owners of these things. We possess nothing; everything is His. The samsar (World) is not mine. He is the maker;

He is the controller. The body, the senses, the mind and intellect as well as the external nature, all belong to Him. He creates, organizes and dispenses everything. When this thought dawns upon a spiritual mendicant, he becomes free from worldly feelings and attachments. He turns Godward faster. This is called truly renouncing samsar. This means, living in samsar but remaining unattached like water droplets on a lotus leaf.

13. **Question-** What is supersensuous state. How to experience it?

Answer- Truth is explained to us by sages in two stages. First, perceived by senses; second, not perceived by senses.

Let us discuss this in detail. Everything is made of five elements, such as- earth, water, fire, air and space. Out of these five elements, while we can see earth, water and fire, we are not able to see air and space. Space appears like a void. So it is also called void. But in reality the space is not empty. It is full of resources. The material universe has come out from the space. Earth is gross. Water is subtler than earth. Fire is subtler than water. Air is still subtler than fire. Space is the subtle-most element. Skin can feel the air but not the space. The sky is blue, we say, but this is not a correct statement. Space (Akash tattva) can be bracketed under supersensuous category.

According to physics, the matter exists in three states such as- Solid, Liquid and Gas. Besides these three states, there is a subtler state which is not perceptible but which is real. In this state, various atomic particles, sub-particles, different powerful rays and waves etc. are there. In other words, this fourth state is the treasury of all energy. From out of all these invisible or supersensuous treasures, everything in this universe is structured and regulated, involving extraordinary intelligence, science and technology!

Thus existing infinite energy or power very systematically undergoes number of ramifications which are further subject to sequential modifications bearing diversified properties. This universe is not a random outcome. In various mythologies, the invisible individual powers are personified as different personal deities. With increased knowledge as well as purified mind with strong inquisitiveness and concentration, this subject can be understood and appreciated better. The scientists can understand these things very well but they remain bounded as they focus their attention only to their fragmented or specific research areas. They have so far not paid much attention to the Consciousness that underlies all our deeds, thoughts, theories, designs, discoveries and inventions. Without Conscious Energy, we would not have existed even.

14. **Question-** Everybody wants to get rid of sufferings. Why sufferings do not go off altogether?

Answer- Sufferings come due to many reasons such as- desire, greed, and infatuation etc. Sufferings also come due to natural calamities and also ignorance-generated pitfalls and hazards. To get rid of sufferings, knowledge is essential by which one can analyse the causes of sufferings and find out ways to wipe those out. One tries day and night to eliminate sufferings but due to lack of proper knowledge, one does not find the appropriate way to get out of sufferings. In fine, as long as one is entangled in samsar, one cannot get rid of sufferings. Without self-knowledge, sufferings cannot be eradicated fully. The sages got rid of sufferings only by means of true knowledge. They said, "Only God is Bliss-Absolute."

15. **Question-** If a man performs his duty well, he can live happily. If so, where is the need for any spiritual knowledge?

Answer- People believe that spiritual subject is different from routine way of living. That is why they raise such questions. If we attach so much importance to our duty, we must know well what our duties are. Many people do not have clear idea about their duties. Before discharging any duty properly, we should have knowledge about what is justice. If we do not know for certain what is justice then how shall we know what Dharma is! Without adequate knowledge about Truth, justice, Dharma and the goal of life, man cannot choose and discharge his duties properly. He does his duties for living with peace and happiness. Further this life has got some noble purpose for which we do karma. We may say we have sufficient knowledge about our duty. If that is so, why there are lapses in our duties. For these lapses we have to suffer. To get rid of sufferings, spiritual knowledge is required. This is because in the spiritual knowledge there is sense of duty, justice, righteousness etc. In the spiritual knowledge, there is bliss and all knowledge pertaining to a divine life that leads us to our destination. If man evinces interest in acquiring spiritual knowledge, he can get peace and happiness sought after by each and everybody. More or less we all have some spiritual knowledge which we have been utilizing in our day to day life. Due to want of sufficient knowledge we are not able to advance much. Therefore everyone should endeavour to increase the level of spiritual knowledge. By doing this one can progress faster on the spiritual path and reach one's destination. It should be remembered that spiritual knowledge is the reservoir of all peace, bliss and freedom. With spiritual knowledge man can make his life simple, beautiful and divine as a result of which he can get rid of all sufferings. It is the foremost duty and Dharma of every human being to acquire spiritual knowledge. In other words, sticking to spiritual practices for the self-development of one and all should be the foremost among all other duties.

16. **Question-** What is Maya? What is to be done to get rid of Maya?

Answer- Whatever all are happening, appearing or disappearing in this Creation are God's greatness which is called His lila or Play. In a magic show, the word 'Maya' or 'Indrajaal' is used. Appearances of different things, disappearance of things and change of something to another thing are all parts of magic show. There the word 'Maya' is used. In various mythologies there are examples of demons assuming different forms and disappearing as and when they willed. In this Creation whatever gets manifested are all due to God's greatness or His lila. Things do happen where the best mind or intellect cannot reach. They are wonderful and beyond our reasoning or perceiving capacities. Many mind-boggling questions remain unanswered. Every moment, something or other happens but we do not know the 'how' and 'why' of it. We are left in illusion, in a world of reflections. Because of ignorance about the Truth, we are placed in an illusory situation not being able to understand and appreciate things properly. This 'not knowing the Truth' is 'Maya'. God's play creates such illusory spell which we humans do not understand. We get befooled by the tricks of the magician; we all live in Maya. We are influenced by Maya. We also suffer due to Maya. In order to get rid of the Maya-generated sufferings, we have to necessarily know the doer of lila. Only by His blessings we shall get divine knowledge to realise the Truth. At that time only the Maya (corollary or even synonym of ignorance) shall vanish. Ultimately Truth and Consciousness shall prevail with resultant Bliss.

17. **Question-** If consciousness is equally present in all beings, why thoughts and actions of different people are different?

Answer- Consciousness is capable of manifesting itself in innumerable ways. Different qualities are found depending upon the level of consciousness. If consciousness manifests as a human, the qualities pertaining to a human will only be seen in him. In a lower animal, the qualities of that specific lower animal shall be seen. When a District Magistrate or any other powerful official is at home, different behaviour will be seen in him. But when he is in his office, he is seen to be in different action mode. In other words, depending on the circumstances, the qualities find expression. Even though the Self-consciousness is uniform everywhere, in different environments and circumstances, manifestation becomes different. Divya Darshan speaks of Truth in four categories. They are Temporal truth, Partial truth, Truth and Supreme Truth. I am now speaking to you or I am writing a book; suddenly there is lightning; lightning vanishes and thunder comes. All these come under temporal truth. Similarly there are partial truth, truth and Supreme Truth. Without consciousness, neither we can see nor hear. It is consciousness that manifests as various experiences, thoughts and expressions. Qualities also vary from persons to persons according to the varying degrees of manifestation of consciousness.

18. **Question-** Without God, whether a man can live with peace and happiness?

    Answer- We do not have adequate knowledge about what God is and who God is. Most men have become materialistic in the name of modernity. Man does not know the true nature of God. Anything in order to be created is preceded by certain truths. To prepare a cake many ingredients are to be kept ready. Those ingredients are truths. Water is truth; flour is truth; sugar is truth; cake is also truth. You may call it truth or 'form'. For creation, sustenance and dissolution also there are some preceding truths. What should be our intake of food are all based on certain truths knowing which is called knowledge. I want to live in peace but if there are bad qualities in me, I cannot get peace. For getting peace, there are some pre-conditions which are truths. Similarly for getting freedom also there are some truths without which it is impossible to attain freedom. Brahman is the Supreme Truth who manifests as different truths. Once we know the related truths, we can destroy something or save a dying man. We have to follow certain truths for happiness, peace and freedom. Truths have to be applied for accomplishing something. Dharma is observance of some truths or the Law of Eternity. Those truths are the laws of God. God himself is the Truth-Absolute. Everything that happens is caused by God. Divya Darshan goes one step further and asserts that God manifests as everything. The entire Creation is a manifestation of Brahman. When Truth is God and God is Truth, how can someone survive without God?

19. **Question-** who is the Creator? What is the purpose of Creation and mystery of Creation?

    Answer- Brahman is the Creator. Upanishad says that Brahman willed to be many. Brahman is named as Brahma, Vishnu and Maheswar while discharging different roles. Now the question arises what was the need for dissolution when Brahman created and also made all sorts of arrangements for sustenance. I am asking you what for do you eat? You are speaking; you are working; you are taking rest. What for all these activities? The answer is- "That is how you express yourselves. Without all these you do not have any existence." "Why Brahman goes for dissolution?" This question has no meaning. This Jagat is a manifestation of Brahman. He expresses Himself like that. That's all. When you feel hungry you have to take food. When you feel sleepy, you have to sleep. Similarly why the man is born? To this question, the answer is man's birth is preceded by some truths. His actions in the previous birth are the reason of his present birth. Everything that happens is controlled and guided by the Law of Eternity. This much can be said here that dissolution is also a changing phase in the grand cycle of change. Dissolution does not mean passing into nothingness. It means some other beginning or reappearance.

20. **Question-** Who is a disgruntled spirit? Is there any etheric world? Where do the etheric bodies exist?

Answer- Man is a bundle of desires. He dies before all his desires are fulfilled. After death the *jivatma* is called *pretatma*. There are many instances where the etheric spirits enter into the gross bodies of others. In other words, they get themselves super-imposed on others. If someone dies after getting Ishta Mantra from a Sadguru, he remembers the Mantra after his death also while he remains in his etheric body. But after a new birth, due to many reasons he forgets the Mantra.

Without getting spiritual knowledge if someone dies, he continues with his hankerings as before and always remains unfulfilled. There is no specific place for the *pretatma*. A *pretatma* can go anywhere as it is free to move in its etheric body. It may go even to the lunar region. Those who are enriched with divine knowledge can move still higher. The sinful *pretatma* cannot go beyond Bhuloka. In other words, such a *pretatma* remains in the lower region i.e. within 50 feet whereas, the wise with divine qualities, move to higher regions. The sinful *pretatma* due to ignorance carries with it many mundane obsessions and is heavier. For this reason it cannot move to higher regions.

21. Question- How will a *pretatma* get liberated?

    Answer- One must consciously acquire virtues instead of indulging in vices. The sinful are reborn as lower creatures. Those, who have taken shelter of Sadguru, get protection as they are aware of divine knowledge and remember Sadguru. They will be born in good environment which will help them move higher and higher spiritually. "How shall I get liberated?" If someone thinks over it, he will find the way towards liberation and will try for the same. Those, who do not know what freedom is, will never make any effort also. The *pretatma*, who has got interest in spirituality, gets opportunity to join satsang (spiritual discourses) and enhance its knowledge by listening to the greatness of God. He or she may, with increase in true knowledge which is divine knowledge, take shelter of God and move on spiritual path. On getting complete knowledge, one may attain liberation.

22. **Question-** Whether fate or destiny is inevitable? If so what is that?

    Answer- We talk of fate or destiny. After birth a *jivatma* expresses himself through a particular pattern. We call the same as nature. We are the makers of our own destiny. We get results from out of the type of actions we perform. Like actions, like results. These results may not come immediately. Some are stored for future and return at appropriate time. When we cannot cognize, identify or correlate the results coming back to us, we call it destiny or fate. It is just like the law of reflection in Physics. Also according to Newton's third Law of Motion, "Every action has equal and opposite reaction." Everything happens strictly in accordance with Law. Many believe that having committed sin if one apologizes or does penance, he will be saved from sin. But it is not so. The Law will take its own course. Even God or Ishwar shall not break the Law. God manifests as Truth, Law and Consciousness. Normally God never intervenes to enhance or trim down the results of past actions. A person by experiencing the results of his own actions should refine his tendencies that decide his future course of actions. When he will be established in monism by acquiring complete knowledge, all reflections shall end along with the end of dualism. This means he would be liberated from the bondage of actions. With the increase in knowledge he would be able to realise that he is different from body, senses, mind and intellect. Consequently, he would be free from the sufferings of the body, senses, mind and intellect.

23. **Question-** When can a disciple realise the powers and blessings of God? What are the symptoms of a good disciple?

Answer- Guru can know the attitude, ability and aspirations of the disciple the moment He comes in his contact. Accordingly, Guru imparts knowledge to the disciple. After taking birth everyone forgets his True Self. Even Lord Rama and Lord Krishna had forgotten their True Self. Only after receiving the knowledge imparted by their respective Gurus, they remembered their True Self. There are some already prepared souls who need not take initiation or Mantra. God or Guru's blessings are raining always. But the deluded man does not realise that. When the disciple bears in mind the presence of Guru, he can realise slowly all happenings in and around him in the kingdom of nature. According to his level of contemplation, a disciple experiences Guru accordingly. Supersensuous state is beyond the ordinary level. Senses, mind or intellect cannot reach there. By knowledge, the supersensuous state can be experienced. He, who possesses divine virtues and unflinching devotion towards Guru, can reach that supersensuous state and realise Guru's blessings. The Sun always shines but the blind cannot see it. Similarly due to ignorance, a person is not able to realise the continued blessings of Sadguru. When divine virtues will overwhelm him, he will be pure and pious. All impurities in him shall be cleaned and he would be eligible for divine blessings. He would realise Guru and enjoy the blissful state where there remains no fear or anxiety. He is free.

24. **Question-** What is my duty?

Answer- We are blessed with this human form to realise our True Self. With lot of good impulses, man is eligible to make self-enquiry and go ahead for realising his true self. Man is gifted with inquisitiveness. Till his death he goes on acquiring knowledge and enriching his good impulses.

Man's duty is to fully utilise his power of inquisitiveness, acquire true knowledge and realise his 'Self'. This is his first and foremost duty. Having a healthy and peaceful living is a pre-requirement of self-realisation. So man should make efforts to acquire divine virtues and true knowledge to achieve his goal of self-realisation. This is his true Dharma.

25. **Question-** Who am I? Why have I come?

Answer- You are pure Atman. You are Bliss-Absolute. You are Sat-Chit-Ananda (Existence, Consciousness and Bliss) but because you are in a human garb, qualities corresponding to the human form are expressed in you. You are playing your role accordingly. On the stage you completely engross yourself in your role. Similarly when you will know about your true identity, you will know that you are different from the body, senses, mind and intellect. Then you will say, "I am Sat-Chit-Ananda Brahman."

❖ Once the spiritual mendicant knows about the fourth state of matter, he can realise Para Shakti. It is subtler than the subtlest. To attain this, sincere spiritual practice as well as Guru's grace is essential.

❖ Union between Atman and Atman is true love. There is nothing to do with the physical appearance or quality.

❖ Above the Sat-Chit-Ananda state, it is unqualified Brahman i.e. Brahman without any quality which is self-conscious awareness. There is nothing other than Him; but by Him or due to His inherent powers everything appears or happens.

❖ If you repeatedly contemplate on Divya Darshan, you can experience everything within yourself and get His blessings to realise 'Self'. Always entertain noble thoughts, walk on righteous path, earn your livelihood sincerely and honestly, observe true spirit of the teachings of scriptures and sages.

❖ I have enkindled the flame of Divya Darshan. You all should keep it ablaze.

❖ Divya Darshan teaches those tricky points regarding the truth and laws by observing which you can be divine and realise the divine Self. The subject matter of the Law of Eternity is there in Divya Darshan. It is not a mere compilation of personal opinions or imaginations.

❖ Divya Darshan teaches that it is essential to possess true knowledge and divine virtues to realise the divinity within. By possessing divine qualities, you can live in the society in peace and happiness. By acquiring true knowledge, you can realise God. This means if you enhance your knowledge and experience, you can realise your True Self.

❖ God cannot be seen by gross eyes. He can be realised by jnana and *bhava*. His all-pervasive nature can be realised by knowledge. Whatever we experience in this visible world are all His manifestations which are illusory. Brahman can at best be described as 'Neti, Neti'.

❖ To walk on the path of Dharma is the right path. Dharma remains ever with us even after we shed our mortal bodies. Dharma protects us, sustains us and gives us peace, happiness and bliss. By Dharma, we can attain liberation. The essence of Dharma is known as punya. Hence everyone should try to accumulate punya. By acquiring true knowledge, Dharma can be understood and observed. Dharma comes from knowledge and liberation from Dharma.

❖ When man is controlled by mind, he is bound to suffer. When he is guided by conscience, he gets peace and happiness. Due to the wayward tendencies of mind and senses, man suffers, Mind is tamasic, intellect rajasic and conscience sattvic. Ego springs up from mind and intellect. One should listen to one's conscience and be guided accordingly. Then only one can be free from ego.

❖ "I am Peace-Absolute, Bliss Absolute." If one thinks of this his sufferings would vanish.

❖ Even before a disciple asks for anything, Sadguru, when pleased with the disciple, bestows upon the disciple His Will Power by which he can cross hurdles and tide over sufferings.

❖ Brahman is one but due to ignorance we consider Him as many. Sadguru clearly explains the existence of the Absolute in all. He also explains the manifestation of Brahman.

- ❖ Brahman is without forms and without qualities. He manifests as all movables and immovable in the universe of names, forms and qualities.

- ❖ Brahman cannot be realised by one's mind and intellect. When a disciple surrenders completely to Guru, Guru overwhelms him by Supreme knowledge. In other words, by His Grace, He can be realised. There is nothing more valuable in this Creation than Sadguru. To attain Gurushakti, self-surrender is essential. When Guru is pleased with a disciple, Gurushakti shall get transmitted to the disciple.

- ❖ We, under various pretexts like want of time, domestic afflictions etc. avoid attending satsang. By this we distance ourselves from God. This results in increased sufferings.

- ❖ The Supreme Truth manifests as Sat, Chit and Ananda. The term Sat refers to His Existence. Chit is Knowledge. By knowledge we realise Sat and experience Bliss.

- ❖ Those, who are being guided by mind and senses, are asleep from spiritual point of view. Those, who are guided by Buddhi, have just woke up. Those, who are guided by conscience, are wakeful. Those, who have attained Atman, are ever awake.

- ❖ To realise Brahman is siddhi. Those, who are possessed of divine qualities, would attain Brahman quicker.

- ❖ Scriptures describe Brahman as both Saguna (with attributes) and Nirguna (attributeless). Some people worship Saguna Brahman and some others worship Nirguna Brahman. From the point of view of true knowledge, the unitary Energy-Absolute manifests as everything in this universe including movables and immovable, Saguna and Nirguna. Therefore, both Saguna and Nirguna constitute the indivisible Brahman.

- ❖ Those, who have strong faith on Sadguru, shall get His blessings. Those, who have not surrendered to Sadguru, cannot attain liberation. They would be undergoing the cycle of births and deaths. It is regrettable that many people are hesitant or they feel ashamed to approach Guru for true knowledge.

❖ When a man would purify himself, he can, by listening to various scriptural instructions about self-knowledge, assimilate the same and realise Brahman.

❖ Vedanta Darshan by Vyasadeva establishes the Truth i.e. the unitary Supreme Brahman. Divya Darshan conforms to this non-dual philosophy. According to it the various powers of the unitary Brahman are named as different personal godheads. We should not only know the personal godheads, but we must know the Brahman also. Liberation comes only after realisation of Brahman.

❖ By surrendering to Sadguru, I am getting knowledge. By surrendering to Dharma not only I am protected, I also get peace, happiness and bliss. By surrendering to Truth, I am moving towards liberation. This thought should be firmed up.

❖ Brahman is 'Om'. He, who realises 'Om', shall be merged with 'Om'. This means, he would be merged with Brahman. You are all created by 'Om' and 'Om' is established in you. You are the gross manifestation of 'Om' or the Self-Absolute.

❖ Those who adore Truth are jnani. Those, who are attracted towards Divya Darshan, are also jnani. Divya Darshan represents Truth and Law of Eternity.

❖ Knowledge is the greatest wealth. Siddhi means attainment of Supreme knowledge, which is attainment of Brahman. The sages and seers who have attained siddhi have attained true knowledge. This is His grace. The more one gets His blessings, the more one gets released from the worldly chains. Divine power comes as knowledge.

❖ Bhakti together with jnana becomes Para-Bhakti. By Para-Bhakti the wise men realise Brahman and enjoy Supreme Bliss.

❖ When heart is filled with divine thoughts, it is to be understood that you are getting divine blessings and God expresses Himself as such. Divine thoughts are God. God is beyond knowledge. Knowledge is the path. Bhava is the lion-gate. Mahabhava is the throne. God is Sat-Chit-Ananda.

❖ Those, who have not surrendered to Sadguru, cannot reach God. By surrendering to Sadguru, the disciples can go up to the doorstep of God or they come to proximity of God. Sadguru imparts instructions to the disciples and explains how to get rid of the illusory attachments.

❖ Mind must be changed first. He, who can change the mind, can control his senses. Thereafter, intellect can be conquered to attain stability. One can reach the level of conscience, once one goes beyond mind and intellect. Those, who are keen to get rid of sufferings and attain liberation, should try to transform their mind. He, who is not able to change his mind, is bound to suffer till death. Hence, one should contemplate, "I am not mind, not intellect even not conscience. I am Self-Absolute." He, who contemplates like this, would sooner or later attain liberation in this birth even.

❖ Dharma protects us. To know Truth is knowledge and to observe the same is Dharma. Every moment you should be inquisitive to know Truth. He, who is trying to know, is really worshipping Him. Observance of Dharma is true sadhana.

❖ Try to meditate daily in the morning and evening for 10-15 minutes. Contemplate on His Greatness. God can be realised by reading, listening, meditating and repeatedly contemplating. During meditation, if anything else other than Guru comes to your mind, it is to be understood that Maya has come to distract you. Try to get rid of all diversified thoughts. If only Guru comes continuously during meditation, then that is real and more effective meditation.

❖ He, who realises Truth, gets His blessings. There is no greater tapa than Truth. He, who takes shelter of Truth and conducts himself in

Truth, attains Him. Support truth, speak to others about truth and express truth in your conduct. Then only you can realise Truth. The greatest achievement of life is attainment of Truth. Hence the best effort is to know about Truth and attain it.

* By surrendering to Sadguru, the weaknesses in the disciple gradually vanish and the latent powers get activated. The disciple gets Guru's grace. This inspires the disciple to proceed on the path of Truth. There is power in Guru's instructions. The disciple becomes more powerful by following Guru's instructions. Those, who have forgotten Guru, distance themselves from Guru and in them Gurushakti remains inert. Those, who remember Guru and repose strong faith on Ishta Mantra, would advance faster.

* If Guru does not love you, then why He has descended from Satya-Loka to Bhulok? He loves you more than God.

* God is peace-Absolute, Bliss-Absolute and Freedom-Absolute. He, who knows Him as such, gets peace, bliss and freedom.

* He, who believes in Guru, reposes faith on Guru, serves Guru and serves his parents, acquires good impulses. For this no academic qualification is necessary.

* Parents are greater God than all pilgrimages. But people without serving their parents visit pilgrimages. He, who gets the blessings of the parents, also gets the blessings from the personal godheads. Those, who get blessings from the personal godheads, also get blessings from God. Hence all great persons and sages respect their parents.

* Knowledge is Guru. Knowledge has been compared with mirror. Objects are reflected on only one side of the mirror, but knowledge shows us all dimensions covering 360 degrees. In other words, the entire movable and immovable universe is seen and understood by knowledge. Knowledge is present everywhere and always. None has created it. Hence the sages call Him as Knowledge-Absolute, Chit- Swarup and Energy-Absolute.

❖ Without taking shelter of a Sadguru, we cannot realise God. Because we are afflicted by greed and infatuation, we are not able to attain God. Only Guru has the power to remove those negative qualities from us to make us pure. This is the truth.

❖ He, who can know how much Guru loves him, would be eligible to get blessings from Guru.

❖ Guru creates the necessary environment to take the disciples to Nitya-Loka. Since we have not understood the greatness of Guru, we are not able to free ourselves from the worldly bondage. In this Creation, everywhere there is the presence of knowledge. He, who can realise the all pervasiveness of knowledge, can realise God.

❖ By merely chanting God's name, one does not get liberation. One has to necessarily possess divine virtues to attain God. The *bhava* behind the name is more important than mere repeating God's name.

❖ The disciple can acquire knowledge in two ways. First, by possessing inquisitiveness; second, by following the instructions of Guru. If the disciple can merge his Atman with Guru's Atman, he can get Guru's blessings. The disciple has to surrender his ego in order to get overwhelmed by Gurushakti.

❖ Guru is there everywhere and always. He, who has strong conviction over this, would get His blessings faster.

❖ Gurushakti is the source of all energy. Guru's grace is no small thing. By His Grace, we can get the blessings of all personal godheads. We can get blessings of parents even with a little effort.

❖ True freedom is where there is no bondage. The sages and seers are totally free. By taking holy dip, one cannot get liberation or freedom. Freedom is a state in which all *vikaras* of the mind get lost, all conflicts are resolved. There does not remain any question or any answer. Only eternal bliss rules.

❖ Man, in order to gain powers, must possess divine virtues which are divine powers. He must acquire the related knowledge.

❖ God is Sat-Chit-Ananda. Sat indicates His Eternal Existence. We exist because He exists. Had there been no God, we would not have come to exist. God is beginningless and endless too. The Creation is there; hence the Creator is also there. Chit means Consciousness. Sat expresses Himself as Consciousness and Bliss, and also this entire Creation.

❖ Trying to acquire knowledge on Truth amounts to doing yoga. By this yogic practice, he can reach supersensuous state. His conduct gets refined and he becomes simple and humble. Whatever is done for the sake of God-realisation is Yoga.

❖ The relation between the Guru and the disciple is such that the disciple gets released from the worldly bondage. Whatever loka the Guru speaks about, the disciple reaches that loka. When Guru talks about Satya-Loka, at that time both the Guru and the disciple are in Satya-Loka. The Guru remains with the disciple till the disciple reaches Nitya-Loka. In the Nitya-Loka there is immergence with Brahman.

❖ The first manifestation of Brahman is knowledge. Generally, knowledge is from mind to conscience. Mind is controlled by intellect, intellect by conscience and Conscience by Atman. All *vikaras* of mind vanish on the advent of self-knowledge which is true knowledge.

❖ Common people may observe some special features in the gross body of a Sadguru. But generally, people cannot recognise a Sadguru. Only one seer can know another seer. Their teachings and gospels give some indications about their level of realisation.

❖ Only when one reaches the supersensuous state, one can realise Para-Shakti. For attaining this state intense spiritual practices are required along with acquisition of knowledge.

❖ Fears and doubts are there in dualism. They vanish on reaching monism or Advaita. The best way is to try to know the Self within.

In this case, there is no question of fear. But if one seeks Him outside, fears and doubts shall be there.

❖ Why some people do not get food to survive? Due to ignorance they do not have sense of duty; hence, they suffer. When, a man would take to spiritual path, the negative qualities such as falsehood, pretensions and crookedness etc. shall go away from him and he would start walking on the path of Dharma. There shall not be any dearth of food for him, who is dutiful and pious.

❖ He, who is keen to acquire knowledge, will one day realise the Supreme Truth. By knowledge one's devotion becomes strong and one attains Para knowledge.

❖ By taking initiation from Sadguru, good impulses get accumulated.

❖ The word 'Guru' connotes knowledge, heaviness, greatness etc. He, who takes shelter of Sadguru, gets rid of all sufferings and attains liberation. Impossible things, in other words, things beyond one's imagination, can be attained if one surrenders to Sadguru. He, who realises the greatness of Sadguru, and always remembers Him, accomplishes his tasks successfully.

❖ We are all children of God. Once this thought comes, one would start enjoying bliss and would attain God who is eternally blissful. God expresses Himself as Love and Bliss. When we love others, it means, we are loving God. If we understand Him in this manner, we would get His Grace and shall be entitled to bliss and freedom.

❖ A person possessing divine virtues, becomes divine. He gets blessings from personal godheads. By these divine qualities he ultimately earns the Grace of Brahman, the Supreme.

❖ Whatever Divya Darshan preaches is all subject matter of the Law of Eternity. According to it, the goal of everyone is self-realisation or attainment of liberation. Possessing divine virtues is the essence of Sanatan Dharma or the Law of Eternity.

❖ Divya Darshan is not a new name. It is not a separate sect, creed or community. Everyone's goal is to realise the Supreme and become divine. Therefore, Divya Darshan is a way of life. It belongs to none but at the same time it belongs to all. He, who knows it, gets it.

❖ Divya Darshan is eternal. It existed in the past; it exists now and it shall be there in future. He, who preaches Divya Darshan, was there in the past, He is present now and He shall be there in future. For the sake of presenting Divya Darshan, He has assumed a form only.

❖ By acquiring divine knowledge, one can attain divinity. That divine existence manifests Himself as the Law of Eternity. Realising or experiencing the same is Darshan which is self-realisation. The Law of Eternity or Sanatan Dharma is presented scientifically in a unique manner in the name of Divya Darshan.

❖ **Dharma:** Self is there within everyone. He eternally expresses Himself. Since Atman is Bliss-Absolute and Freedom-Absolute, we all wish to enjoy bliss and freedom. One must search for Atman within. He, who does not know himself, how can he know others? Acquiring self-knowledge is Dharma; knowing the Self is Dharma. He, who does not evince interest to know Self, is ignorant. He is bound to commit sins and undergo sufferings. Therefore, every human being should light the candle of knowledge within.

✿ ✶ ✿

Epilogue

How much do we know about the destination or true goal of our life? How much we know about our true identity? In fact, very little do we know how to properly conduct ourselves in this world constantly keeping the goal in mind so as to rid ourselves of all sufferings and attain bliss and freedom. If these questions bother us anytime, then it can be inferred that our journey has truly begun. It is said that a journey of thousand steps begins with one small step. The journey to self-identity begins with being inquisitive about self.

Then we search for a master, who can guide us; who has completed this journey and has found right answer. What does He do? He enhances our capability to understand things hitherto not understood. He is like a beacon who guides in our journey. The journey has to be undertaken by self only. There is no substitute for that.

And what does Divya Darshan do? How does it help? Divya Darshan is the philosophy of life that states the purpose of life and its great destination. Divya Darshan lays stress on living in the society with harmony, inculcating divine virtues and practising self-knowledge. Divva Darshan asserts that we are intrinsically divine but as we have taken human forms we have forgotten our True Self. By spiritual efforts and Guru's grace, we can realise our true nature.

This Creation is a continuous process. And it is changing every moment. The only Eternal Truth behind all changes is the unchanging Creator who remains unknown though. That infinite existence has manifested as this Creation.

This book, which is a compilation of Sadguru Sri Sri Arjun's teachings is a modest step towards making mankind conscious of their true goal of life and showing them the ways to attain the same. Literatures are aplenty on this subject. But here in this book the style of presentation is simple and hence it is expected that this will be easy to realise what ails us and how to get rid of Sins and sufferings. Silence cannot be explained by words. Likewise, infinity cannot be comprehended by finite; every book has its limitations. Hence he, who follows the great teachings and contemplates deeply, may by His grace realise True Self in this birth itself.

Reference to Divyadhara (Oriya)

13. Divyadhara -3, Karma Sidhanta o Daivi Guna, Page -45

14. Divyadhara -19, Amrita Bindu-103, Page -36

15. Divyadhara -2, Divya Darshan ra Darshan Kana, Page -48

16. Divyadhara -19, Darshan Chart, Page -20

17. Divyadhara -14, Divya Darshan ra Sapta Ranga, Page -28

18. Divyadhara -18, Amriit Bindu 32, Page -19

19. Divyadhara -18, Amriit Bindu 123, Page -22

Divya Darshan

20. Divyadhara -10, Divya Darsan, Page -24

21. Divyadhara -8, Divya Darsana Sambandhare, Page -52

22. Divyadhara -2, Dukha ra Karana, Page -3

23. Divyadhara -2, Dharma Kan, Page -18

24. Divyadhara -4, Divya Darshan ra Abirbhava o Udeshya, Page -33

25. Divyadhara -4, Divya Darshan ra Visesatwa, Page -36

26. Divyadhara -8, Jiva o Iswara, Page -7

27. Divyadhara -4, Divya Darshan ra Lakhya, Page -38

28. Divyadhara -16, Sanatan Dharma ra Mahatva o Divya Darshan, Page -48

29. Divyadhara -2, Divya Darshan ra Darshan Kan, Page -31

30. Divyadhara -4, Sanatan Dharma, Page -27

31. Divyadhara -2, Divya Darshan ra Yoga, Page -34

32. Divyadhara -2, Divya Darshan ra Lakhya, Page -36

33. Divyadhara - 20, Divya Darshan ra Lakhya-2, Page - 46

34. Divyadhara -2, Divya Darshana ra Gurutva, Page -38

35. Divyadhara -19, Amrita Bindu-66, Page -33

Spiritual Practice (Sadhana)

60. Divyadhara -14, Bhaktibhavara Eka Stithi, Page -24

61. Divyadhara -14, Divya Darshan ra Sikhyadana Pranali, Page -36

62. Divyadhara -15, Shanka o Samadhana-3, Page -35

63. Divyadhara -18, Guru Kavacha, Page -7

64. Divyadhara -18, Samaja re Mahapurusa manaka Prabhaba, Page -43

65. Divyadhara -15, Atma Jnana, Page 19

66. Divyadhara - 20, Sadhana O Ashirvachan, Page -23

67. Divyadhara - 20, Amritbindu–51, Page -50

Message to Spiritual Aspirants

68. Divyadhara -17, Sadgurudeva nka sandesha-1, Page -71

69. Divyadhara -7, Prakriti Tatva, Page -40

70. Divyadhara -17, Sadguru nka Sandesha, Page -3

71. Divyadhara -6, Sadguru Ashirvachan, Page -19

72. Divyadhara -19, Upadesh, Page -14

73. Divyadhara -8, Sisya Sisyaanka Udesyre Sadguru Debanka Divya Sandesh, Page -30

74. Divyadhara -8, Sanghabadha Hua, Page -33

75. Divyadhara -6, Ashrama ra Abasakyata o Upadeyata, Page -24

76. Divyadhara -12, Asirbachan, Page -58

77. Divyadhara -18, Sandesha, Page -63

78. Divyadhara -19, 50th Guru Jayanti, Page -18

79. Divyadhara -18, 53rd Guru Jayanti re Sadgurudeba nka Pravachan, Page -12

80. Divyadhara -18, 55th Guru Jayanti re Sadgurudeba nka Pravachan, Page -17

81. Divyadhara -16, Sukhma Sarira, Page -39

Theory of Rebirth

Doubts & Clarifications

Nectarine Drops

ఴ⋆ఴ